WILLIAMS-SONOMA

Meats & Poultry

The Best of Williams-Sonoma Kitchen Library

Meats & Poultry

GENERAL EDITOR
CHUCK WILLIAMS

RECIPE PHOTOGRAPHY
ALLAN ROSENBERG

Oxmoor
House®

Contents

Introduction

Meat and poultry are at the heart and soul of many cooking cultures. The centerpiece of countless meals, frequent soloist on the grill, and the toast of festive gatherings—whether you're serving steaks, chops, roasts, or barbecue—meat and poultry have always provided the essential focus of many menus, no matter the occasion. The holiday season brings splendid turkeys, roasted golden brown; summertime picnics offer the promise of baskets of crispy fried chicken.

As our diets turn toward the lean and protein-oriented, meat and poultry emerge as vital players. It is easy to get started. Consult the Williams-Sonoma Kitchen Library's *Meats & Poultry* and transform humble beef chuck, braised in red wine, into a celebration-worthy Beef Bourguignon. Pair your bird with fragrant herbs and savory meats and prepare Chicken Breasts Stuffed with Herbs, Green Peppercorns, and Prosciutto. Give pork loin a sweet and delicious makeover with the addition of fruit and serve up Roast Pork with Figs. Throughout these pages, you will find recipes drawn from all over the globe. Beef, for instance, takes on new twists, making stops in France (Steak au Poivre), Germany (Sauerbraten), and the United States (Kansas City Beef Brisket), as well as southern climates (Latin American Grilled Steak with Avocado Salsa), and Asian cultures (Korean Grilled Short Ribs). Get ready to take a trip into the world of meat cookery. Enjoy the ride, and bring on the main course—meat and poultry.

CHOICE CUTS FOR EVERY OCCASION

Beef, veal, pork, and lamb

In the world of meat, hearty, flavorful and multi-faceted beef reigns supreme. Not only an excellent and easily accessible source of protein, modern cuts are rich in vitamins and much leaner than they were twenty years ago.

Beef can be roasted, broiled, grilled, fried, ground, braised, rolled, and poached. Select a piece in which the lean portions are bright red (vacuum-packed beef and the interior of ground beef are a darker, purplish red because the meat has been exposed to little air), and use it within a few days unless you freeze it. A good butcher can also help you select the cut that is right for you and lead you through the labyrinth of terminology, grades, and labels. The U.S. Department of Agriculture (USDA) grades meat as prime, choice, or select (or good) for retail sale. The greater the amount of marbling, or flecks of fat, in the beef muscle, the higher the grade—with prime as the highest—because marbling makes the meat tender and juicy.

Roasts are one of the most popular ways to prepare a cut of beef. Try Pot-Roasted Top Sirloin for a hearty weekday supper or the Old-Fashioned Rib Roast for an impressive main course at a family gathering. Begin with a tender cut suited for high, dry heat. Prime rib, with or without the bones, is juicy enough to withstand the penetrating temperatures, even if it is cooked until it is well done. The whole tenderloin and the whole strip, or shell, also make succulent roasts. Depending on the tenderness of the cut, a roast can be nestled among vegetables (Beef with Rosemary and Red Potatoes) or braised slowly in a saucy marinade (Bourbon-Marinated Chuck Roast).

Quick, tasty, and in hot competition with roasts, steaks can be as effortless as setting the right cut in a pan and simply making sure that you have cooked it to your desired level of doneness. Look for strip, shell, club, New York, top loin, T-bone or porterhouse steaks at a reputable market or butcher. Rib-eye steaks and hanger or skirt steaks also work beautifully in such varied recipes as Gingered Skirt Steaks and Grilled Steak with Balsamic Vinegar and Black Pepper.

Ground beef and beef chucks have also stood the test of time as reliable favorites. Pick 80 percent ground chuck for the juiciest burgers, and choose brisket, round, rump, and chuck cuts for stewing. Before you

stew or braise, brown the meat to release its many flavor compounds and bring out the best in your beef.

Beef easily shares the spotlight with other meats such as veal, pork, and lamb. Prized for its rich, tender texture and pale color, milk-fed veal can be substituted with the rosier, chewier, naturally reared calf. Select tender cuts like the loin and the rib for Grilled Veal Loin Chops with Tarragon, Mushrooms, and Cream. Pick the tougher shoulder, neck, and leg portions for Paprika Veal Stew with Dumplings; and rely on thin slices of veal leg for Veal Rollatini.

Look to pork for an inexpensive, lean, flavorful, and remarkably useful meat, one that's been bred, raised, and butchered to be increasingly leaner over the years. Cook it quickly to avoid dryness, and avoid preparing it to a state of gray well-doneness. The meat is notable for its chameleon-like qualities—think of it as an alternative to chicken. Try such varied dishes as Curried Pork Satay, Moroccan-Style Grilled Pork Chops, Barbecued Spareribs, and Winter Casserole of Pork, Sauerkraut, and Potatoes.

Last but definitely not least, and far from meek and mild, lamb provides a wonderful change of pace thanks to its strong, vivid flavor. The meat is favored in European, African, and Middle Eastern dishes. Use

leg portions for Saffron Lamb Kabobs, go for ribs when preparing Herbed Rack of Lamb, and select the shoulder for Rosemary-Smoked Lamb Chops.

POULTRY, ANY TIME AND ANY PLACE
Chicken, turkey, and other poultry
Chicken, America's fair fowl, ranks high as a favorite source of protein. Since the advent of the modern chicken farm after World War II, the chicken has only increased in popularity. Chicken is also a great source of iron, chromium, copper, selenium, phosphorus, potassium, magnesium, and zinc as well as thiamin, riboflavin, niacin, and vitamins B6 and B12.

Poultry will prove to be a lean, mild-tasting, readily available, and versatile component of any meal. Consider it an empty canvas, ready to be transformed by your culinary imagination. Chicken thrives when roasted, poached, braised, broiled, grilled, fried, sautéed, steamed, or stir-fried. Simply choose the perfect bird for the technique. Broiler-fryers—young, tender chickens that are about seven weeks old—can be grilled, broiled, or fried. Capons—neutered male chickens that are fattened—are juicy, sweet, and ideal for roasts. Roasters—older chickens—offer more meat and are best, of course, roasted, poached, and braised. Stewing hens—mature laying hens that are 10 to

18 months old—benefit from long, slow cooking times in moist heat. Cornish hens—1- or 2-pound broiler-fryers—are tender and juicy and are usually roasted whole and served individually. Whole chickens are a festive—and practical—way to feed a family or small party. Roasted, poached, grilled, or smoked, they demand little preparation time and offer moist, delightful results. A cut-up whole chicken works well for a group because everyone can usually get their favorite piece of the bird. Sample the extravagant yet subtle Chicken with Forty Cloves of Garlic or the fragrant Rosemary Chicken with Potatoes.

Chicken breasts are simple to prepare and can be cooked in minutes. A marinade is an easy way to add flavor. Use bold spices, herbs, and seasonings such as onions, ginger, shallots, fresh cilantro (coriander), peppercorns, or mustard. Take them to Jamaica, with jerk sauce and plantains; Mexico, with chiles and limes; or China, with five spices and sesame seed oil—just be certain not to overcook them. Sauté the breasts and bring out the fresh, delicate taste of the herbs in Chicken Breast Sauté with Vinegar-Tarragon Sauce, one of this book's many convenient after-work evening meal ideas.

Though not as popular as chicken breasts, the other parts of the bird can provide an easy, economical way to feed a crowd, while offering the option of dark meat rather than white. Flavorful boneless chicken thighs can stand in for boneless chicken breasts in a pinch. And they shine on their own in recipes treasured in Asia, North Africa, India, the Middle East, southern France, and southern Italy. Turn to thighs for Chicken Paillards or Paprika Chicken. Wings, another favorite part, make fun finger food at lively gatherings. Cook up a big batch of Buffalo Wings and watch them disappear.

Other types of poultry, such as turkey, duck, quail, and squab, are invaluable on special occasions and, in the case of turkey, increasingly for casual meals. Large, lean, and easily cooked, turkey is capable of satisfying a crowd, making it essential during the holidays. But it also provides a nice change from chicken in Turkey Kabobs with Peanut Dipping Sauce and Turkey Burgers with Apple-Mint Relish. Quail, squab, and duck are perfect for entertaining. Look to Thyme and Mustard Quail, Herbed Butterflied Squab, and Duck in Red Wine with Apricots and Prunes. Cornish hens are actually small chickens, though they are sometimes assumed to be different. Regardless, their compact size and savory qualities make them ideal for dinner with company. Try Citrus-Marinated Cornish Hens, a dish that will surely please your guests.

THE GRAND FINALE

Grilled, sautéed, roasted, fried, braised, and now demystified and deconstructed, meat and poultry are vital elements in the vibrant tapestry of world cuisine. Beef—alongside veal, pork, and lamb—continues to reign over the dinner table, lending itself to roasts, steaks, and ground chuck recipes, and delighting all with its versatility and widespread availability. Meanwhile, chicken rules the proverbial roost with its leanness and versatility.

Be sure to check out the basic recipes and techniques sections as well as the informative glossary at the back of the volume. You will find Chicken Stock and Beef Stock, essential for soups. The marinades are bound to enhance all your grilled foods. Sauces such as Pesto and Tomato-Cranberry Salsa will add spice to your table, while relishes such as Plum and Ginger Chutney and spreads such as Tapenade will complement your favorite meat and poultry dishes.

Just pair these succulent meat dishes with your favorite vegetable side dishes or salads for a complete meal. Accompany All-American Beef Short Ribs with dandelion greens or try Smothered Chicken with Mushrooms and Onions next to steamed leeks and broccoli rabe. Let your imagination take wing with *Meats & Poultry's* classic, essential recipes. *Bon appétit!*

Marinades, Sauces & Chutneys

Red or White Wine Marinade

This recipe can be prepared with dry red wine for beef and lamb or dry white wine for poultry. Large roasts and whole chickens can marinate from 1–3 days; the longer they marinate, the more flavor they will gain.

1 bottle (3 cups/750 ml) dry red or white wine

1/2 cup (4 fl oz/125 ml) olive oil

1 yellow onion, finely chopped

1/4 cup (1/3 oz/10 g) chopped fresh flat-leaf (Italian) parsley

2 large cloves garlic, minced

1 tablespoon chopped fresh thyme, rosemary, or tarragon, or 2 teaspoons dried herb of choice

1 teaspoon salt

1/2 teaspoon freshly ground pepper

In a nonaluminum bowl, stir together all the ingredients. Use immediately or refrigerate in a tightly covered jar for up to 2 days.

Makes about 5 cups (40 fl oz/1.25 l), enough for a large roast, leg of lamb, or whole chicken

Citrus Marinade

Citrus juice gives a clean, satisfying flavor to chicken or veal. Let steaks and chops marinate for at least 1 hour, or all day if you wish. Large cuts of meat can marinate for 1–2 days.

1/2 cup (4 fl oz/125 ml) olive oil

1/4 cup (2 fl oz/60 ml) lemon juice

1 clove garlic, minced

2 tablespoons finely chopped shallots or green (spring) onions

2 teaspoons chopped fresh thyme, tarragon, dill, or sage, or 1 teaspoon dried herb of choice

1/2 teaspoon salt

1/2 teaspoon freshly ground pepper

In a nonaluminum bowl, stir together all the ingredients. Use immediately or refrigerate in a tightly covered jar for up to 2 days.

Makes about 1 cup (8 fl oz/250 ml), enough for 2–3 lb (1–1.5 kg) veal, pork chops, or steaks

Dry Rubs

Dry mixtures of salt, pepper, herbs, and spices rubbed over food several hours before grilling are good flavor enhancers. Brush the food lightly with oil before coating it with the rub. Made with fresh herbs, these mixtures will keep for up to 3 days if tightly covered and refrigerated. Made with dried herbs, they will keep for several weeks stored airtight in a cupboard.

FOR LAMB AND BEEF:

2 tablespoons chopped fresh rosemary or 2 teaspoons dried rosemary

2 large cloves garlic, minced

1 1/2 teaspoons salt

1 teaspoon freshly ground pepper

Finely grated zest of 1 lemon or lime

FOR CHICKEN:

1 teaspoon salt

1 teaspoon freshly ground pepper

1 teaspoon dried sage

1/2 teaspoon dried thyme

1/2 teaspoon cayenne pepper

1 clove garlic, minced

FOR PORK:

2 tablespoons chopped fresh thyme or 2 teaspoons dried thyme

1 tablespoon chopped fresh sage or 1 teaspoon dried sage

2 teaspoons salt

1 teaspoon freshly ground pepper

1/4 teaspoon ground allspice or cloves

2 cloves garlic, minced

In a small bowl, stir together all the ingredients until well blended.

Each recipe makes enough for 4–5 lb (2–2.5 kg) beef, pork, or lamb, or 2 lb (1 kg) chicken

Soy-Ginger Marinade

Here, soy sauce, sherry, and ginger are combined to make a version of teriyaki marinade, which is good on flank steak, skirt steak, chicken, and pork. Marinate steaks, chops, or chicken in the refrigerator for at least 3 hours, or up to all day. Large pieces of meat or poultry can marinate, in a covered nonaluminum dish in the refrigerator, for 1–2 days.

1/2 cup (4 fl oz/125 ml) soy sauce

1/2 cup (4 fl oz/125 ml) dry sherry

1/3 cup (3 fl oz/80 ml) vegetable oil

2 tablespoons sugar

2 cloves garlic, minced

1 tablespoon peeled and grated fresh ginger

In a nonaluminum bowl, combine the soy sauce, sherry, oil, sugar, garlic, and ginger. Whisk until blended. If possible, let stand at room temperature for about 1 hour before using to allow the flavors to blend.

Makes about 1 1/3 cups (11 fl oz/345 ml), enough for 3 lb (1.5 kg) meat or poultry

Compound Butters

A slice of flavored butter that is placed on a hot-from-the-grill steak, juicy hamburger, chop, or piece of chicken melts to form a delicious, instant sauce. Store the butters in tightly covered bowls, or shape them into logs and tightly wrap in plastic, then refrigerate and slice into thin rounds for serving. They will keep for up to 4 days in the refrigerator or about 1 month in the freezer. Bring to room temperature before serving.

HERB BUTTER:

1/2 cup (4 oz/125 g) unsalted butter, at room temperature

2 tablespoons chopped fresh tarragon, sage, or cilantro (coriander), or 2 teaspoons dried tarragon or sage

2 tablespoons chopped fresh flat-leaf (Italian) parsley

1/2 teaspoon salt

1/2 teaspoon freshly ground pepper

LEMON BUTTER:

1/2 cup (4 oz/125 g) unsalted butter, at room temperature

1/4 cup (1/3 oz/10 g) chopped fresh flat-leaf (Italian) parsley

2 tablespoons fresh lemon juice

2 teaspoons finely grated lemon zest

1/2 teaspoon salt

1/4 teaspoon freshly ground pepper

MUSTARD BUTTER:

1/2 cup (4 oz/125 g) unsalted butter, at room temperature

3 tablespoons Dijon mustard

2 tablespoons chopped shallots or green (spring) onions

1 tablespoon chopped fresh flat-leaf (Italian) parsley

1–2 tablespoons fresh lemon juice

1/2 teaspoon salt

1/4 teaspoon freshly ground pepper

In a large bowl, beat the butter with a wooden spoon or hand-held electric mixer until smooth, then gradually beat in all the remaining ingredients. Form the butter mixture into a rough log about 4 inches (10 cm) long and 1 inch (2.5 cm) in diameter. Wrap in plastic wrap and chill until firm. To serve, cut into slices 1/2 inch (12 mm) thick.

Serves 6–8

ROQUEFORT BUTTER:

Delicious on steaks and veal chops, or tucked into hamburgers.

3 oz (90 g) Roquefort cheese

6 tablespoons (3 oz/90 g) unsalted butter, at room temperature

2 tablespoons Cognac

1 teaspoon freshly ground pepper

1/4 cup (1 oz/30 g) chopped walnuts (optional)

Place the cheese, butter, Cognac, and pepper in a blender or food processor and process until smooth. Alternatively, place in a bowl and beat with a whisk or a hand-held electric mixer until smooth. Transfer to a bowl and fold in the walnuts, if using.

Serves 6–8

PROVENÇAL OLIVE BUTTER:

Steaks and veal chops are wonderful served with this butter. It is also tasty when tucked under the skin of chicken before broiling.

1 cup (5 oz/155 g) green or black olives, pitted

Grated zest of 1 orange

2 tablespoons Cognac

2 shallots, finely minced

2 teaspoons finely minced thyme

1 teaspoon finely minced garlic

1 tablespoon anchovy fillets packed in olive oil, drained and finely minced

3/4 cup (6 oz/180 g) unsalted butter, at room temperature

Freshly ground pepper

Place the olives in a blender or food processor and pulse just to chop. Add the orange zest, Cognac, shallots, thyme, garlic, and anchovies and pulse just to combine. Add the butter and process until combined but still lightly textured. Season to taste with pepper.

Serves 12

MUSTARD-CHIVE BUTTER:

This is great on steaks or veal chops, as well as broiled chicken.

1 tablespoon dry mustard

1/2 teaspoon sugar

2 tablespoons distilled white vinegar or water

1/4 cup (2 oz/60 g) Dijon mustard

1/2 cup (4 oz/125 g) plus 2 tablespoons unsalted butter, at room temperature

1/4 cup (11/2 oz/45 g) minced fresh chives

Salt and freshly ground pepper

In a small bowl, dissolve the dry mustard and sugar in the vinegar or water. Stir in the Dijon mustard until well blended. Transfer to a food processor or blender, add the butter and chives, and process until smooth. Alternatively, transfer to a bowl and beat with a whisk or hand-held electric mixer until smooth and well blended. Season to taste with salt and pepper.

Serves 12

Cold Horseradish Cream

Ideal for serving hot or cold with boiled beef. Also goes well with cold rare roast beef or broiled steak. This sauce can be warmed gently over low heat and spooned over hot rib-eye or fillet steaks. You may use 5 tablespoons (3 oz/90 g) prepared horseradish for making this sauce, but the fresh root is hotter and has better flavor. If you use prepared horseradish, you may not need as much vinegar or salt.

1/2 cup (4 oz/125 g) thinly sliced, peeled fresh horseradish

3–4 tablespoons (about 2 fl oz/60 ml) distilled white vinegar

3 tablespoons finely minced white onion

11/2 cups (12 fl oz/375 ml) sour cream

1/2 cup (4 fl oz/125 ml) heavy (double) cream

1 teaspoon salt

1/2 teaspoon freshly ground pepper

3 tablespoons chopped fresh dill or chives (optional)

Place the horseradish and 3 tablespoons vinegar in a blender or food processor and process until smooth. Transfer to a bowl. Stir in the remaining ingredients until well mixed, adding another tablespoon vinegar if needed for tartness.

Makes about 2 cups (16 fl oz/500 ml)

Mustard Cream Sauce

Here is a creamy sauce that complements roast beef, sautéed fillet of beef, or broiled veal chops. It is delectable with sautéed or roast chicken, or roast pork loin. The sauce is rich but tangy and provides a nice accent to a host of vegetables as well, including beets, carrots, green beans, or simple boiled potatoes. It can be prepared a few hours in advance and reheated gently over low heat. Tarragon and chives have a natural affinity for mustard-based sauces and either one can be added at the last minute.

2 tablespoons unsalted butter

2 tablespoons all-purpose (plain) flour

1 cup (8 fl oz/250 ml) chicken broth, heated

5–6 tablespoons (about 3 oz/90 g) Dijon mustard

1 cup (8 fl oz/250 ml) heavy (double) cream

2 tablespoons chopped fresh tarragon or chives (optional)

Salt and freshly ground pepper

Melt the butter in a saucepan over medium heat. Add the flour and cook, stirring, for 3–4 minutes. Gradually add the broth, whisking constantly. Whisk in the mustard and cream and simmer until slightly thickened, about 5 minutes. Stir in the herbs, if using. Season to taste with salt and pepper. Serve hot.

Makes about 2 cups (16 fl oz/500 ml)

All-Purpose Stir-Fry Sauce

Here is a great sauce to have around for last-minute stir-fry dishes. It works with any meat, seafood, or vegetable. Simply add it near the end of cooking. This amount is sufficient to season about 1 lb (500 g) of ingredients, but you can make the sauce in whatever quantity you like. The sauce will keep in a jar with a tight-fitting lid for up to 1 week in the refrigerator. If you make it in advance, add the green onion just before using.

3 tablespoons soy sauce

1 teaspoon finely chopped, peeled fresh ginger

1 small clove garlic, minced

1 green (spring) onion, including tender green tops, finely chopped

1/2 teaspoon chili oil (below)

In a small bowl, combine the soy sauce, ginger, garlic, green onion, and chili oil and stir well.

Makes about 1/4 cup (2 fl oz/60 ml)

Chili Oil

Use this both as a seasoning for cooking and as a table condiment. Do not lean directly over the pan as the oil heats, because the red pepper flakes release very pungent fumes that may irritate your eyes. If you like, leave the pepper flakes in the oil; they will make it hotter the longer it stands. The chili oil keeps indefinitely in a small glass jar with a tight-fitting lid in the refrigerator.

1/4 cup (1 oz/30 g) red pepper flakes

1 cup (8 fl oz/250 ml) peanut, canola, or safflower oil

In a small saucepan over medium heat, combine the red pepper flakes and oil. Bring almost to a boil, then turn off the heat and let cool. Strain into a glass container with a lid.

Makes 1 cup (8 fl oz/250 ml)

Basic Barbecue Sauce

This traditional American barbecue sauce is good on chicken, spareribs, and hamburgers. Because the sauce contains sugar, it burns easily and should only be brushed on for the last 10–15 minutes of cooking. Pass any remaining sauce at the table.

2 tablespoons vegetable oil

1 yellow onion, finely chopped

3 cloves garlic, minced

1 1/2 cups (12 oz/375 g) tomato ketchup

1/2 cup (4 fl oz/125 ml) cider vinegar

1/4 cup (2 fl oz/60 ml) Worcestershire sauce

1/3 cup (3 oz/90 g) sugar

1 tablespoon chili powder

1/2 teaspoon cayenne pepper, or to taste

Heat the oil in a nonaluminum saucepan over moderate heat and add the onion and garlic. Cook gently, stirring, for about 5 minutes. Add the ketchup, vinegar, Worcestershire sauce, sugar, chili powder, and cayenne to taste (the more cayenne you use, the hotter it will be). Reduce the heat and simmer, partially covered, until the sauce has thickened slightly, about 20 minutes.

Makes about 2 1/2 cups (20 fl oz/625 ml)

Midwestern Barbecue Sauce

The U.S. Midwest abounds with thick barbecue sauces that are both hot and sweet, and wonderful on pork ribs, beef brisket, or chicken. Because the sauces contain sugar and can burn easily, they are usually brushed on during the last 15–20 minutes of cooking. This is also a good dipping sauce to pass at the table.

2 tablespoons vegetable oil

1 yellow onion, chopped

1/2 cup (2 1/2 oz/75 g) finely chopped celery

1 1/4 cups (10 fl oz/310 ml) tomato ketchup

1/2 cup (4 fl oz/125 ml) cider vinegar

1/2 cup (4 fl oz/125 ml) water

1/3 cup (3 oz/90 g) sugar

1/2 teaspoon cayenne pepper

1/2 teaspoon salt

In a nonaluminum saucepan over medium-high heat, warm the oil. Add the onion and celery and cook, stirring, until the vegetables have softened, about 7 minutes. Add the ketchup, vinegar, water, sugar, cayenne, and salt and stir well. Bring the mixture to a boil, then reduce the heat to low, cover partially, and simmer until the sauce has thickened slightly, 15–20 minutes.

Remove from the heat and let cool. Use immediately, or transfer to a container, cover tightly, and refrigerate for up to 5 days.

Makes about 2 1/4 cups (18 fl oz/560 ml), enough for 5–6 lb (2.5–3 kg) meat or poultry

Red or White Wine Barbecue Sauce

You can use this herbal, wine-based mixture as a marinade or a baste for chicken, pork, lamb, or beef.

1 1/2 cups (12 fl oz/375 ml) dry red or white wine

1/2 cup (4 fl oz/125 ml) red or white wine vinegar

1/3 cup (3 fl oz/80 ml) olive oil

1 yellow onion, finely chopped

2 tablespoons Worcestershire sauce

2 tablespoons chopped fresh rosemary or thyme, or 2 teaspoons dried rosemary or thyme

2 teaspoons finely grated lemon zest

1/2 teaspoon salt

Pinch of red pepper flakes

In a nonaluminum saucepan over high heat, combine the wine, wine vinegar, olive oil, onion, Worcestershire sauce, rosemary, lemon zest, salt, and red pepper flakes. Bring to a boil, stirring once or twice to combine the ingredients. Reduce the heat to low, cover partially, and simmer until the onion has wilted and the sauce has reduced slightly, about 15 minutes. Remove from the heat and let cool. Use immediately or transfer to a container, cover tightly, and refrigerate for up to 4 days.

Makes about 2 cups (16 fl oz/500 ml), enough for about 4 lb (2 kg) meat or poultry

Spicy Mop Sauce

This flavorful concoction belongs to the family of vinegar-based Carolina mop sauces, named for their popularity in North and South Carolina and are traditionally swabbed over a slab of meat with an old-fashioned string mop. The sauces vary from sweet and tangy to fiery hot. This one is at once slightly sweet and moderately hot, but you can adjust the amount of sugar and pepper to suit your taste. It makes a great marinade for beef, pork, or chicken.

1 teaspoon black peppercorns

1 1/4 cups (10 fl oz/310 ml) cider vinegar

2/3 cup (5 fl oz/160 ml) water

3 tablespoons sugar

1/2 teaspoon salt

1 teaspoon red pepper flakes

Place the peppercorns on a work surface and crush them coarsely by firmly pressing and rolling the bottom of a heavy pan over them.

In a nonaluminum saucepan over high heat, combine the crushed peppercorns, vinegar, water, sugar, salt, and red pepper flakes. Bring to a boil, stirring once or twice. Remove from the heat and let stand, uncovered, for at least 1 hour before using, to allow the flavors to blend. For longer storage, let cool completely, transfer to a glass container, cover tightly, and refrigerate for up to 1 week.

Makes about 2 cups (16 fl oz/500 ml), enough for about 4 lb (2 kg) meat or poultry

Basic Tomato Sauce

Tomato sauce is an invaluable addition to the basic pantry. As fresh tomatoes vary dramatically in quality and flavor, for the most consistent year-round sauce, use canned plum tomatoes, preferably those prepared in the Italian style, which usually come packed in tomato purée. Adding more canned tomato purée assures you of a thick sauce with excellent coating properties. This sauce can be stored in a covered container in the refrigerator for about 1 week. Add chopped fresh herbs at serving time, if you like.

2 cans (28 oz/875 g each) plum (Roma) tomatoes

1 cup (8 fl oz/250 ml) canned tomato purée

3 tablespoons unsalted butter or olive oil

Salt and freshly ground pepper

Place the tomatoes with some of their juices in a blender or food processor and process until finely chopped. Transfer the tomatoes to a heavy, nonaluminum saucepan. Place over low heat and stir in the tomato purée. Cook, stirring often, until the sauce thickens slightly, about 10 minutes. Stir in the butter or olive oil and season to taste with salt and pepper.

Makes about 6 cups (48 fl oz/1.5 l)

Caper Sauce

This sauce is excellent on cold or hot beef dishes. For a less tart taste, use fresh lemon juice in place of some of the vinegar.

1 cup (1½ oz/45 g) chopped fresh flat-leaf (Italian) parsley

⅓ cup (1½ oz/45 g) drained capers, coarsely chopped

½ cup (2½ oz/75 g) finely minced white onion

⅓ cup (3 fl oz/80 ml) red or white wine vinegar

1¼ cups (10 fl oz/310 ml) olive oil

1–2 tablespoons anchovy fillets packed in olive oil, drained and finely minced

2–4 cornichons, finely minced (optional)

½ cup (2 oz/60 g) fine dried bread crumbs (optional)

Salt and freshly ground pepper

In a large bowl, stir together all the ingredients, including salt and pepper to taste, until well mixed.

Makes about 2½ cups (20 fl oz/625 ml)

Green Parsley Sauce

1 cup (8 fl oz/250 ml) chicken stock

3 tablespoons chopped fresh flat-leaf (Italian) parsley

2 tablespoons well-drained capers, coarsely chopped

Salt and freshly ground pepper

Pour the stock into a bowl. Stir in the parsley and capers, mixing well. Season to taste with salt and pepper.

Makes about 1 cup (8 fl oz/250 ml)

Horseradish-Mustard Sauce

1 cup (8 fl oz/250 ml) heavy (double) cream

1 teaspoon Dijon mustard

2 teaspoons prepared horseradish

1 tablespoon fresh lemon juice

1 tablespoon chopped fresh tarragon

Freshly ground pepper

In a bowl, whip the cream until stiff peaks form. Using a tablespoon, fold in the mustard and horseradish. Stir in the lemon juice and tarragon and season to taste with pepper.

Makes about 1 cup (8 fl oz/250 ml)

Red Pepper Sauce

2 red bell peppers (capsicums), seeded and coarsely chopped

1 clove garlic

1 tablespoon red wine vinegar

½ cup (4 fl oz/125 ml) olive oil

Salt and freshly ground pepper

Put the bell peppers in a blender or food processor. Add the garlic and vinegar and process until smooth. Place the purée in a small saucepan over high heat and boil, stirring, until the liquid evaporates, 1–2 minutes. Add the olive oil and simmer for 1 minute. Season to taste with salt and pepper. Serve at room temperature.

Makes about 1 cup (8 fl oz/250 ml)

Peanut Dipping Sauce

Slightly sweet and slightly hot, this Asian-influenced sauce complements grilled pork or poultry right from the fire. Pass it in a bowl at the table.

½ cup (4 fl oz/125 ml) water

1 teaspoon cornstarch (cornflour)

½ cup (5 oz/155 g) smooth or chunky peanut butter

¼ cup (2 fl oz/60 ml) fresh lime juice

⅓ cup (3 fl oz/80 ml) soy sauce

¼ cup (2 fl oz/60 ml) Asian sesame oil

2–3 tablespoons sugar

½–1 teaspoon red pepper flakes

¼ teaspoon Chili Oil (page 17)

¼ cup (⅓ oz/10 g) chopped fresh cilantro (fresh coriander)

¼ cup (¾ oz/20 g) chopped green (spring) onion

In a saucepan, combine the water and cornstarch and stir until the cornstarch dissolves. Add the peanut butter, lime juice, soy sauce, sesame oil, sugar, red pepper flakes, and chili oil and whisk until smooth. Bring to a boil over medium-high heat, whisking frequently. Reduce the heat to low and simmer, uncovered, until the sauce thickens slightly, about 3 minutes.

Remove from the heat and let cool. Stir in the cilantro and green onion. Use immediately, or transfer to a container, cover tightly, and refrigerate for up to 3 days.

Makes about 1¾ cups (14 fl oz/440 ml)

Honey-Mustard Dipping Sauce

This sweet and tangy dipping sauce is a perfect partner for Chicken Kabobs (page 228), and Chicken Paillards (page 243). The yogurt in it acts as a cooling agent, which comes in handy when served with the spicy Jamaican Jerk Chicken (page 253). Mustard has a natural affinity for pork, making this sauce suitable for a number of pork dishes.

2/3 cup (5 oz/155 g) low-fat plain yogurt

1/4 cup (3 oz/90 g) honey

2 tablespoons Dijon mustard

2 tablespoons water

1/2 teaspoon salt

Pinch of freshly ground pepper

In a small bowl, combine the yogurt, honey, mustard, water, salt, and pepper. Using a whisk or fork, stir until blended and smooth. Store in a tightly covered jar in the refrigerator for up to 3 days.

Makes about 1 1/4 cups (10 fl oz/310 ml)

Yogurt and Herb Dressing

The pleasing tang of this dressing lends itself to a variety of lamb dishes. It also complements beef, and can be paired with Moroccan Meatballs (page 78) or Hamburgers with Grilled Tomatoes (page 70) in place of their respective sauces. For a creamier dressing, substitute a few tablespoons of mayonnaise, either reduced-fat or regular, for part of the yogurt.

1 cup (8 oz/250 g) low-fat plain yogurt

3 tablespoons white wine vinegar or cider vinegar

1 teaspoon salt

Pinch of freshly ground pepper

2 tablespoons chopped fresh dill, tarragon, parsley, or chives

In a small bowl, combine the yogurt, vinegar, salt, pepper, and herb of choice. Using a whisk or fork, stir until blended and smooth. Store in a tightly covered jar in the refrigerator for up to 3 days.

Makes about 1 1/4 cups (10 fl oz/310 ml)

Pesto

This fragrant sauce is the gift of Liguria, Italy, to the food world. It pairs well with grilled or broiled poultry dishes.

2 cups (2 oz/60 g) firmly packed fresh basil leaves

2 teaspoons finely chopped garlic

2 tablespoons pine nuts or walnuts, toasted (page 326)

2 teaspoons freshly ground pepper

About 1 cup (8 fl oz/250 ml) olive oil, plus extra for topping pesto

1/2 cup (2 oz/60 g) freshly grated Parmesan cheese (optional)

About 1 teaspoon salt

In a blender or food processor, combine the basil, garlic, nuts, pepper, and 1/2 cup (4 fl oz/ 125 ml) of the olive oil. Pulse or blend briefly to form a coarse paste. With the motor running, slowly add as much of the remaining oil as needed to form a thick purée.

Do not overmix; the purée should contain tiny pieces of basil leaf.

Add the Parmesan cheese, if using, and process briefly to mix. Taste and add the salt; you may need less than 1 teaspoon if the cheese is salty. If you are not adding cheese, add 1 teaspoon salt.

Transfer the pesto to a jar and pour a film of olive oil onto the surface to preserve the bright green color. Cover and refrigerate for up to 1 month.

Makes about 2 1/2 cups (20 fl oz/625 ml)

Tapenade

For the true taste of Provence, seek out Niçoise olives, although Kalamata olives can be used in their place and are easier to pit. To pit the olives, hit each one with a meat pounder to loosen the flesh, then pick the pit out. An olive pitter will not work on Niçoise olives, as they are too small.

1 cup (5 oz/155 g) pitted Niçoise olives

2 tablespoons drained capers, rinsed and chopped

1 tablespoon minced garlic

2 teaspoons anchovy fillets packed in olive oil, drained and chopped

1/2 teaspoon freshly ground pepper

4–6 tablespoons (2–3 fl oz/ 60–90 ml) olive oil

1 tablespoon finely grated lemon zest (optional)

2 tablespoons Armagnac or other brandy (optional)

In a blender or food processor, combine the olives, capers, garlic, anchovies, pepper, and 4 tablespoons (2 fl oz/60 ml) of the olive oil, and the lemon zest and Armagnac, if using. Process to form a rough purée or paste. Add more oil if the mixture is too thick; it should have a spreadable consistency. Taste and adjust the seasonings, then transfer to a bowl or jar, cover tightly, and refrigerate for up to 3 weeks. Bring to room temperature before using.

Makes about 1 1/4 cups (10 fl oz/310 ml)

Tomato-Cranberry Salsa

Easily prepared, this salsa complements nearly any type of cooked meat. It will also perk up leftover chicken that you might want to serve cold.

2 cups (8 oz/250 g) fresh cranberries

1/2 cup (2 oz/60 g) coarsely chopped red onion

4 tomatoes, coarsely chopped

1 jalapeño chile, stemmed

2 tablespoons fresh lemon juice

Salt

Put the cranberries and onion in a food processor. Pulse to chop. Add the tomatoes and jalapeño and purée. Transfer to a nonaluminum bowl. Stir in the lemon juice and salt to taste. Allow the flavors to blend for 1 hour before serving.

Makes about 3 cups (24 fl oz/750 ml)

Pear and Mustard Chutney

Most chutneys are simple to make and can be an excellent way to enjoy the fruit in season. This one calls for crisp fall pears and gives both sweet and sour dimensions to foods. Use it with your favorite pork or lamb dishes.

6 large, firm but ripe pears, preferably Bosc or Comice, peeled, quartered, and cored

1/4 cup (2 oz/60 g) whole-grain mustard

3/4 cup (6 fl oz/180 ml) white wine vinegar

1/2 cup (3 1/2 oz/105 g) firmly packed brown sugar

1/2 cup (2 1/2 oz/75 g) minced yellow onion

1/2 teaspoon ground cloves

1/2 teaspoon ground nutmeg

1/2 teaspoon ground allspice

Place all of the ingredients in a nonaluminum bowl, stir well, cover, and marinate overnight at room temperature.

The next day, transfer the mixture to a nonaluminum saucepan and bring to a boil. Reduce the heat to low and simmer, uncovered, until the mixture thickens, 1 1/2–2 hours.

Transfer to clean, sterilized jars with tight-fitting lids, let cool, cover, and refrigerate for up to 3 weeks.

Makes about 2 cups (1 1/4 lb/625 g)

Plum and Ginger Chutney

Both Indian and English cooks alike take great pride in the making of chutneys—condiments based on fruits or vegetables cooked with sugar, vinegar, and spices to form a jamlike consistency. This fragrant version is a flavorful accompaniment to any pork or lamb dish. Any type of plum will work well.

3/4 cup (6 fl oz/180 ml) cider vinegar

1/2 cup (3 1/2 oz/105 g) firmly packed brown sugar

3 cloves garlic, minced

1 small yellow onion, minced

1/2 teaspoon ground cinnamon

3 tablespoons peeled and grated fresh ginger

1/4 cup (2 oz/60 g) granulated sugar

2 lb (1 kg) plums, pitted and coarsely chopped

In a nonaluminum saucepan over high heat, combine all the ingredients. Stir well and bring to a boil. Reduce the heat to low and simmer, uncovered, until the mixture thickens, 1 1/2–2 hours.

Transfer to clean, sterilized jars with tight-fitting lids, let cool, cover, and refrigerate for up to 3 weeks.

Makes about 2 cups (1 1/4 lb/625 g)

Beef

Beef Bourguignon

In a frying pan over medium heat, sauté the salt pork until the fat is rendered (melted), 8–10 minutes. Using a slotted spoon, transfer the pork to paper towels to drain; set aside.

Add enough oil to the fat in the pan to measure ¼ cup (2 fl oz/60 ml). Add the shallots, diced onions, carrots, and garlic. Sauté until the vegetables are slightly soft, about 10 minutes. Using a slotted spoon, transfer to a large, heavy pot.

On a plate, mix the flour and salt, pepper, and nutmeg to taste. Coat the beef cubes with the flour mixture. Add oil as needed to the fat in the frying pan, place over high heat, add the beef cubes, and brown well on all sides, about 15 minutes. Using a slotted spoon, transfer the beef to the large pot. Add the Cognac and a little of the stock to the frying pan and deglaze over high heat by stirring with a wooden spoon to dislodge any browned bits from the bottom. Add to the beef along with the thyme, all but ½ cup (4 fl oz/125 ml) of the remaining stock, the wine, and the bay leaf. Bring to a boil, reduce the heat to low, cover, and simmer on the stove top or in an oven preheated to 325°F (165°C) until the beef is tender, about 3 hours.

Meanwhile, peel the pearl onions (page 326). In a frying pan over medium heat, melt 2 tablespoons of the butter. Add the onions in a single layer and sprinkle with the sugar. Cook, stirring, until onions are tender and golden, 8–10 minutes; add only enough of the ½ cup reserved stock to prevent scorching. Transfer to a bowl and set aside.

In the same pan over medium heat, melt the remaining 3 tablespoons butter. Add the mushrooms and sauté until browned, about 5 minutes; set aside.

Add the mushrooms and pearl onions to the beef during the last 30 minutes of cooking. Taste and adjust the seasoning. Remove the thyme and bay leaf, and discard. Sprinkle with the salt pork and parsley and serve.

Serves 6

½ lb (250 g) salt pork, cut into ¼-inch (6-mm) dice

Olive oil as needed

8 shallots, minced

2 yellow onions, finely diced

2 carrots, peeled and finely diced

2 cloves garlic, minced

About 2 cups (10 oz/315 g) all-purpose (plain) flour

Salt, freshly ground pepper, and freshly grated nutmeg

3 lb (1.5 kg) well-marbled stewing beef, cut into 2-inch (5-cm) cubes

¼ cup (2 fl oz/60 ml) Cognac

2 cups (16 fl oz/500 ml) Beef Stock (page 314)

2 fresh thyme sprigs

3 cups (24 fl oz/750 ml) dry red wine

1 bay leaf

18–24 unpeeled pearl onions

5 tablespoons (2½ oz/75 g) unsalted butter

2 tablespoons sugar

1 lb (500 g) white or cremini mushrooms, brushed clean and stemmed

Chopped fresh flat-leaf (Italian) parsley for garnish

Chinese Beef Stew with Five-Spice Powder

The ingredients in this recipe are easily found in well-stocked markets that carry Asian foods. The Chinese radish is sweeter than its more popular cousin, the Japanese daikon. Any mild turnip may be substituted.

1 tablespoon olive or canola oil

1¹/₂ lb (750 g) beef sirloin tip, cut into strips ¹/₂ inch (12 mm) thick and 3 inches (7.5 cm) long

2 cups (16 fl oz/500 ml) Beef Stock (page 314)

¹/₄ cup (2 fl oz/60 ml) soy sauce

2 tablespoons dry sherry or rice wine

1 unpeeled piece fresh ginger, about 1 inch (2.5 cm) long, sliced lengthwise into julienne

¹/₂–³/₄ teaspoon Chinese five-spice powder

¹/₂ lb (250 g) Chinese radish, peeled, cut in half lengthwise and then cut crosswise into 2-inch (5-cm) pieces

4 green (spring) onions, including tender green tops, cut into 2-inch (5-cm) lengths

5 or 6 leaves napa cabbage, cut crosswise into strips 2 inches (5 cm) wide

In a Dutch oven over medium-high heat, heat the oil. Working in batches, add the beef strips and brown well on all sides, about 5 minutes per batch. Add the beef stock and deglaze the pot, stirring with a wooden spoon to dislodge any browned bits. Add the soy sauce, sherry, ginger, five-spice powder to taste, Chinese radish, and green onions. Bring to a simmer, reduce the heat to medium-low, cover, and simmer gently until the meat falls apart when tested with a fork, about 3 hours.

Using a large spoon, skim the fat from the surface of the stew. Add the cabbage, cover, and continue to simmer over medium-low heat until the cabbage is very soft and wilted but not mushy, about 30 minutes longer.

Spoon into warmed shallow bowls and serve.

Serves 4–6

Paprika Veal Stew with Dumplings

Hungarian paprika gives this well-known dish an especially vibrant color and superior flavor. To reheat the stew, use low heat and do not allow it to boil or the sour cream will curdle.

2 tablespoons olive oil

1¹/₂ lb (750 g) boneless veal shoulder, cut into 1-inch (2.5-cm) cubes

1 large sweet white onion, cut in half lengthwise and then crosswise into slices ¹/₄ inch (6 mm) thick

1 tablespoon sweet Hungarian paprika

¹/₂ teaspoon dried thyme

1 can (28 oz/875 g) whole plum (Roma) tomatoes in purée

Old-Fashioned Dumplings, steamed on a plate (page 316)

1 cup (8 oz/250 g) sour cream, at room temperature

Salt and freshly ground pepper

Fresh thyme sprigs (optional)

In a Dutch oven over medium-high heat, heat the olive oil. Working in batches, add the veal cubes and brown on all sides, about 5 minutes per batch. Add the onion slices and sauté, stirring, until they are softened and the browned bits from the pot bottom begin to cling to them, about 5 minutes. Stir in the paprika, thyme, and tomatoes with the purée, breaking up the tomatoes with a wooden spoon. Bring to a simmer, reduce the heat to medium-low, cover, and simmer gently until the veal is tender, 40–60 minutes.

About 20 minutes before the veal is done, steam the dumplings. When the veal is done, remove the pot from the heat and stir in the sour cream. Season to taste with salt and pepper.

Spoon the stew into warmed shallow bowls and slide the dumplings on top. Garnish with the thyme sprigs, if desired, and serve immediately.

Serves 4

Beef Stew with Tomatoes

The addition of brown sugar, ginger, and cinnamon imparts a mild sweetness to this aromatic stew. Serve it over a bed of Steamed White Rice (page 317) or crusty country bread, if you like.

In a Dutch oven over medium-high heat, heat the olive oil. Working in batches if necessary, add the beef and brown well on all sides, about 5 minutes per batch. Add the onion slices and sauté, stirring, until they are softened, 2–3 minutes. Add the tomatoes with the purée, the vinegar, brown sugar, cinnamon, ginger, and bay leaf and stir well. Bring to a simmer, reduce the heat to medium-low, cover, and simmer gently for 30 minutes.

Add the carrots and potatoes and continue to simmer gently until the meat and vegetables are tender, about 1 hour longer. Discard the bay leaf and season to taste with salt and pepper.

To serve, transfer the meat to a cutting board. Cut across the grain into thick slices. Place the slices in warmed bowls and spoon the vegetable mixture over the top.

Serves 4

2 tablespoons olive oil

1½ lb (750 g) beef bottom round

1 large sweet white onion, cut in half and then into slices ½ inch (12 mm) thick

1 can (28 oz/875 g) whole plum (Roma) tomatoes in purée

1 tablespoon red wine vinegar

2 tablespoons firmly packed golden brown sugar

1 teaspoon ground cinnamon

½ teaspoon ground ginger

1 bay leaf

4 large carrots, peeled and cut into 1-inch (2.5-cm) pieces

4 white boiling potatoes, peeled and cut into 1-inch (2.5-cm) cubes

Salt and freshly ground pepper

Beef Stew in a Pumpkin

A sugar pumpkin, a mildly sweet pumpkin variety, provides a beautiful as well as interesting serving container for this chunky stew. Bourbon, an American whiskey, adds a touch of sweet, smoky flavor.

Preheat the oven to 350°F (180°C).

Cut a circle 4 inches (10 cm) in diameter around the stem of the pumpkin and lift it off. Discard the pumpkin top or set it aside to use as a lid. Scoop out and discard all of the seeds. Line the bottom and sides of a shallow baking pan with aluminum foil and spray it with vegetable-oil cooking spray or coat with vegetable oil. Place the pumpkin in the baking pan and set aside.

In a Dutch oven over medium-high heat, heat the olive oil. Working in batches if necessary, add the beef cubes and brown well on all sides, about 5 minutes per batch. Using a slotted spoon, transfer the beef to a dish. Pour the stock into the pot and, using a large spoon, deglaze the pot over medium-high heat by stirring with a wooden spoon to dislodge any browned bits from the bottom. Pour the liquid over the beef, then wipe the pot clean.

In the same pot over medium heat, melt the butter. Add the onions and parsnips and sauté, stirring, until the onions are lightly browned, about 15 minutes.

Return the beef and liquid to the pot and add the cinnamon, nutmeg, and bourbon. Mix well and then carefully spoon the beef mixture into the pumpkin. Sprinkle the brown sugar over the top. Bake until the pumpkin is soft when pierced with a fork and the meat is tender, 2–2 1/2 hours. About 45 minutes before the stew is done, place the pumpkin lid, if using, in the baking pan and bake until tender, about 45 minutes. Season the stew to taste with salt and pepper and top with the pumpkin lid, if using.

Spoon into warmed bowls at the table and serve immediately.

Serves 4

1 sugar pumpkin, about 5 lb (2.5 kg)

1 tablespoon olive oil

1 lb (500 g) beef top round, trimmed of fat and cut into 1/2-inch (12-mm) cubes

1 3/4 cups (14 fl oz/440 ml) Beef Stock (page 314)

1 tablespoon unsalted butter

3 yellow onions, cut in half and then into slices 1/2 inch (12 mm) thick

3 small parsnips, peeled and coarsely chopped

1/2 teaspoon ground cinnamon

1/4 teaspoon freshly grated nutmeg

1/4 cup (2 fl oz/60 ml) bourbon or other whiskey

2 tablespoons firmly packed brown sugar

Salt and freshly ground pepper

Corned Beef

Serve this classic dish with hot mustard and boiled new potatoes. Traditionalists may add thick wedges of green cabbage to the pot during the last 15 minutes of cooking. Any leftover beef makes great sandwiches.

1 corned beef brisket, 4–5 lb (2–2.5 kg)

3 qt (3 l) boiling water

2 yellow onions, each stuck with 3 whole cloves

2 carrots, peeled

2 bay leaves

3 fresh flat-leaf (Italian) parsley sprigs

12 peppercorns, crushed

12 coriander seeds

1 cinnamon stick, about 1 inch (2.5 cm) long

Put the corned beef in a Dutch oven and add cold water to cover. Bring to a boil, reduce the heat to low, cover, and simmer for 1 hour. Pour off the water.

Add the boiling water, onions, and carrots. Bring to a boil and skim off any scum from the surface. Add all the bay leaves, parsley, peppercorns, coriander, and cinnamon stick. Reduce the heat to low, cover, and simmer until tender, 2–4 hours. After 2 hours, occasionally test the beef with a skewer for doneness. When the meat can be pierced easily, it is ready.

Drain the meat. Discard the other solids. Place the beef on a platter and let stand for about 10 minutes. Slice across the grain and serve.

Serves 6

Braised Brisket of Beef

Brisket is one of the best cuts of beef to use for pot roast because the meat is marbled with fat and remains tender and moist during long, slow cooking. Carrots and mushrooms make fine accompaniments.

1 beef brisket, 3–4 lb (1.5–2 kg)

2 teaspoons sweet Hungarian paprika

Salt and freshly ground pepper

4 tablespoons (2 oz/60 g) unsalted butter

4 large yellow onions, diced

2 cups (16 fl oz/500 ml) canned tomato purée

8 large carrots, peeled and cut into 3-inch (7.5-cm) lengths (optional)

1 lb (500 g) fresh white or cremini mushrooms, brushed clean, cut into quarters if large (optional)

Pat the brisket dry with paper towels. Rub the brisket on both sides with the paprika, $1/2$ teaspoon salt, and 1 teaspoon pepper.

In a large, heavy frying pan over high heat, melt 2 tablespoons of the butter. Add the brisket and brown on both sides, about 15 minutes. Set aside.

In a Dutch oven over medium heat, melt the remaining 2 tablespoons butter. Add the onions and cook, stirring, until soft and golden, about 15–20 minutes. Place the brisket on top of the onions and cover the pot. Reduce the heat to low and simmer for $1^{1}/2$ hours. The meat will give off quite a bit of liquid.

Add the tomato purée, cover, and continue to simmer until the meat is tender, about 1 hour longer. If desired, add the carrot and mushrooms during the last 30 minutes of cooking.

Transfer the meat to a platter and let stand for about 10 minutes. If you have added the carrots and mushrooms, transfer them with a slotted spoon to a serving bowl or the platter. Taste the pan juices, adjust the seasoning, and pour into a bowl. Slice the brisket crosswise and serve with the vegetables and pan juices.

Serves 6

Kansas City Beef Brisket

Brisket of beef, a flavorful but none-too-tender cut, is a perfect choice for slow roasting in a covered grill. Here it is prepared Kansas City–style, with plenty of spices and barbecue sauce.

Soak 3 handfuls (about 5 oz/155 g) hickory chips in water to cover for about 1 hour.

Prepare a fire for indirect-heat cooking in a charcoal grill with a cover (page 326), or preheat a gas grill to low.

In a small cup or bowl, stir together the paprika, 1 1/2 teaspoons salt, 1/2 teaspoon black pepper, and the cayenne pepper. Pat the brisket dry with paper towels. Rub the entire surface of the brisket with the olive oil, then rub the paprika mixture over the meat.

Scoop half of the soaked wood chips out of the water and sprinkle them on the fire. If using a gas grill, place the chips in an aluminum packet, poke holes in the bottom, and place on top of the lava rocks. Place the brisket on the grill rack over indirect heat, cover the grill, and open the vents slightly less than halfway, or enough to maintain slow, steady heat. Cook for 1 hour. Turn the brisket, scoop the remaining wood chips from the water, and drop them onto the fire. Replenish the charcoal fire with fresh coals. Cook for 1 hour longer. Brush the meat lightly with the barbecue sauce, then turn the brisket and cook, repeating 2 or 3 times, until the brisket is well browned and has formed a crust on the outside, about 3 1/2 hours total. Add fresh coals to the charcoal fire every hour or so.

Remove the meat from the grill and let rest for 10 minutes. To serve, carve into thin slices across the grain; the slices will likely crumble a little. Alternatively, pull the meat apart with 2 forks. Arrange the meat on a warmed platter and spoon some of the barbecue sauce over the top. Pass the remaining sauce at the tabe.

2 teaspoons sweet Hungarian paprika

Salt and freshly ground black pepper

1/2 teaspoon cayenne pepper

1 beef brisket, 4–5 lb (2–2.5 kg), trimmed of excess fat

2 tablespoons olive oil

Double recipe Midwestern Barbecue Sauce (page 17)

Sweet-and-Sour Brisket

This mouthwatering dish can be simmered on top of the stove. It can be made up to 3 days in advance and refrigerated. Make sure you buy a first-cut brisket, which is less fatty than other cuts.

Pat the brisket dry with paper towels. In a large Dutch oven over medium-high heat, place the brisket, fat side down. Brown, turning once, until deep brown on both sides, about 6 minutes per side. Pour off the fat from the pot.

Cut the onions in half lengthwise, then crosswise into slices about $1/2$ inch (12 mm) thick. Add the onions, celery, chili sauce, brown sugar, mustard, vinegar, soy sauce, molasses, paprika, and beer to the pot. Stir well and bring to a simmer. Reduce the heat to medium-low, cover, and simmer gently for 3 hours.

Using a large spoon, skim off as much fat as possible from the top of the stew. Add the potatoes, carrots, and cabbage and return to a simmer. Simmer the stew gently, uncovered, over medium-low heat until the brisket falls apart easily when tested with a fork and the vegetables are tender, about 1 hour.

To serve, transfer the brisket to a cutting board and cut across the grain into slices $1/2$ inch (12 mm) thick. Stir the caraway seeds into the cabbage mixture. Spoon the cabbage onto a warmed platter. Place the meat slices on the cabbage and arrange the vegetables alongside. Spoon any remaining pan juices over the top.

Serves 8

1 beef brisket, 5–6 lb (2.5–3 kg)

2 large sweet white onions

4 celery stalks, cut into slices $1/2$ inch (12 mm) thick

1 cup (8 fl oz/250 ml) chili sauce

$1/2$ cup ($3^1/2$ oz/105 g) firmly packed golden brown sugar

$1/3$ cup (3 oz/90 g) Dijon mustard

$1/4$ cup (2 fl oz/60 ml) red wine vinegar

$1/4$ cup (2 fl oz/60 ml) soy sauce

3 tablespoons light molasses

$1/2$ teaspoon sweet Hungarian paprika

1 can (12 fl oz/375 ml) beer

4 white boiling potatoes, peeled and thickly sliced

4 carrots, peeled and cut into 1-inch (2.5-cm) pieces

1 small head green cabbage, cored and tough outer leaves removed, cut into slices 1 inch (2.5 cm) thick

1 tablespoon caraway seeds

Sesame Flank Steak

Because flank steaks are thin, the flavor of the sesame marinade will permeate
them thoroughly, producing a wonderfully aromatic result. Grilled baby bok choy
and yellow bell peppers (capsicums) are good accompaniments.

FOR THE MARINADE:

1/4 cup (2 fl oz/60 ml)
olive oil

1/4 cup (2 fl oz/60 ml) Asian
sesame oil

1/4 cup (2 fl oz/60 ml) soy
sauce

2 tablespoons fresh lemon
juice

2 tablespoons peeled and
grated fresh ginger

1 flank steak, about 1 1/2 lb
(750 g)

To make the marinade, in a small bowl, whisk together the olive oil, sesame oil, soy
sauce, lemon juice, and ginger. Reserve 1/4 cup (2 fl oz/60 ml) of the marinade. Put
the steak in a shallow nonaluminum dish large enough for it to lie flat. Pour the
remaining marinade over the steak and turn to coat evenly. Cover and refrigerate,
turning the meat often, for at least 3 hours, or all day if you wish.

Prepare a fire in a charcoal grill, or preheat a gas grill or broiler (grill).

Remove the steak from the marinade and pat it dry with paper towels. Place the
steak on the grill rack or broiler (grill) pan. Grill or broil 4–6 inches (10–15 cm)
from the heat source, brushing with the reserved marinade and turning at least
2 or 3 times, about 12 minutes for medium-rare.

Remove the steak from the grill and transfer to a cutting board. Let rest for about
3 minutes. To serve, cut into thin crosswise slices on the diagonal. Arrange the
slices on a warmed platter and serve at once.

Serves 4

Beef with Orange-Chile Sauce

This dish can be quite spicy. Be sure to warn your guests not to eat the chiles, as they are very hot. Serve with Steamed White Rice (page 317) or any other variation such as Vegetable Fried Rice (page 317), if you like.

In a small bowl, combine the stock, soy sauce, orange zest, and cornstarch and stir to dissolve the cornstarch. Set aside.

In a wok or large frying pan over medium-high heat, heat 1 tablespoon of the oil. Add the dried chiles and stir-fry until they turn dark red, about 1 minute. Watch carefully so they do not burn. Transfer to a bowl and set aside.

Raise the heat to high and add another 1 tablespoon oil to the pan, swirling to coat the bottom and sides. When the oil is almost smoking, add the carrot and bell pepper and stir-fry until they begin to soften, about 2 minutes. Add to the bowl holding the chiles.

Add another 1 tablespoon oil to the pan, again swirling to coat. When it is almost smoking, add half of the beef strips and stir-fry until browned but still slightly pink inside, 2–3 minutes. Be sure to distribute the meat evenly in the pan so it comes into maximum contact with the heat and cooks evenly. Add to the bowl holding the vegetables. Add the remaining 1 tablespoon oil to the pan and cook the rest of meat in the same manner.

Return the vegetables and meat to the pan. Quickly stir the reserved sauce and add it to the pan. Stir-fry over medium-high heat until the sauce begins to thicken, about 2 minutes. Stir in the orange segments and green onions and serve.

Serves 4

1/3 cup (3 fl oz/80 ml) Chinese Style Chicken Stock (page 315)

2 tablespoons soy sauce

Finely grated zest of 1 orange

2 teaspoons cornstarch (cornflour)

4 tablespoons (2 fl oz/60 ml) peanut oil

12 small dried red chiles

1 carrot, peeled and cut into thin strips 2 inches (5 cm) long and 1/2 inch (12 mm) wide

1/2 small red bell pepper (capsicum), seeded, deribbed, and cut into strips 2 inches (5 cm) long and 1/2 inch (12 mm) wide

1 lb (500 g) flank steak, sliced in half horizontally and then cut into thin strips about 2 inches (5 cm) long and 3/4 inch (2 cm) wide

1 orange, peeled with all white pith removed, then divided into segments and each segment cut in half crosswise

3 green (spring) onions, including tender green tops, thinly sliced

Beef, Asparagus, and Red Bell Peppers

Tender flank steak is accented with green asparagus and red bell peppers, all bound together in a simple soy-and-ginger sauce. You can substitute turkey breast meat for the beef, if you prefer. Serve with Steamed White Rice (page 317).

3 tablespoons peanut oil

¹/₂ lb (250 g) asparagus, trimmed, cut on the diagonal into 1¹/₂-inch (4-cm) lengths, parboiled for 2 minutes, drained, rinsed in cold water, and drained again

1 lb (500 g) flank steak, sliced in half horizontally and then cut into thin strips 2 inches (5 cm) long and ¹/₄ inch (6 mm) wide

1 red bell pepper (capsicum), seeded, deribbed, and cut into strips about 2 inches (5 cm) long and ¹/₄ inch (6 mm) wide

2 teaspoons cornstarch (cornflour) dissolved in 3 tablespoons water

All-Purpose Stir-Fry Sauce (page 17)

In a wok or large frying pan over high heat, heat 1 tablespoon of the oil, swirling to coat the bottom and sides of the pan. When the oil is almost smoking, add the asparagus and stir-fry until lightly browned, about 2 minutes. Transfer to a dish.

Add another 1 tablespoon oil to the pan over high heat, again swirling to coat the pan. When the oil is almost smoking, add half of the beef strips and stir-fry until lightly browned but still slightly pink inside, 2–3 minutes. Be sure to distribute the meat evenly in the pan so it comes into maximum contact with the heat and cooks evenly. Transfer to a bowl. Add the remaining 1 tablespoon oil to the pan and cook the remaining beef in the same manner.

Return the first batch of beef to the pan and add the bell pepper. Stir-fry over high heat until the bell pepper begins to soften, 1–2 minutes. Quickly stir in the cornstarch mixture along with the sauce. Stir-fry until the sauce thickens, 1–2 minutes. Return the asparagus to the pan, toss to coat evenly with the sauce, and serve.

Serves 4

Ginger Beef Stir-Fry

This Asian-inspired dish is fast, easy, and economical. The oil used to cook the beef is poured off, so the finished dish is not oily at all. Serve with Steamed White Rice (page 317).

1 lb (500 g) flank steak, cut across the grain into slices about 2½ inches (6 cm) long and ⅛ inch (3 mm) thick

1 tablespoon soy sauce

1 tablespoon Asian sesame oil

1 tablespoon cornstarch (cornflour)

¼ lb (125 g) fresh ginger, peeled and cut into matchstick strips

1 teaspoon salt

1 cup (8 fl oz/250 ml) peanut oil

1 lb (500 g) asparagus, trimmed and cut on the diagonal into slices ¼ inch (6 mm) thick (optional)

3 tablespoons water, if using asparagus

1 clove garlic, minced (optional)

3 tablespoons sherry or rice wine

1 teaspoon sugar

Put the flank steak slices in a bowl and add the soy sauce, sesame oil, and cornstarch. Mix well and let stand at room temperature for about 30 minutes.

In a separate bowl, toss together the ginger strips and salt. Let stand until the ginger softens, about 20 minutes. Rinse and pat dry with paper towels.

In a wok or large sauté pan over high heat, heat the peanut oil. Add the beef and stir-fry until the beef changes color, 1–2 minutes. Transfer to a plate.

Pour off all but 3 tablespoons of the oil and heat in the wok or sauté pan over high heat. If using the asparagus, add the slices and the water and stir-fry until the water evaporates and the asparagus is almost cooked, about 2 minutes. Add the reserved ginger, garlic (if using), beef, sherry, and sugar. Stir-fry until the beef is heated through, 1–2 minutes. Serve at once.

Serves 4

Beef with Caramelized Onions and Red Bell Pepper

This dish works well when served on its own with a green vegetable or on top of a bed of Steamed White Rice (page 317). For a touch of citrus flavor, add 1 teaspoon grated orange zest with the vinegar and sugar.

In a nonaluminum bowl, combine the sherry, soy sauce, and 2 teaspoons cornstarch and stir well. Add the beef strips, toss to coat, and let stand at room temperature for 15 minutes.

In a wok or large frying pan over medium-high heat, heat 1 tablespoon of the oil, swirling to coat the bottom and sides of the pan. Add half of the beef strips and stir-fry until browned but still slightly pink inside, 2–3 minutes. Be sure to distribute the meat evenly in the pan so that it comes into maximum contact with the heat and cooks evenly. Transfer to a bowl. Add another 1 tablespoon oil to the pan, if needed, and cook the remaining beef in the same manner. Transfer to the bowl.

Add the remaining 2 tablespoons oil to the pan over medium-high heat, again swirling to coat the pan. When the oil is hot, add the onion and stir-fry until softened, 5–7 minutes. Be sure to distribute the onion evenly in the pan so that it comes into maximum contact with the heat and cooks evenly. Add the bell pepper and stir-fry until it begins to soften, 2 minutes longer.

Add the vinegar and sugar and stir-fry until the onion begins to caramelize, about 2 minutes longer. Add the stock, bring to a boil over high heat, and cook for 2 minutes. If you want a thicker sauce, add the optional cornstarch mixture.

Return the beef to the pan and stir-fry until heated through, about 30 seconds. Taste and adjust the seasoning. Serve immediately.

Serves 4

1 tablespoon dry sherry

1 tablespoon soy sauce

2 teaspoons cornstarch (cornflour)

1 lb (500 g) flank steak, sliced in half horizontally and then cut into thin strips about 2 inches (5 cm) long and 3/4 inch (2 cm) wide

4 tablespoons (2 fl oz/60 ml) peanut oil

1 large yellow onion, thinly sliced

1 red bell pepper (capsicum), seeded, deribbed, and thinly sliced

2 tablespoons balsamic vinegar

1 teaspoon sugar

1/2 cup (4 fl oz/125 ml) Beef Stock (page 314)

1 teaspoon cornstarch (cornflour) dissolved in 3 tablespoons water (optional)

Spicy Beef Salad

This refreshing Asian-inspired salad is substantial enough to serve as a main course. Those who like their food spicy should be generous with the chili oil. Garnish with cherry tomato halves, if you like.

To make the dressing, in a small bowl, whisk together the mustard, soy sauce, vinegar, and salt and pepper to taste. Gradually whisk in the olive oil until blended.

In a large bowl, combine the sherry and beef strips, tossing to coat evenly. Let stand at room temperature for 15 minutes.

Tear the escarole and spinach into bite-sized pieces. Place in a large bowl, add the dressing, and toss until evenly coated. Divide the greens evenly among 6 dinner plates and set aside.

In a wok or large frying pan over high heat, heat 2 tablespoons of the peanut oil, swirling to coat the sides of the pan. When it is almost smoking, add the onions and ginger and stir-fry until the onions just begin to soften, 2–3 minutes. Add the garlic and stir-fry for 30 seconds longer. Transfer to a bowl.

Add another 1 tablespoon oil to the pan over high heat, again swirling to coat the pan. When the oil is almost smoking, add half of the beef strips and stir-fry until tender but still pink inside, 2–3 minutes. Be sure to distribute the beef evenly in the pan so it comes into maximum contact with the heat and cooks evenly. Transfer to the bowl holding the onion mixture. Repeat with the remaining beef.

Add the corn kernels and soy sauce to the pan over medium-high heat and stir-fry until the corn is just tender, 1–2 minutes. Return the beef mixture to the pan and stir-fry to heat through, about 30 seconds.

Spoon the mixture on top of the greens, dividing evenly among individual plates. Drizzle with the chili oil and serve.

Serves 6

FOR THE DRESSING:

1 tablespoon Dijon mustard

2 teaspoons soy sauce

3 tablespoons rice vinegar

Salt and freshly ground pepper

1/3 cup (3 fl oz/80 ml) olive oil

1 tablespoon dry sherry

1 lb (500 g) flank steak, sliced in half horizontally and then cut into thin strips about 2 inches (5 cm) long and 1/2 inch (12 mm) wide

1 head escarole, cored

1 bunch spinach, stemmed, well washed and dried

4 tablespoons (2 fl oz/60 ml) peanut oil

2 red onions, finely chopped

1 tablespoon peeled and minced fresh ginger

2 cloves garlic, minced

1/2 cup (3 oz/90 g) corn kernels (about 1 ear)

1 tablespoon soy sauce

1/2–1 teaspoon Chili Oil (page 17)

Latin American Grilled Steak with Avocado Salsa

This simple onion and citrus marinade accents the beefiness of the steak. Serve with black beans and tortillas, corn on the cob, or roasted potatoes topped with sour cream, chopped roasted chiles, tomatoes, and green (spring) onions.

2 lb (1 kg) flank steak, or 4 rib-eye steaks, about 1/2 lb (250 g) each

1 yellow onion

2 cloves garlic, finely minced

2 teaspoons *each* ground cumin and black pepper

1/2 cup (4 fl oz/125 ml) fresh lemon juice

FOR THE AVOCADO SALSA:

2 avocados

4 plum (Roma) tomatoes

1 teaspoon *each* jalapeño chile and garlic, minced

1/4 cup (2 oz/60 g) finely chopped green bell pepper (capiscum)

3 tablespoons finely minced red onion

2 tablespoons red wine vinegar or fresh lemon juice

2 tablespoons minced fresh cilantro (fresh coriander)

1/2 cup (4 fl oz/125 ml) olive oil

Salt and freshly ground pepper

Olive oil for brushing

Put the steak(s) in a shallow nonaluminum dish. Coarsely chop the yellow onion. In a blender or food processor, combine the onion, garlic, cumin, pepper, and lemon juice. Pulse a few times to chop. Pour over the steak(s), cover, and let stand at room temperature for at least 1 hour.

Meanwhile, prepare the salsa: Peel and pit the avocados, cut into 1/2-inch (12-mm) chunks, and place in a bowl. Peel and seed the tomatoes, cut into 1/2-inch (12-mm) chunks, and add to the bowl with the avocados. Add the jalapeño, garlic, bell pepper, red onion, vinegar, cilantro, olive oil, and salt and pepper to taste and mix well. Set aside at room temperature.

Prepare a fire in a charcoal grill, or preheat a gas grill or broiler (grill). Remove the steak(s) from the marinade. Brush lightly with oil and sprinkle with salt. Place on the grill rack or on a broiler (grill) pan. Grill or broil 4–6 inches (10–15 cm) from the heat source for about 4 minutes on each side for medium-rare. If using flank steak, slice crosswise on the diagonal. Serve at once and pass the salsa at the table.

Serves 4

Peppery Flank Steak

The delicious flavor of the marinade penetrates this thin, flank steak completely. Serve this peppery beef rare, with grilled green onions and tomatoes, and baked potatoes.

FOR THE MARINADE:

Grated zest of 1 lime

2 tablespoons fresh lime juice

2 cloves garlic, minced

1/2 teaspoon Chili Oil (page 17)

1/4 cup (2 fl oz/60 ml) olive oil

1 teaspoon red pepper flakes

1/2 cup (4 fl oz/125 ml) dry red wine

2 tablespoons soy sauce

1 tablespoon sugar

11/2 lb (750 g) flank steak

To make the marinade, in a small bowl, stir together all the lime zest and juice, garlic, chili oil, olive oil, red pepper flakes, wine, soy sauce, and sugar. Reserve $1/4$ cup (2 fl oz/60 ml) of the marinade. Put the meat in a shallow nonaluminum bowl. Pour the remaining marinade over the steak, cover with plastic wrap, and marinate in the refrigerator for at least 2 hours or up to all day, turning the meat occasionally in the marinade.

Prepare a fire in a charcoal grill, or preheat a gas grill or broiler (grill). Remove the steak from the marinade and pat it dry with paper towels. Place the steak on the grill rack or on a broiler (grill) pan. Grill or broil 4–6 inches (10–15 cm) from the heat source for 10–12 minutes, turning once and brushing 2 or 3 times with the reserved marinade; the meat should be on the rare side.

Cut the steak crosswise and on the diagonal into thin slices. Serve at once.

Serves 4

Red Wine–Marinated Fillets

Pan-broiling is a simple technique for cooking meat or fish in a heavy frying pan with little or no oil or butter. A cast-iron pan works best. Serve with scalloped potatoes and grilled mushrooms.

To make the marinade, pour the wine into a small saucepan and bring to a simmer over medium heat. Add the bay leaf, peppercorns, garlic, cloves, allspice, thyme, and orange zest and simmer for 15 minutes. Remove from the heat and let cool.

Place the beef in a shallow nonaluminum bowl and pour the marinade over the top. Cover and marinate at room temperature for up to 4 hours, or in the refrigerator for as long as overnight.

Meanwhile, pour the stock into a small saucepan, bring to a boil, and cook until reduced by half, about 20 minutes. Remove from the heat and set aside.

Preheat a broiler (grill). Remove the beef from the marinade, reserving the marinade. Pat dry with paper towels and sprinkle with a little salt. Heat a heavy flameproof frying pan over high heat. Add the beef and broil 4–6 inches (10–15 cm) from the heat source, turning the meat once, about 3 minutes on each side for rare. Remove the beef from the pan and keep warm.

Pour 1 cup (8 fl oz/250 ml) of the marinade into the frying pan over high heat and deglaze by stirring with a wooden spoon to dislodge any browned bits from the bottom. Boil until reduced by half. Add the reduced beef stock and boil to reduce again by half. Swirl in the butter to smooth out the sauce and thicken it a bit. Spoon over the beef and serve.

Serves 4

FOR THE MARINADE:

2 cups (16 fl oz/500 ml) dry red wine

1 bay leaf

6 peppercorns, lightly crushed

2 cloves garlic, smashed

2 whole cloves

1 whole allspice, lightly crushed

2 fresh thyme sprigs

2 strips orange zest, each about 3 inches (7.5 cm) long

4 slices beef fillet, each about 1/2 lb (250 g) and 1 1/2 inches (4 cm) thick

1 cup (8 fl oz/250 ml) Beef Stock (page 314)

Kosher salt

2 tablespoons unsalted butter

Beef Stroganoff

In this version of the classic Stroganoff, the beef fillet medallions are quickly seared and the sauce is spooned on top. Serve with kasha, fried potatoes, or potato pancakes.

8 slices beef fillet, each about ¹/₂ inch (12 mm) thick

Salt and freshly ground pepper

6 tablespoons (3 oz/90 g) unsalted butter

2 cups (7 oz/220 g) sliced yellow onions

1 tablespoon sweet Hungarian paprika

2 tablespoons canned tomato purée

5 cups (1 lb/500 g) sliced fresh white or cremini mushrooms

1 cup (8 fl oz/ 250 ml) Beef Stock (page 314)

1 tablespoon olive oil

1 cup (8 oz/250 g) sour cream, at room temperature

Minced fresh flat-leaf (Italian) parsley or dill for garnish (optional)

Place the fillet slices between 2 sheets of plastic wrap and pound gently with a meat pounder until they are about ¹/₄ inch (6 mm) thick. Season lightly with pepper and set aside.

In a large sauté pan over medium heat, melt 2 tablespoons of the butter. Add the onions and sauté until tender, about 10 minutes. Stir in the paprika and tomato purée and cook 1 minute longer. Transfer to a bowl and set aside.

In the same sauté pan over high heat, melt 3 tablespoons of the butter. Add the mushrooms and sauté just until barely tender, 1–2 minutes. Return the onion mixture to the pan, pour in the stock, and bring to a simmer. Season to taste with salt and pepper. Remove from the heat and keep warm.

In a heavy frying pan over high heat, melt the remaining 1 tablespoon butter with the olive oil. Add the fillet slices and sear, turning once, about 2 minutes on each side for medium-rare.

Divide the fillet slices among individual plates. Swirl the sour cream into the warm mushroom sauce. Taste and adjust the seasoning and spoon over the cooked fillets. Sprinkle with the parsley, if desired.

Serves 4

Steak au Poivre

Pepper and steak have a natural affinity. This well-loved classic never goes out of style. Serve it with shoestring potatoes or French fries and green beans or carrots.

Spread the peppercorns on a plate or cutting board. Press the fillet slices into the cracked peppercorns, turning to coat both sides. Push the peppercorns into the meat with the heel of your hand. Let stand at room temperature for 30 minutes.

Sprinkle the fillets with salt. In a large, heavy sauté pan, melt the butter with the olive oil over high heat. When the butter foam begins to subside, add the fillets. Sear, turning once, for 3 minutes on each side for rare. Transfer to a warmed platter and keep warm.

Pour off the excess fat from the pan and place over high heat. Pour in the Cognac and deglaze the pan, stirring with a wooden spoon to dislodge any browned bits from the bottom. Add the stock, the mustard (if using), and the cream and cook to reduce by half. Pour over the fillets. Serve at once.

Serves 4

5 tablespoons coarsely cracked peppercorns

4 slices beef fillet, each about 1/2 lb (250 g) and about 1 1/2 inches (4 cm) thick

Salt

1/4 cup (2 oz/60 g) unsalted butter

1 tablespoon olive oil

1/2 cup (4 fl oz/125 ml) Cognac or Armagnac

1/2 cup (4 fl oz/125 ml) Beef Stock (page 314)

2 tablespoons Dijon mustard (optional)

1 cup (8 fl oz/250 ml) heavy (double) cream

Beef Kabobs with Pineapple Relish

The marinade used for these kabobs recalls the Indonesian dish satay, except cubes of beef, rather than thin strips, are used here. Serve with Steamed White Rice (page 317).

1½ lb (750 g) beef fillet or sirloin, cut into 1-inch (2.5-cm) cubes

¼ cup (2 oz/60 g) grated yellow onion

1 tablespoon minced garlic

2 tablespoons ground coriander

1 tablespoon ground caraway

2 teaspoons curry powder

½ cup (4 fl oz/125 ml) coconut milk

2 tablespoons soy sauce

2 tablespoons lemon juice

FOR THE PINEAPPLE RELISH:

1 small pineapple

1 tablespoon peanut oil

1 yellow onion, thinly sliced

2 red chiles, minced

¼ cup (2 oz/60 g) firmly packed golden brown sugar

1 teaspoon ground cinnamon

Grated zest and juice of 1 lemon

Put the beef in a shallow nonaluminum bowl. In a small bowl, stir together the grated onion, garlic, coriander, caraway, curry powder, coconut milk, soy sauce, and 2 tablespoons lemon juice. Pour over the beef and toss to coat on all sides. Let stand at room temperature for about 1–2 hours.

Meanwhile, prepare the relish: Peel and core the pineapple. Cut into 1-inch (2.5-cm) cubes. Set aside. In a sauté pan over low heat, heat the oil. Add the onion and chiles and sauté until the onion softens, 5 minutes. Add the pineapple, brown sugar, cinnamon, and lemon zest and juice and cook over medium heat until the pineapple is tender and translucent, about 10 minutes. Remove from the heat, let cool, and chill before serving.

Prepare a fire in a charcoal grill, or preheat a gas grill or broiler (grill). Thread the beef onto skewers. Arrange the skewers on the grill rack or on a broiler (grill) pan. Grill or broil 4–6 inches (10–15 cm) from the heat source, turning to cook the meat evenly on all sides, 7–8 minutes for medium-rare. Serve the kabobs with the pineapple relish on the side.

Serves 4

Pot-Roasted Top Sirloin

To ensure a succulent finish, pot-roasted beef must be cooked at a low, gentle simmer, as boiling will toughen the meat. A heavy Dutch oven is the best vessel to use for this dish.

In a small bowl, combine the wine, orange zest, onion, garlic, 1 teaspoon salt, the peppercorns, cloves, and thyme. Stir well and set aside.

Rub flour over the roast. In a Dutch oven, melt the butter with the oil. Add the roast and brown evenly on all sides, about 10 minutes.

Remove the roast from the pot and pour off all but a light film of fat. Heat the pot over high heat. Pour in the wine mixture and deglaze the pot by stirring with a wooden spoon to scrape up any browned bits from the bottom of the pot. Return the meat to the pot and turn to coat with the liquid. Bring to a boil, reduce the heat to low, cover, and simmer gently until tender, about 1 1/2 hours.

Transfer the meat to a platter and cover to keep warm. Strain the pan juices through a fine-mesh sieve into a small bowl. Spoon off the fat and discard. Reheat the juices and pour into a serving bowl. Slice the meat crosswise and arrange on the platter. Pass the pan juices at the table.

Serves 10

1/2 cup (4 fl oz/125 ml) dry red wine

3 strips orange zest, each about 3 inches (7.5 cm) long and 1 inch (2.5 cm) wide

1 small yellow onion, sliced

2 cloves garlic, halved

Salt

6 peppercorns

2 whole cloves

1/2 teaspoon dried thyme

All-purpose (plain) flour for rubbing

1 top sirloin beef roast, about 5 lb (2.5 kg)

2 tablespoons unsalted butter

1 tablespoon olive oil

Sauerbraten

Rich and savory, this German sweet-and-sour pot roast is best served with braised red cabbage, potato pancakes, and applesauce or sautéed apple slices. Plan ahead: The meat must marinate for 2–3 days.

2 teaspoons dry mustard

1 teaspoon salt

1/2 teaspoon freshly ground pepper

1/2 teaspoon ground cloves

3 tablespoons firmly packed golden brown sugar

3 tablespoons red wine vinegar

2 cups (16 fl oz/500 ml) dry red wine

2 cups (16 fl oz/500 ml) Beef Stock (page 314)

1/4 cup (2 fl oz/60 ml) canned tomato purée

1 teaspoon Worcestershire sauce

8 gingersnaps, crushed, plus more if needed to thicken pan juices

2 yellow onions, thinly sliced

3 cloves garlic, minced

1 top round (rump) roast, 3–4 lb (1.5–2 kg)

1 cup (6 oz/185 g) raisins (optional)

In a large, nonaluminum bowl, combine the mustard, salt, pepper, cloves, and brown sugar. Whisk in the vinegar and wine until blended. Add the stock, tomato purée, Worcestershire sauce, 8 gingersnaps, onions, and garlic. Mix well, add the beef, and turn to coat. Cover and refrigerate for 2–3 days, turning the beef often.

Place the beef and all of the marinade in a Dutch oven. Bring to a boil, reduce the heat to low, cover, and simmer until the meat is tender, about 2 1/2 hours. Add the raisins, if using, during the last 30 minutes.

Transfer the beef to a platter, tent with aluminum foil, and let stand for 10 minutes. If the pan juices are thin, crumble in a few more gingersnaps and cook over high heat to reduce. Taste and adjust the seasoning. Pour the juices into a bowl and serve alongside the beef. Slice the beef crosswise and serve hot.

Serves 6

Steak Sandwiches with Chive Butter

These delectable open-face sandwiches are topped with a pat of chive butter that melts slowly over the steak, forming an instant herb sauce. Watercress provides a crisp, peppery counterpoint to the rich flavors.

To make the chive butter, in a small bowl, combine the butter, chives, lemon juice, salt, and pepper. Using a wooden spoon, beat vigorously until blended. Transfer to a sheet of plastic wrap and shape into a log about 2 inches (5 cm) long and 1 inch (2.5 cm) in diameter. Wrap in the plastic wrap and refrigerate until firm, about 1 hour, or refrigerate for up to 3 days.

Prepare a fire in a charcoal grill, or preheat a gas grill or broiler (grill).

Sprinkle the steaks lightly with salt and pepper. Place the steaks on the grill rack or broiler (grill) pan. Grill or broil 4–6 inches (10–15 cm) from the heat source, turning every 2 minutes, for a total of about 9 minutes for medium-rare. About 4 minutes before the steaks are done, arrange the bread slices on the rack and grill, turning once, until lightly browned, about 2 minutes on each side.

To serve, transfer the bread slices to individual plates. Divide the watercress among the bread slices and top each with a steak. Cut the chive butter into 4 equal slices and place a slice on each steak. Serve at once.

Serves 4

FOR THE CHIVE BUTTER:

1/4 cup (2 oz/60 g) unsalted butter, at room temperature

2 tablespoons minced fresh chives, or 2 teaspoons dried chives

2 teaspoons fresh lemon juice

1/2 teaspoon salt

1/4 teaspoon freshly ground pepper

4 beef tenderloin steaks, about 6 oz (185 g) each

Salt and freshly ground pepper

4 slices firm-textured white sandwich bread

1–1 1/2 cups (1–1 1/2 oz/30–45 g) watercress, large stems removed

Tenderloin Pepper Steaks

If you like black pepper, you will love this dish. Any tender steak, such as T-bone or New York, may be prepared this way. To coarsely crush peppercorns, place them in a sturdy plastic bag and smash them with the bottom of a heavy saucepan.

4 beef tenderloin steaks,
6–8 oz (185–250 g) each

Salt

4 tablespoons coarsely crushed peppercorns

1/2 recipe Herb Butter or Mustard Butter (page 15)

Sprinkle each steak lightly with salt, then rub about $^{1}/_{2}$ tablespoon coarsely crushed peppercorns into each side, pressing the pepper firmly into the meat.

Prepare a fire in a charcoal grill, or preheat a gas grill or broiler (grill). Place the steaks on the grill rack or on a broiler (grill) pan. Grill or broil about 4–6 inches (10–15 cm) from the heat source, turning every 1 or 2 minutes, for a total cooking time of about 9 minutes for medium-rare. Top each steak with a slice of flavored butter before serving.

Serves 4

Marinated Beef Tenderloin with Tarragon Butter

Tenderloin tends to be more costly than other cuts of beef, but it's the most succulent, with no bone and no waste. Have the butcher trim it for you, and plan ahead so you can marinate it for at least a day.

Prepare the marinade. Place the beef in a large lock-top plastic bag and pour in the marinade. Press out the air and seal the bag tightly. Massage the bag gently to distribute the marinade evenly. Place in a large bowl and refrigerate, turning and massaging the bag occasionally, for several hours, or all day if you prefer.

Meanwhile, in a nonaluminum bowl, combine the butter, tarragon, parsley, lemon juice, $^1/_2$ teaspoon salt, and $^1/_2$ teaspoon pepper. Using a wooden spoon, stir until combined. Shape into a rough log about 4 inches (10 cm) long and 1 inch (2.5 cm) wide, wrap in plastic wrap and chill until firm.

Prepare a fire for indirect-heat cooking in a charcoal grill with a cover (page 326) or preheat a gas grill. Position the grill rack 4–6 inches (10–15) above the heat.

Remove the meat from the marinade and pat it dry with paper towels.

Place the meat over the indirect heat, cover the grill and open the vents halfway. Grill, turning frequently to brown all sides and an instant read thermometer registers 130°F (55°C) for rare or 140°F (60°C) for medium.

Remove the tenderloin from the grill and transfer to a cutting board. Cover loosely with aluminum foil and let rest for 10 minutes. To serve, carve into slices $^3/_4$–1 inch (2–2.5 cm) thick and arrange on a warmed platter or individual plates. Top each serving with a pat of tarragon butter.

Serves 6–8

Red Wine Marinade (page 14)

1 beef tenderloin (fillet), about 4 lb (2 kg) after trimming

$^1/_2$ cup (4 oz/125 g) unsalted butter, at room temperature

2 tablespoons chopped fresh tarragon or 2 teaspoons dried tarragon

2 tablespoons chopped fresh flat-leaf (Italian) parsley

1 tablespoon fresh lemon juice

Salt and freshly ground pepper

Grilled Steak with Balsamic Vinegar and Black Pepper

Flank steak can stand in for sirloin steak in this simple and tasty dish, if you like. Serve with your favorite potato preparation and with broiled mushrooms or radicchio basted with some of the marinade.

Put the steak in a shallow nonaluminum bowl. In a small bowl, stir together the vinegar, olive oil, honey, and 1 tablespoon pepper. Pour over the steak. Let stand at room temperature for 1–2 hours.

Prepare a fire in a charcoal grill, or preheat a gas grill or broiler (grill). Sprinkle the steak lightly with salt. Place the steak on the grill rack or on a broiler (grill) pan. Grill or broil 4–6 inches (10–15 cm) from the heat source for about 4 minutes on each side for medium-rare. Slice and serve at once.

Serves 4

1 sirloin steak, 1 1/2 lb (750 g)

1/3 cup (3 fl oz/80 ml) balsamic vinegar

2 tablespoons olive oil

2 tablespoons honey

Salt and freshly ground pepper

Steak Fajitas

Tuck these flavorful meat strips into flour tortillas that have been wrapped in aluminum foil and warmed briefly on the grill. Offer tomato salsa, guacamole, and sour cream as accompaniments.

FOR THE MARINADE:

1/3 cup (3 fl oz/80 ml) tequila

1/4 cup (2 fl oz/60 ml) fresh lime juice

2 tablespoons olive oil

2 cloves garlic, minced

1/2 teaspoon salt

1/2 teaspoon red pepper flakes

2 lb (1 kg) skirt steak or flank steak

2 red or yellow onions, sliced 1/2 inch (12 mm) thick

3 red or green bell peppers (capsicums), seeded, deribbed, and cut crosswise into rings 1/2 inch (12 mm) thick

Olive oil for brushing

Salt

12 or more flour tortillas, each 8–10 inches (20–25 cm) in diameter, warmed

Fresh cilantro (fresh coriander) sprigs for garnish

To make the marinade, in a bowl, whisk together the tequila, lime juice, olive oil, garlic, salt, and red pepper flakes. Reserve 1/4 cup (2 fl oz/60 ml) of the marinade. Place the meat in a shallow nonaluminum bowl large enough for it to lie flat. Pour the remaining marinade over the steak and turn to coat both sides. Cover and refrigerate, turning the meat occasionally, for at least 3 hours, or all day if you wish.

Prepare a fire in a charcoal grill, or preheat a gas grill or broiler (grill).

Remove the meat from the marinade and pat it dry with paper towels.

Brush the onion slices and bell pepper rings with olive oil and sprinkle with salt. Grill or broil for 3 minutes, then brush with oil, turn, and grill until lightly browned, about 3 minutes longer. Transfer to a warmed platter, separating the onion slices into rings; set aside while you cook the meat.

Place the steak on the grill rack or on a broiler (grill) pan. Grill or broil 4–6 inches (10–15 cm) from the heat source, turning and brushing with the reserved marinade every 2 minutes, until done to your liking, about 9 minutes for medium-rare.

To serve, cut the steak into thin crosswise slices on the diagonal. Mound the steak slices on the platter with the onions and peppers. At the table, place the sliced steak on warm tortillas and garnish with the cilantro sprigs.

Serves 6

Gingered Skirt Steaks

Skirt steak has a rich, beefy flavor, which is accented here with a zesty marinade. Served with grilled onions on a crusty French roll, the steaks make a great sandwich.

To make the marinade, in a small bowl, stir together the wine, soy sauce, ginger, lime zest and juice, garlic, sugar, and Tabasco. Reserve $^1/_4$ cup (2 fl oz/60 ml) of the marinade. Put the meat in a shallow nonaluminum bowl large enough for it to lie flat. Pour the remaining marinade over the steak and turn to coat both sides. Cover tightly and refrigerate, turning the meat occasionally, for at least 3 hours, or all day if you wish.

Prepare a fire in a charcoal grill, or preheat a gas grill or broiler (grill). Remove the meat from the marinade and pat it dry with paper towels. Place the steaks on the grill rack or on a broiler (grill) pan. Grill or broil 4–6 inches (10–15 cm) from the heat source for 6–8 minutes, turning and brushing with the reserved marinade every minute or so. Skirt steak is best served rare and will toughen if overcooked. Divide into 6 pieces and serve.

Serves 6

FOR THE MARINADE:

$^1/_2$ cup (4 fl oz/125 ml) dry red wine

$^1/_3$ cup (3 fl oz/80 ml) soy sauce

2 tablespoons peeled and grated fresh ginger

Grated zest and juice of 1 lime

2 cloves garlic, minced

1 tablespoon sugar

Dash of Tabasco sauce

3 lb (1.5 kg) beef skirt steak, trimmed of fat and silver skin

Grilled Steak with Sauce Poivrade

This traditional French sauce can be made 1 day ahead of time, up to the point where the butter is added. Freshly grated nutmeg can be substituted for the mace, if desired.

1 yellow onion, finely diced

1 carrot, peeled and finely diced

2 cloves garlic, minced

1/2 cup (4 fl oz/125 ml) red wine vinegar

1/2 cup (4 fl oz/125 ml) Beef Stock (page 314)

1 cup (8 fl oz/250 ml) dry red wine

1/4 teaspoon ground mace

1 teaspoon chopped thyme

1 tablespoon freshly ground pepper, plus pepper to taste

Salt

4 rib-eye or New York strip steaks, about 1/2 lb (250 g) each

Olive oil for brushing

6 tablespoons (3 oz/90 g) unsalted butter

Chopped fresh flat-leaf (Italian) parsley for garnish

In a saucepan, combine the onion, carrot, garlic, and vinegar. Place over high heat and cook to reduce the liquid by half, 3–4 minutes. Add the stock, wine, mace, and thyme; boil again until reduced by half. Add the 1 tablespoon pepper and salt to taste and set aside.

Prepare a fire in a charcoal grill, or preheat a gas grill or broiler (grill). Brush the steaks with olive oil and sprinkle lightly with salt and pepper. Place the steaks on the grill rack or on a broiler (grill) pan. Grill or broil 4–6 inches (10–15 cm) from the heat source, 3–4 minutes on each side for medium-rare. Transfer to a platter.

Bring the sauce to a boil, reduce the heat to low, and swirl in the butter. Spoon the sauce over the steaks and top with the parsley.

Serves 4

Beef with Rosemary and Red Potatoes

Rosemary is the special touch that gives this beef stew its distinctive taste. Beef bottom round becomes tender through long cooking, and readily absorbs the other flavors.

In a large Dutch oven over medium-high heat, heat the olive oil. Add the garlic and beef cubes and cook, stirring, until the beef is lightly browned and the garlic is golden but not dark brown, 3–4 minutes.

Pour in the wine and deglaze the pot by stirring with a wooden spoon to dislodge any browned bits from the bottom. Add the stock and stir well.

Add the potatoes and sprinkle with the rosemary. Bring to a simmer. Reduce the heat to medium-low, cover, and simmer gently until the beef and potatoes are tender when pierced with a fork, 25–30 minutes. Season to taste with salt and pepper.

Spoon into warmed bowls and serve.

Serves 4

2 tablespoons olive oil

2 cloves garlic, minced

1½ lb (750 g) beef bottom round, cut into 1-inch (2.5-cm) cubes

½ cup (4 fl oz/125 ml) dry red wine

1 cup (8 fl oz/250 ml) Beef Stock (page 314)

10 unpeeled small red potatoes

2 tablespoons fresh rosemary leaves or 2 teaspoons dried rosemary

Salt and freshly ground pepper

Hamburgers with Grilled Tomatoes

For cheeseburgers, place a slice of Swiss or Cheddar cheese on each patty about 1 minute before removing it from the grill. Serve on toasted sourdough, onion, or Kaiser rolls.

2/3 cup (5 oz/165 g) mayonnaise

1 tablespoon prepared horseradish

2 lb (1 kg) lean ground (minced) beef

2 tablespoons Dijon mustard

2 tablespoons Worcestershire sauce

Salt and freshly ground pepper

3 firm but ripe tomatoes, cut into slices 1/2–3/4 inch (12 mm–2 cm) thick

3–4 tablespoons (about 2 fl oz/60 ml) olive oil

Prepare a fire in a charcoal grill, or preheat a gas grill or broiler (grill).

In a small bowl, stir together the mayonnaise and horseradish. Cover and refrigerate until serving.

In a bowl, combine the beef, mustard, Worcestershire sauce, 1 teaspoon salt, and 2 teaspoons pepper. Using a fork, stir to combine. Divide the meat into 6 equal portions and press each portion into a patty about 3 inches (7.5 cm) in diameter and 1 inch (2.5 cm) thick; don't worry about making them perfectly round.

Place the patties on the grill rack or a broiler (grill) pan. Grill or broil 4–6 inches (10–15 cm) from the heat source, turning every 2 minutes, 9 minutes for medium-rare. About 4 minutes before the burgers are done, brush the tomato slices with some of the olive oil and sprinkle with salt to taste. Grill or broil, oiled side down, for 2 minutes. Brush the tops with olive oil, turn, and grill or broil until the tomatoes are very lightly browned on both sides, about 2 minutes longer.

To serve, transfer the burgers to a warmed platter and place the tomato slices atop and around them. Pass the horseradish mayonnaise at the table.

Serves 6

Bourbon-Marinated Chuck Roast

Marinating the meat in bourbon and spices for at least 24 hours yields a flavorful and interesting roast. Serve with roasted autumn vegetables and Steamed White Rice (page 317) or rice pilaf.

To make the marinade, in a bowl, whisk together the whiskey, olive oil, vinegar, mustard, 1 teaspoon salt, and ¹/₂ teaspoon pepper. Reserve ¹/₄ cup (2 fl oz/60 ml) of the marinade. Place the beef in a large lock-top plastic bag and pour in all of the remaining marinade. Press out the air and seal the bag tightly. Massage the bag gently to distribute the marinade. Place in a large bowl and refrigerate, turning and massaging the bag occasionally, for at least 1 day, or for up to 3 days if you wish.

Prepare a fire for indirect-heat cooking in a charcoal grill with a cover (page 326) or preheat a gas grill. Position the grill rack 4–6 inches (10–15 cm) above the heat.

Remove the meat from the marinade and pat it dry with paper towels.

Place the meat over the indirect heat, cover the grill, and open the vents halfway. Cook, brushing with the reserved marinade and turning, until the roast is well browned and an instant-read thermometer inserted into the thickest part registers 135°F (57°C) for medium-rare, about 50 minutes.

Remove the roast from the grill and transfer to a cutting board. Cover loosely with aluminum foil and let rest for 10 minutes. To serve, carve crosswise into thin slices and arrange on a warmed platter or individual plates.

Serves 6–8

FOR THE MARINADE:

²/₃ cup (5 fl oz/160 ml) bourbon whiskey

¹/₃ cup (3 fl oz/80 ml) olive oil

¹/₃ cup (3 fl oz/80 ml) cider vinegar

1 tablespoon Dijon mustard

Salt and freshly ground pepper

1 boneless beef chuck roast, 3–3¹/₂ lb (1.5–1.75 kg)

Texas Beef Chili

Some chili lovers add the beans to the meat, but purists serve the beans on the side. Serve with warm corn tortillas, sour cream, sliced avocado, and salsa. Finely minced onion and cilantro (coriander) may be sprinkled on top, if desired.

FOR THE BEANS:

1 cup (7 oz/220 g) dried pinto or kidney beans

1 yellow onion, chopped

2 cloves garlic, minced

1 teaspoon dried oregano

Salt

4 tablespoons (2 fl oz/60 ml) olive oil or melted lard

2 lb (1 kg) beef chuck, cut into ½-inch (12-mm) dice

2 yellow onions, chopped

4 cloves garlic, minced

3 tablespoons chili powder

1 tablespoon *each* dried oregano and ground cumin

Salt and freshly ground black pepper

½ teaspoon cayenne pepper

1 can (6 oz/185 g) tomato paste

2 cups (12 oz/375 g) canned diced plum (Roma) tomatoes, with their juices

1½ cups (12 fl oz/375 ml) beer, water, or Beef Stock (page 314)

To prepare the beans, pick over them and discard any stones; rinse well. Put the beans in a bowl, add water to cover by 2 inches (5 cm), and let soak for 4 hours or overnight. Drain and place in a saucepan. Add water to cover by 2 inches (5 cm). Add the onion, garlic, and oregano. Bring to a boil, reduce the heat to low, and simmer until tender, about 1 hour. Add salt to taste and set aside.

In a large, heavy pot over medium heat, heat 2 tablespoons of the olive oil. Working in batches, add the meat and brown on all sides, 8–10 minutes. Set aside.

In another large, heavy pot over medium heat, heat the remaining 2 tablespoons olive oil. Add the onions and cook until soft and pale gold, 15–20 minutes. Add the garlic, chili powder, oregano, cumin, 1 teaspoon salt, 1 teaspoon black pepper, and cayenne pepper; simmer for 1–2 minutes. Stir in the tomato paste and the tomatoes with their juices. Add the reserved beef and the beer; bring to a boil, reduce the heat to low, cover, and simmer until the beef is tender, about 1 hour.

Divide the beef mixture among warmed individual bowls and serve the beans on the side. Alternatively, stir the beans into the chili and simmer together for about 15 minutes.

Serves 6

Sumatran Beef Ragout

This rich and flavorful beef curry is called *kalio* in its place of origin, the island of Sumatra. Serve over Steamed White Rice (page 317) and accompany with green beans seasoned with ginger or toasted coconut.

Place a large frying pan over high heat and pour in enough peanut oil to form a film on the bottom. Working in batches, add the beef and fry over high heat until browned on all sides, 10–15 minutes per batch. Set aside.

In a Dutch oven over medium heat, heat the 3 tablespoons peanut oil. Add the onions and cook until soft, 10–15 minutes. Add the ginger, garlic, jalapeño, turmeric, coriander, bay leaves, and lemon zest and cook 5 minutes longer.

Add the beef to the pot along with the coconut milk and stock. Bring to a simmer, cover, and cook until the meat is very tender, about 3 hours.

Discard the bay leaves and lemongrass (if used). Season to taste with salt and pepper, and serve.

Serves 6

Peanut oil as needed, plus 3 tablespoons

3 lb (1.5 kg) stewing beef such as chuck, cut into 1$\frac{1}{2}$-inch (4-cm) cubes

4–5 cups (1–1$\frac{1}{4}$ lb/ 500–625 g) diced yellow onions (about 3 large)

3 tablespoons peeled and grated fresh ginger

2 tablespoons minced garlic

1 teaspoon minced jalapeño chile, or to taste

1 teaspoon ground turmeric

2 tablespoons ground coriander

2 bay leaves

2 long strips lemon zest, or 2 stalks fresh lemongrass, white part only, peeled, crushed, and cut into 3-inch (7.5-cm) lengths

3 cups (24 fl oz/750 ml) coconut milk

2 cups (16 fl oz/500 ml) Beef Stock (page 314)

Salt and freshly ground pepper

Stuffed Cabbage

This is one of those homey peasant dishes that everyone loves, though it's rarely found on restaurant menus. It is best made the day before and reheated. Serve with good dark bread to soak up the juices.

2 green cabbages, about 2 lb (1 kg) total weight

FOR THE FILLING:

1 yellow onion, coarsely chopped

2 eggs

1½ lb (750 g) ground (minced) beef chuck

2 cups (14 oz/440 g) long-grain white rice

Salt and freshly ground pepper

1 yellow onion, diced

1 cup (8 fl oz/250 ml) Beef Stock (page 314) or water

3 cups (24 fl oz/750 ml) canned tomato purée

½ cup (4 fl oz/125 ml) fresh lemon juice, or more to taste

1 cup (7 oz/220 g) firmly packed golden brown sugar, or more to taste

Salt and freshly ground pepper

Bring a large pot of salted water to a boil. Using a sharp knife, remove the central tough core of the cabbages, leaving them whole. Drop the cabbages, one at a time, into the boiling water. Simmer until the leaves loosen and are pliable, about 10 minutes. Transfer to a colander. When the cabbages are cool enough to handle, pull off the largest leaves, being careful not to tear them, and set aside. You'll need about 24 leaves. (Reserve the remainder for another use, such as adding to a soup.)

To make the filling, in a blender or a food processor, combine the chopped onion and eggs and purée until smooth. Put the beef and rice in a bowl, add the egg mixture, and mix well. Season to taste with salt and pepper. Place 1 or 2 heaping tablespoons of filling on each cabbage leaf. Fold in the sides, roll up, and skewer closed with a toothpick.

In a Dutch oven, combine the diced onion, stock, tomato purée, lemon juice, and brown sugar. Bring to a simmer over medium heat, stirring to dissolve the sugar. Slip in the cabbage rolls and wait until the liquid returns to a gentle simmer. Cover and simmer over low heat on the stove top or in an oven preheated to 325°F (165°C) until the filling is fully cooked, about 2½ hours. Baste the cabbage rolls often with the cooking liquid.

Using a slotted spoon, transfer the rolls to a warmed platter or individual bowls. Carefully remove the toothpicks. Adjust the sweet-and-sour flavor of the pan juices, if necessary, with more sugar and lemon juice. Season to taste with salt and pepper. Spoon the pan juices over the rolls and serve.

Serves 6–8

Beef Paprikash

Sautéed bell peppers (capsicums) and fresh dill make a colorful, tasty garnish for this hearty Hungarian ragout. Serve with buttered egg noodles or simple boiled potatoes.

In a heavy frying pan over high heat, melt $1/4$ cup (2 oz/60 g) of the butter. Sprinkle the beef with salt and pepper and 1 tablespoon of the paprika. Working in batches, add the meat to the pan and brown on all sides, about 15 minutes per batch. Remove from the heat and set aside.

In a Dutch oven over medium heat, melt the remaining $1/4$ cup butter. Add the onions and sauté until soft, 10–15 minutes. Add the garlic and the remaining 4 tablespoons paprika and cook until fragrant, about 2 minutes. Add the tomato paste, stock, and reserved beef. Bring to a boil, reduce the heat to low, cover, and simmer until the beef is tender, about $2^{1}/_{2}$ hours.

Taste and adjust the seasoning. Remove from the heat and stir in the sour cream and dill. Serve at once.

Serves 6

$1/2$ cup (4 oz/125 g) unsalted butter or lard

3 lb (1.5 kg) beef chuck, cut into 2-inch (5-cm) cubes

Salt and freshly ground pepper

5 tablespoons sweet Hungarian paprika

2 large yellow onions, chopped

3 cloves garlic, minced

2 tablespoons tomato paste

2 cups (16 fl oz/500 ml) Beef Stock (page 314)

1–$1^{1}/_{2}$ cups (8–12 fl oz/ 250–375 ml) sour cream, at room temperature

$1/2$ cup ($3/4$ oz/20 g) minced fresh dill

Moroccan Meatballs

The beef for this recipe should not be too lean or the meatballs will be dry. Serve these spicy, fragrant meatballs atop a bed of couscous. Fresh mint or cilantro (coriander) may be substituted for the parsley.

1 lb (500 g) ground (minced) beef chuck

4 teaspoons ground cumin

1 tablespoon paprika

1/2 teaspoon cayenne pepper

1/2 teaspoon ground cinnamon

1/4 teaspoon ground ginger

3/4 cup (11/2 oz/25 g) minced fresh flat-leaf (Italian) parsley

3 tablespoons minced fresh cilantro (fresh coriander)

3 small yellow onions, chopped

Salt and freshly ground pepper

4 tablespoons (2 fl oz/60 ml) olive oil

2 cups (1 lb/500 g) canned plum (Roma) tomatoes

4 cloves garlic, minced

1 cup (8 fl oz/250 ml) canned tomato purée

In a bowl, combine the beef, 2 teaspoons of the cumin, the paprika, 1/2 teaspoon cayenne pepper, cinnamon, ginger, 1/4 cup (1/3 oz/10 g) of the parsley, the cilantro, 1 of the onions, 1 teaspoon salt, and 1/2 teaspoon black pepper. Using your hands, mix well. Form into balls 1 inch (2.5 cm) in diameter.

In a frying pan over high heat, heat 2 tablespoons of the olive oil. Add the meatballs and brown on all sides, 8–10 minutes. Remove from the heat and set aside.

Place the tomatoes and some of their juice from the can in a food processor and process until finely chopped. Set aside. In a large sauté pan over medium heat, heat the remaining 2 tablespoons oil. Add the remaining 2 onions and sauté until soft, 10–15 minutes. Add the garlic, the remaining 2 teaspoons cumin, cayenne pepper to taste, 1/2 teaspoon black pepper, and the remaining 1/2 cup (3/4 oz/20 g) parsley and sauté for 5 minutes longer. Add the browned meatballs, reserved tomatoes, and tomato purée and cook for 15 minutes longer. Serve at once.

Serves 4

Tomato-Glazed Meat Loaf

This is a basic, old-fashioned, crowd-pleasing meat loaf. Serve with mashed potatoes and a green vegetable. If there are leftovers, make meat loaf sandwiches with a little chili sauce spread on the bread.

Preheat the oven to 350°F (180°C). Grease a baking pan.

In a bowl, combine the meat, bread, eggs, onion, herbs, parsley, and salt and pepper to taste. Mix well with your hands. Form the meat mixture into an oval loaf. If you like, place the hard-boiled eggs in a row in the center of your loaf as you form it. Place the loaf in the pan and pour the tomato sauce over the top.

Bake the meat loaf until no longer pink in the center, about 1 1/4 hours. Let stand for 15 minutes, then slice and serve hot.

Serves 4

2 lb (1 kg) ground (minced) beef chuck

3 slices bread, soaked in tomato juice or milk just to cover and squeezed dry

2 eggs

1 large yellow onion, finely chopped

1 tablespoon mixed dried herbs such as sage, oregano, and thyme, or 3 tablespoons chopped fresh herbs of choice

4 tablespoons chopped fresh flat-leaf (Italian) parsley

Salt and freshly ground pepper

2 or 3 hard-boiled eggs (optional)

1 cup (8 fl oz/250 ml) Basic Tomato Sauce (page 18) or chili sauce

Onion-Stuffed Beef Kefta

While Indian-style ground-meat kabobs are traditionally made with lamb, they may also be made with beef. Serve with pita bread and a raita made of plain yogurt, diced tomatoes, and cucumbers flavored with toasted cumin seeds.

FOR THE FILLING:

2 tablespoons unsalted butter

1 large yellow onion, finely chopped

2 teaspoons peeled and grated fresh ginger

1 teaspoon minced jalapeño chile, or to taste

1/4 cup (1/3 oz/10 g) minced fresh mint

Grated zest of 1 lemon

Salt and freshly ground black pepper

1 lb (500 g) ground (minced) beef chuck

1 tablespoon minced garlic

2 teaspoons ground cumin

1 teaspoon ground cinnamon

1 teaspoon salt

1/2 teaspoon *each* freshly ground black pepper and ground ginger

1/4 teaspoon cayenne pepper

Olive oil for frying

Salt

To make the filling, in a sauté pan over medium heat, melt the butter. Add the onion and sauté until translucent, 3–5 minutes. Add the ginger and jalapeño and sauté until fragrant, 1–2 minutes longer. Remove from the heat and mix in the mint and lemon zest. Season to taste with salt and black pepper. Transfer to a bowl, let cool, cover, and refrigerate until chilled, about 1 hour.

In a bowl, combine the beef, garlic, cumin, cinnamon, 1 teaspoon salt, 1/2 teaspoon black pepper, 1/2 teaspoon ginger, and cayenne and mix well with your hands. Cover and refrigerate until chilled, about 1 hour.

Divide the meat mixture in half. Form one half into 4 patties, each about 1/2 inch (12 mm) thick. Make a well in the center of each patty and stuff one-fourth of the onion filling into the well. Top each patty with one-fourth of the remaining meat. Shape each portion into an oval about 3 inches (7.5 cm) long.

Lightly oil a large, heavy frying pan with olive oil and heat until very hot. Sprinkle lightly with salt. When the salt starts to brown, add the meat ovals. Fry, turning once, until crusty and browned, about 3 minutes on each side. Do not overcook; the kabobs should be quite juicy.

Serves 4

Beef Strudel

This dish, a sort of fancy meat loaf encased in pastry, is ideal for buffet suppers. Serve with a dollop of yogurt or sour cream. Steamed or sautéed cucumbers with chives or dill are also a nice accompaniment.

In a large frying pan over medium heat, melt the 3 tablespoons butter. Add the onion and sauté until soft, 8–10 minutes. Add the garlic, parsley, dill, oregano, cinnamon, allspice, and beef. Cook, stirring occasionally and breaking up the beef with a wooden spoon, until the meat is cooked through, about 10 minutes. Transfer to a bowl and let cool slightly. Stir in the egg and bread crumbs and season to taste with salt and pepper. Let cool for 30 minutes or longer.

Preheat the oven to 350°F (180°C). Butter a baking sheet. Place 1 filo sheet on a clean, dry surface with a long side facing you. Brush with some of the melted butter. Top with a second sheet, brush with more of the melted butter, and top with a third sheet. Repeat until 6 sheets have been used. Place half of the meat mixture in a strip along the long edge nearest you, leaving a 1-inch (2.5-cm) border. Fold in the ends and, beginning from the long edge nearest you, roll up like a jelly roll. Repeat with the remaining sheets and meat mixture to make a second roll. If making the strudel ahead, cover with plastic wrap and refrigerate for up to 12 hours.

Place the filo rolls on the prepared baking sheet. Brush with the remaining melted butter. Bake until golden, about 40 minutes. Cut into slices $1/2$ inch (12 mm) thick and serve hot.

Serves 6

3 tablespoons unsalted butter or olive oil, plus 1/2 cup (4 oz/125 g) unsalted butter, melted

1 large yellow onion, finely chopped

1 teaspoon minced garlic

3 tablespoons minced fresh flat-leaf (Italian) parsley

3 tablespoons minced fresh dill

1 teaspoon dried oregano

1 teaspoon ground cinnamon

1/2 teaspoon ground allspice or freshly grated nutmeg

1 lb (500 g) ground (minced) beef

1 egg, beaten

1/4 cup (1 oz/30 g) fine dried bread crumbs (page 324)

Salt and freshly ground pepper

12 sheets filo pastry (about 1/2 lb/250 g)

Beef Top Round with Jalapeño Marinade

Top round, sometimes labeled London broil, is a tasty cut of beef, but be careful not to overcook it or it can toughen. Accompany this dish with grilled fennel and endive or an assortment of other vegetables.

FOR THE MARINADE:

3 jalapeño chiles

2/3 cup (5 fl oz/160 ml) dry red wine

1/3 cup (3 fl oz/80 ml) olive oil

2 large cloves garlic

Handful of fresh flat-leaf (Italian) parsley sprigs

1 teaspoon salt

1/2 teaspoon freshly ground pepper

1 top-round beef steak, about 2 1/2 lb (1.25 kg)

To make the marinade, halve the chiles and remove their stems, seeds, and ribs. In a blender or a food processor, combine the chiles, wine, olive oil, garlic, parsley, salt, and pepper. Process until smooth. Reserve 1/4 cup (2 fl oz/60 ml) of the marinade.

Using a sharp knife, score the surface of the steak with crisscross cuts about 1/8 inch (3 mm) deep and 2 inches (5 cm) apart. Place in a large lock-top plastic bag and pour in the remaining marinade. Press out the air and seal the bag tightly. Massage the bag gently to distribute the marinade evenly. Place the bag in a large bowl and refrigerate, turning and massaging the bag occasionally, for at least 6 hours or for up to 2 days.

Prepare a fire in a charcoal grill, or preheat a gas grill or broiler (grill). Remove the steak from the marinade and pat it dry with paper towels. Place the steaks on the grill rack or on a broiler (grill) pan. Grill or broil 4–6 inches (10–15 cm) from the heat source, turning and brushing with the reserved marinade 3 or 4 times, about 17 minutes for medium-rare.

To serve, carve crosswise into thin slices on the diagonal. Arrange on a warmed platter and serve at once.

Serves 6

Deviled Short Ribs

Zesty oven-barbecued short ribs are best served with simple side dishes such as baked potatoes and greens. Marinate the ribs for at least 6 hours, or preferably overnight.

In a large nonaluminum bowl, combine the mustard, chili powder, 1 tablespoon salt, the brown sugar, lemon zest and juice, garlic, onion, allspice, 2 teaspoons pepper, and the olive oil. Mix well, add the ribs, cover, and refrigerate for at least 6 hours, or up to overnight, turning the ribs often.

Preheat the oven to 450°F (230°C). Drain the ribs and reserve the marinade. Place in a flameproof roasting pan and bake until browned, about 30 minutes. Reduce the temperature to 350°F (180°C). Pour the reserved marinade evenly over the ribs and cook until tender, about 1 1/2 hours longer.

Transfer the ribs to a platter and keep warm. Drain off the excess fat from the pan and place the pan on the stove top over high heat. Pour in the stock and deglaze the pan by stirring with a wooden spoon to dislodge any browned bits on the bottom. Boil for about 2 minutes. Taste and adjust the seasoning with salt and pepper and add more mustard, if you like. Pour the sauce over the short ribs and serve at once.

Serves 6

1/2 cup (4 oz/125 g) Dijon mustard, or more to taste

2 tablespoons chili powder

Salt and freshly ground pepper

4 teaspoons firmly packed golden brown sugar

1 tablespoon grated lemon zest

1/4 cup (2 fl oz/60 ml) fresh lemon juice

4 cloves garlic, minced

2 cups (8 oz/250 g) diced yellow onion

1 teaspoon ground allspice, or 1/2 teaspoon ground cloves

1/2 cup (4 fl oz/125 ml) olive oil

6 lb (3 kg) short ribs, cut into serving pieces

1 cup (8 fl oz/250 ml) Beef Stock (page 314)

Old-Fashioned Rib Roast

If you like beef prepared simply, this classic dish is for you. Serve it with
onion wedges, brushed with oil and placed on the grill rack around the roast
for the last 20 minutes or so of cooking.

4 teaspoons coarse or kosher salt

3 tablespoons minced fresh thyme or 2 teaspoons dried thyme

1½ teaspoons freshly ground pepper

2 large cloves garlic, minced

Finely grated zest of 1 lemon or lime

1 beef rib roast, 6–7 lb (3–3.5 kg), trimmed of excess fat and tied at 1-inch (2.5-cm) intervals

2 tablespoons olive oil

Prepare a charcoal fire for indirect-heat cooking in a grill with a cover (page 326) or preheat a gas grill to low.

In a small bowl, stir together the salt, thyme, pepper, garlic, and lemon zest.

Pat the roast dry with paper towels. Rub with the olive oil, then rub the salt mixture over the surface of the meat.

Place the roast, rib side down, on the grill rack over indirect heat. Cover the grill and open the vents halfway. Cook for 45 minutes. Replenish the charcoal fire with fresh coals. Turn the roast rib side up and cook until an instant-read thermometer inserted into the thickest portion of the roast away from the bone registers 135°F (57°C) for medium-rare, about 15 minutes longer.

Remove the roast from the grill and transfer to a cutting board. Cover loosely with aluminum foil and let rest for 10 minutes. To serve, snip and discard the strings. Carve the meat into slices 3/4–1 inch (2–2.5 cm) thick and arrange on a warmed platter or individual plates.

Serves 6

Korean Grilled Short Ribs

Korean short ribs are rubbed with sugar to tenderize them, then marinated in a spicy paste before grilling. Serve with Steamed White Rice (page 317) and spinach sprinkled with toasted sesame seeds.

4 lb (2 kg) beef short ribs

1/3 cup (3 oz/90 g) sugar

1/2 cup (2 oz/60 g) sesame seeds

1/4 cup (2 fl oz/60 ml) Asian sesame oil

1/2 cup (4 fl oz/125 ml) plus 2 tablespoons soy sauce

3 cloves garlic, minced

2 teaspoons red pepper flakes

1 tablespoon peeled and grated fresh ginger

3 tablespoons all-purpose (plain) flour

Make deep cuts through the meat on the ribs at regular intervals. Rub the sugar into the meat and let stand at room temperature for 30 minutes.

In a small, dry frying pan over medium-low heat, toast the sesame seeds, stirring, until golden, about 3 minutes. Transfer immediately to a plate to cool, then pulverize using a mortar and pestle.

In a bowl, stir together the ground sesame seeds, the sesame oil, soy sauce, garlic, red pepper flakes, ginger, and flour. Coat the ribs with the mixture and let stand for about 1 hour.

Prepare a fire in a charcoal grill, or preheat a gas grill or broiler (grill) until very hot. Place the ribs on the grill rack or a broiler (grill) pan. Grill or broil 4–6 inches (10–15 cm) from the heat source until well browned on the outside but still somewhat rare in the center, about 5 minutes per side. Serve at once.

Serves 4 or 5

All-American Beef Short Ribs

Short ribs benefit from long, slow cooking, so that the meat practically falls off the bone. At the table, moisten the ribs with plenty of tangy barbecue sauce and serve with cool cole slaw.

To make the marinade, in a small bowl, whisk together the pineapple juice, olive oil, soy sauce, brown sugar, and chili powder. Reserve ¹/₄ cup (2 fl oz/60 ml) of the marinade and set aside. Place the ribs in a large lock-top plastic bag and pour in the remaining marinade. Press out the air and seal the bag tightly. Massage the bag gently to distribute the marinade evenly. Place in a large bowl and refrigerate for at least 4 hours, or for up to 2 days if you wish.

Prepare a fire for indirect-heat cooking in a charcoal grill with a cover (page 326) or preheat a gas grill to low. Position the grill rack 4–6 inches (10–15 cm) above the fire.

Remove the ribs from the marinade and pat them dry with paper towels. Place the ribs on the grill rack over indirect heat. Cover the grill and open the vents halfway. Cook for 1 hour, then turn and brush with the reserved marinade. Replenish the charcoal fire with fresh coals. Continue to cook, brushing with the marinade and turning every 20–30 minutes, until the meat is well browned and begins to shrink from the bone, 1–2 hours longer.

To serve, transfer the ribs to a warmed platter or individual plates. Pass the barbecue sauce at the table.

Serves 4

FOR THE MARINADE:

1 cup (8 fl oz/250 ml) unsweetened pineapple juice

¹/₄ cup (2 fl oz/60 ml) olive oil

¹/₄ cup (2 fl oz/60 ml) soy sauce

¹/₄ cup (2 oz/60 g) firmly packed golden brown sugar

1 tablespoon chili powder

4 lb (2 kg) beef short ribs, trimmed of excess fat

Midwestern Barbecue Sauce (page 17)

Veal Rollatini

These rolls may be refrigerated for up to 12 hours before cooking. To toast and skin hazelnuts, place them in a 325°F (165°C) oven until lightly colored, 5–10 minutes, then rub off the skins with a kitchen towel.

4 tablespoons (2 oz/60 g) unsalted butter

4 shallots, minced

2 cloves garlic, minced

¼ lb (125 g) white or cremini mushrooms, brushed clean and coarsely chopped

6 fresh sage leaves, minced

24 hazelnuts (filberts), toasted and skinned (page 326), and then finely chopped

Salt and freshly ground pepper

¼ teaspoon freshly grated nutmeg

12 slices veal scallops (1½ lb/750 g total), each about ⅓ inch (8 mm) thick

6 thin slices prosciutto

¼ cup (2 fl oz/60 ml) olive oil, or equal parts olive oil and unsalted butter

1 cup (8 fl oz/250 ml) Beef Stock (page 314)

1 cup (8 fl oz/250 ml) Marsala

Chopped fresh flat-leaf (Italian) parsley for garnish

In a sauté pan over medium heat, melt 2 tablespoons of the butter. Add the shallots and sauté until softened, about 5 minutes. Add the garlic and mushrooms and cook until most of the mushroom liquid evaporates, about 10 minutes. Add the sage and hazelnuts, reserving some of the chopped nuts for garnish, and simmer for 1 minute. Season to taste with salt and pepper and stir in the nutmeg. Remove from the heat and let cool.

Place the veal scallops between 2 sheets of plastic wrap and pound gently with a meat pounder until they are ¼ inch (6 mm) thick. Cut the prosciutto slices in half and place 1 piece on each veal scallop. Top each with a heaping spoonful of the mushroom mixture. Roll up and securely tie with kitchen twine or skewer closed with wooden toothpicks.

Preheat the oven to 350°F (180°C). In a large sauté pan over high heat, heat the olive oil. Add the rolls and cook, browning them on all sides, until tender, 6–8 minutes. Transfer to a baking dish and place in the oven to keep warm.

Meanwhile, pour off the excess fat from the pan and place over high heat. Pour in the stock and deglaze the pan by stirring with a wooden spoon to dislodge any browned bits from the bottom. Boil until reduced by half, 3–5 minutes. Add the Marsala and reduce again by half. Swirl in the remaining 2 tablespoons butter. Remove the rolls from the oven; discard the skewers. Add the rolls to the sauce and toss gently. Transfer with the sauce to a platter. Serve at once, topped with the parsley and the reserved hazelnuts.

Serves 4

Veal Ragout with Mushrooms and Cream

For a deeper mushroom flavor, add ¼ cup (½ oz/15 g) dried porcini mushrooms, soaked to soften and drained, with the fresh mushrooms. Meat cut from the shank can be substituted for the veal shoulder.

On a large plate, mix the flour and salt, pepper, and nutmeg to taste. Cut the veal into 2-inch (5-cm) cubes. Coat the veal pieces with the seasoned flour. In a frying pan, heat 4 tablespoons (2 fl oz/60 ml) of the olive oil. Working in batches, add the veal and brown on all sides, about 10 minutes, adding more oil as needed. Set aside.

In a Dutch oven over low heat, heat 2 tablespoons of the remaining olive oil. Add the diced onion and sauté until soft, 10–15 minutes. Add the garlic and 1 teaspoon of the thyme and sauté for 2 minutes. Add the veal and 5 cups (40 fl oz/ 1.25 l) of the stock. Bring to a boil, reduce the heat to low, cover, and simmer until the veal is tender, 1–1¼ hours.

Meanwhile, peel the pearl onions (page 326). In a saucepan, bring the remaining 1 cup (8 fl oz/250 ml) stock to a boil, add the pearl onions, reduce the heat to low, cover, and cook until tender, 10–15 minutes. Meanwhile, in a frying pan, heat the remaining 3 tablespoons oil. Add the mushrooms and brown quickly, 2–3 minutes.

Add the pearl onions and mushrooms and their liquid and the remaining 1 tea-spoon thyme to the veal during the last 10 minutes of cooking. Just before serving, stir together the egg yolks (if using), the cream, and the lemon juice, then stir into the veal. Simmer, stirring, to thicken a bit. Do not boil if egg yolks have been added. Taste and adjust the seasoning, sprinkle with the parsley, and serve.

Serves 6

About 1 cup (5 oz/155 g) all-purpose (plain) flour

Salt, freshly ground pepper, and freshly grated nutmeg

3 lb (1.5 kg) veal shoulder

9 tablespoons (4½ fl oz/ 145 ml) olive oil

1 large yellow onion, diced

1 teaspoon minced garlic

2 teaspoons chopped fresh thyme

6 cups (48 fl oz/1.5 l) Chicken Stock (page 314)

18–24 unpeeled pearl onions

1 lb (500 g) small fresh white, cremini, or wild mushrooms, brushed clean and stemmed

2 egg yolks (optional)

½–1 cup (4–8 fl oz/ 125–250 ml) heavy (double) cream

3 tablespoons fresh lemon juice, or to taste

Minced fresh flat-leaf (Italian) parsley for garnish

Grilled Veal Loin Chops
with Tarragon, Mushrooms, and Cream

This elegant dish could hardly be easier: Simply grill or broil the veal chops and top with the rich mushroom-laden tarragon sauce. Serve with sautéed seasonal vegetables. Garnish with fresh tarragon sprigs.

Prepare a fire in a charcoal grill, or preheat a gas grill or broiler (grill).

To prepare the sauce, in a sauté pan over medium heat, melt the butter. Add the shallots and sauté until soft, about 5 minutes. Raise the heat to medium-high, add the mushrooms, and sauté, stirring often, until the mushrooms are tender and give off a little liquid, 1–2 minutes. Add the tarragon, wine, and cream and cook to reduce slightly. Season to taste with salt and pepper; set aside and keep warm.

Brush the veal chops lightly with olive oil and sprinkle with salt and pepper. Place on the grill rack or on a broiler (grill) pan. Grill or broil 4–6 inches (10–15 cm) from the heat source, 4 minutes on each side for medium-rare. Place the chops on warmed plates and spoon the warm sauce over the top.

Serves 6

FOR THE SAUCE:

6 tablespoons (3 oz/90 g) unsalted butter

6–8 shallots, diced

3/4 lb (375 g) white or cremini mushrooms, brushed clean and sliced 1/4 inch (6 mm) thick

2 tablespoons minced fresh tarragon or 1 tablespoon dried tarragon

1/2 cup (4 fl oz/125 ml) dry white wine

1 cup (8 fl oz/250 ml) heavy (double) cream

Salt and freshly ground pepper

6 bone-in veal loin chops, each about 3/4 lb (375 g)

Olive oil for brushing

Salt and freshly ground pepper

Pork

Sausage and White Bean Stew

This hearty stew can be made ahead of time and then reheated just before serving. Serve with toasted slices of country-style bread rubbed with garlic and brushed with extra-virgin olive oil.

Pick over the beans and discard any stones; rinse well. Place in a bowl and add water to cover by 2 inches (5 cm). Soak for at least 4 hours or as long as overnight.

Drain the beans and put them in a large saucepan. Add the quartered onion, allspice, cloves, stock, and water to cover by 3 inches (7.5 cm). Bring to a boil over high heat, reduce the heat to medium-low, and simmer, uncovered, for 30 minutes. Remove the quartered onion and discard. Set the beans aside.

In a large sauté pan over medium heat, heat the olive oil. Add the chopped onion, bell pepper, garlic, and sausages and cook, stirring occasionally, until the onion is very tender, about 10 minutes. Add the beans and their liquid and bring to a boil. Reduce the heat to low and simmer gently, uncovered, until the beans are tender and the liquid has thickened, about 30 minutes. Season to taste with salt and pepper.

To serve, remove the sausages from the pan and cut on the diagonal into thin slices. Return the slices to the pan and heat thoroughly. Spoon into warmed bowls and serve immediately.

Serves 6

1½ cups (10½ oz/330 g) dried small white (navy) or Great Northern beans

1 small yellow onion, quartered, plus 1 medium yellow onion, finely chopped

¼ teaspoon ground allspice

¼ teaspoon ground cloves

6 cups (48 fl oz/1.5 l) Chicken Stock (page 314)

¼ cup (2 fl oz/60 ml) olive oil

1 red bell pepper (capsicum), seeded, deribbed, and cut into ½-inch (12-mm) dice

4 cloves garlic, minced

6 sweet pork sausages, about 1½ lb (750 g) total weight, pricked with a fork

Salt and freshly ground pepper

Pork Tenderloin Stuffed with Onion Marmalade

3 large pork tenderloins,
3/4–1 lb (375–500 g) each,
trimmed of excess fat

1 tablespoon olive oil

3 cloves garlic, minced

1/4 teaspoon ground cumin

1/4 teaspoon cayenne pepper

1/4 teaspoon ground cloves

Salt and freshly ground
black pepper

FOR THE ONION MARMALADE:

2 tablespoons olive oil

2 yellow onions, thinly sliced

1 teaspoon grated orange zest

3/4 cup (6 fl oz/180 ml) fresh
orange juice

1/3 cup (2 oz/60 g) golden
raisins (sultanas)

1/4 cup (2 fl oz/60 ml) sherry
vinegar or white wine vinegar

2 teaspoons sugar

1 cup (8 fl oz/250 ml) water

Salt and freshly ground pepper

1/2 cup (4 fl oz/125 ml) dry
white wine

2 cups (16 fl oz/500 ml) Chicken
Stock (page 314)

Fresh flat-leaf (Italian) parsley
sprigs for garnish (optional)

Butterfly the pork tenderloins by making a long slit down the length of each one, cutting just deep enough so that the tenderloin opens up to lay flat; do not cut all the way through. Flatten the tenderloins and pound gently with a meat pounder. Place in a single layer in a baking dish. In a bowl, combine the olive oil, garlic, cumin, cayenne, cloves, and salt and pepper to taste. Rub the pork with the mixture, cover, and refrigerate for 1 hour or as long as overnight.

To make the onion marmalade, in a frying pan over medium heat, heat the olive oil. Add the onions and sauté, stirring occasionally, until lightly golden, about 15 minutes. Add the orange zest, orange juice, raisins, vinegar, sugar, water, and salt and pepper to taste. Cover and cook over low heat until the onions are very soft, about 30 minutes. Uncover, raise the heat to medium-high, and cook until the onions are dry, about 10 minutes.

Lay the pork tenderloins cut side up, on a work surface. Spread the onion mixture over the pork, distributing it evenly. Close the tenderloins and using kitchen twine, tie at 1-inch (2.5-cm) intervals.

Place the pork in a Dutch oven and add the wine and stock. Cover, bring to a boil, reduce the heat to very low, and simmer until the pork is firm to the touch and pale pink when cut in the thickest portion, about 30 minutes. Transfer the pork to a cutting board; cover loosely with aluminium foil and keep warm. Raise the heat to high and, stirring occasionally, cook to reduce the liquid by half, about 10 minutes. Strain the sauce and keep warm.

Remove the twine from the tenderloins and cut the meat crosswise into slices 1/2 inch (12 mm) thick. Arrange on warmed plates and spoon the sauce on top. Garnish with the parsley sprigs, if desired, and serve.

Serves 6

Pork with Prunes and Apple Brandy

Dried fruit, fresh vegetables, and pork tenderloin are spiked with apple brandy in this delicious stew, ideal for a hearty, cold-weather supper. Serve with a green salad and crusty bread.

1 tablespoon olive oil

1¹/₂ lb (750 g) lean pork tenderloin, trimmed of excess fat and cut into 1¹/₂-inch (4-cm) cubes

¹/₂ cup (4 fl oz/125 ml) Calvados or other apple brandy

1 tablespoon unsalted butter

1 large sweet white onion, cut in half lengthwise and then crosswise into slices ¹/₄ inch (6 mm) thick

4 carrots, peeled and cut into 1-inch (2.5-cm) pieces

1 cup (8 fl oz/250 ml) apple juice

2 cups (12 oz/375 g) pitted prunes

Salt and freshly ground pepper

In a Dutch oven over medium-high heat, heat the olive oil. Working in batches if necessary, add the pork cubes and brown lightly on all sides, 3–4 minutes per batch. Transfer the pork to a dish and set aside. Pour off the oil from the pot and place the pot over medium-high heat. Add the apple brandy and deglaze the pot by stirring with a wooden spoon to dislodge any browned bits from the bottom. Pour the deglazing liquid over the pork, then wipe the pot clean.

In the same pot, melt the butter over medium heat. Add the onion and sauté until translucent, about 5 minutes. Return the pork and any accumulated juices to the pot. Add the carrots, apple juice, and prunes and bring to a simmer. Reduce the heat to medium-low, cover, and simmer gently until the pork and vegetables are tender, about 40 minutes. Season to taste with salt and pepper.

Spoon into warmed shallow bowls or plates and serve.

Serves 4–6

Pork and Parsnips in Sherry

The combination of maple syrup and dry sherry provides a mildly sweet and wonderfully mellow accent. Serve over Steamed White Rice (page 317) or cooked egg noodles and garnish with a sprinkling of chopped parsley.

In a Dutch oven over medium-high heat, heat the olive oil. Working in batches if necessary, add the pork cubes and brown lightly on all sides, 3–4 minutes per batch. Transfer the pork to a dish. Pour the sherry into the pot and deglaze over medium-high heat by stirring with a wooden spoon to dislodge any browned bits from the bottom. Pour the liquid over the pork, then wipe the pot clean.

In the same pot, melt the butter over medium heat. Add the shallots, parsnips, and sweet potatoes and sauté until the shallots are golden brown, about 10 minutes. Return the pork and juices to the pot and add the stock and maple syrup. Stir well and bring to a simmer. Reduce the heat to medium-low, cover, and simmer gently until the pork is tender, 40–45 minutes. Season to taste with salt and pepper.

Spoon into warmed shallow bowls, garnish with the parsley, and serve.

Serves 6

2 tablespoons olive oil

2 lb (1 kg) pork tenderloin, trimmed of excess fat and cut into 1-inch (2.5-cm) cubes

2/3 cup (5 fl oz/160 ml) dry sherry

1 tablespoon unsalted butter

4 shallots, minced

6 small parsnips, peeled and quartered

4 sweet potatoes or yams, peeled and cut into bite-sized pieces

2 1/2 cups (20 fl oz/625 ml) Chicken Stock (page 314)

2 tablespoons pure maple syrup

Salt and freshly ground pepper

Minced fresh flat-leaf (Italian) parsley for garnish

Pork and Papaya

Peaches can be substituted for the papayas in this recipe; use 4 peaches, peeled, pitted and sliced, and omit the lime juice. Creamy mashed potatoes make a delicious bed for this colorful stew.

Place the flour on a large plate and dredge the pork cubes in it. In a Dutch oven over medium-high heat, melt the butter. Add the pork and brown on all sides, about 5 minutes.

Meanwhile, in a bowl, toss the shallots and papayas with the lime juice. When the pork is browned, add the shallots and papayas, bouquet garni, stock, and wine to the pot. Bring to a simmer, reduce the heat to medium-low, cover, and simmer gently until the pork is tender, 35–40 minutes. If desired, add the green beans during the last 15 minutes of cooking.

When the stew is ready, remove the bouquet garni and discard. Add the hot-pepper sauce and season to taste with salt and pepper.

To serve, spoon into warmed shallow bowls or plates and garnish with the chives.

Serves 4

1/4 cup (1 1/2 oz/45 g) all-purpose (plain) flour

1 lb (500 g) pork tenderloin, trimmed of excess fat and cut into 1-inch (2.5-cm) cubes

2 tablespoons unsalted butter

2 shallots, minced

2 papayas, peeled, halved lengthwise, seeded, and cut crosswise into slices 1/2 inch (12 mm) thick

2 tablespoons fresh lime juice

Bouquet garni (page 316), substituting 6 whole cloves for the garlic

1 1/2 cups (12 fl oz/375 ml) Chicken Stock (page 314)

1/2 cup (4 fl oz/125 ml) sweet white wine

1/2 lb (250 g) green beans, trimmed and cut into 2-inch (5-cm) lengths (optional)

3 or 4 dashes Tabasco sauce

Salt and freshly ground pepper

Minced fresh chives for garnish

Pork and Endive with Juniper Berries

A combination of slightly sweet and bitter flavors accents succulent pork tender-loin in this simple-to-assemble dish. Juniper berries can be found in well-stocked markets and specialty food stores.

2 tablespoons unsalted butter

1 lb (500 g) pork tenderloin, trimmed of excess fat and cut into 1-inch (2.5-cm) cubes

2 large sweet white onions, cut in half and then into slices ¹/₂ inch (12 mm) thick

2 cups (16 fl oz/500 ml) Chicken Stock (page 314)

1 tablespoon juniper berries

4 heads Belgian endive (chicory/witloof)

2 tablespoons firmly packed golden brown sugar

1 teaspoon soy sauce

Salt and freshly ground pepper

In a Dutch oven over medium heat, melt the butter. Add the pork cubes and brown on all sides, 3–5 minutes. Add the onions and sauté, stirring, until they are slightly soft and the browned bits from the pot bottom begin to cling to them, 6–8 minutes.

Pour in the stock and add the juniper berries, mixing well. Add the endives, pushing them down into the liquid so they are fully immersed. Bring to a simmer, reduce the heat to medium-low, cover, and simmer gently until the pork is cooked through and the endives are tender, 30–40 minutes.

Add the brown sugar and soy sauce and stir until well mixed. Season to taste with salt and pepper.

Spoon into warmed bowls and serve.

Serves 4

Pork Medallions with Lemon and Capers

Pork medallions cook quickly and make a simple but impressive main course. Serve this dish with roasted potatoes seasoned with a little fresh lemon juice, olive oil, and rosemary.

2 pork tenderloins, about ³/₄ lb (375 g) each, trimmed of excess fat

¹/₂ cup (2¹/₂ oz/75 g) all-purpose (plain) flour

Salt and freshly ground pepper

About 4 tablespoons (2 fl oz/60 ml) olive oil

4 cloves garlic, minced

¹/₂ teaspoon minced fresh rosemary

¹/₂ cup (4 fl oz/125 ml) dry white wine

2 cups (16 fl oz/500 ml) Chicken Stock (page 314)

¹/₄ cup (2 oz/60 g) drained capers, rinsed

1–2 tablespoons fresh lemon juice

Lemon wedges for garnish

Cut the tenderloins crosswise into slices ¹/₂ inch (12 mm) thick. Place each slice between 2 sheets of plastic wrap and, using a meat pounder, pound the pork gently until it is evenly ¹/₄ inch (6 mm) thick.

On a plate, combine the flour and salt and pepper to taste. In a large frying pan or sauté pan over medium-high heat, heat 2 tablespoons of the olive oil. Coat the pork with the seasoned flour, shaking off the excess. Working in batches, add the pork to the pan in a single layer and sauté, turning once, until golden brown, 1–2 minutes on each side per batch, adding the remaining olive oil if needed. Transfer to a platter and keep warm.

Reduce the heat to low, add the garlic and rosemary, and sauté for 30–60 seconds. Raise the heat to high, add the wine, and deglaze the pan by stirring with a wooden spoon to dislodge any browned bits from the bottom. Boil until reduced by half, about 1 minute. Add the stock and boil until reduced by half, about 5 minutes. Stir in the capers, lemon juice, and salt and pepper to taste.

Pour the sauce over the pork and garnish with the lemon wedges. Serve at once.

Serves 6

Pork Tenderloin with Braised Cabbage

Lean and boneless, pork tenderloins are cooked with cabbage on the stove top in this simple dish. Mashed or boiled potatoes are all that is needed to round out the menu.

Remove any bruised outer leaves from the head of cabbage and discard. Cut the head into quarters through the stem end and then remove the central core from each wedge. Slice the wedges crosswise into thin shreds. You should have about 10 cups (30 oz/940 g) shredded cabbage. Set aside.

In a large nonstick frying pan over medium-high heat, heat the oil until almost smoking. Add the tenderloins, sprinkle lightly with salt and pepper to taste, and cook, turning frequently, until browned on all sides, about 10 minutes. Remove from the pan and set aside.

Return the pan to medium-high heat. Add the cabbage, 1 teaspoon salt, and ¼ teaspoon pepper. Cook, stirring and tossing several times, until the cabbage is slightly wilted, about 5 minutes. Add the vinegar and sprinkle on the sugar; stir and toss to combine. Reduce the heat to low and return the pork to the pan, pressing the tenderloins down slightly into the cabbage. Cover and cook until the cabbage is tender, the pork is firm to the touch and pale pink when cut in the thickest portion, and an instant-read thermometer inserted into the thickest part of a tenderloin reads 150°F (66°C), about 20 minutes.

Transfer the tenderloins to a cutting board. Mound the cabbage on a platter or on 6 individual plates. Cut the tenderloins on the diagonal into thin slices and arrange over the cabbage. Serve at once.

Serves 6

1 large head green cabbage

1 tablespoon olive oil

2 pork tenderloins, about ¾ lb (375 g) each, trimmed of excess fat

Salt and freshly ground pepper

2 tablespoons cider vinegar

1 tablespoon sugar

Pork Noisettes with Peppers and Balsamic Vinegar

Pork tenderloin is made extra flavorful here with a bell-pepper stuffing and a rich olive sauce. Serve this dish as a main course, accompanied with oven-roasted red potatoes seasoned with garlic cloves and chopped rosemary and thyme.

Cut the roasted bell peppers lengthwise into strips 3/4 inch (2 cm) wide. Put in a bowl and add 1 tablespoon of the balsamic vinegar and salt and pepper to taste. Toss well.

Butterfly the pork tenderloins by making a long slit down the length of each one, cutting just deep enough so that the tenderloin opens up to lay flat; do not cut all the way through. Flatten the tenderloins and pound gently with a meat pounder. Season with salt and pepper to taste. Place the bell pepper strips side by side down the center of each tenderloin. Close up the tenderloins and, using kitchen twine, tie at 1-inch (2.5-cm) intervals so they assume their original shape.

In a large frying pan or sauté pan over medium-high heat, heat the olive oil. Add the pork and brown on all sides, about 5 minutes. Reduce the heat to medium-low, cover, and continue to cook, turning occasionally, until the meat is firm to the touch and pale pink when cut in the thickest portion, 15–18 minutes. Transfer the tenderloins to a platter, cover loosely with aluminum foil, and keep warm. Raise the heat to high and add the stock, remaining 1 tablespoon balsamic vinegar, and olives. Cook, stirring occasionally, until reduced by half, about 5 minutes.

Remove the twine from the tenderloins. Cut the meat crosswise into slices 1 inch (2.5 cm) thick. To serve, arrange the pork slices on warmed plates and spoon the sauce over them. Garnish with the thyme sprigs and serve immediately.

Serves 6

1 red and 1 yellow bell pepper (capsicum), roasted and peeled (page 326)

2 tablespoons balsamic vinegar

Salt and freshly ground pepper

3 pork tenderloins, about 3/4 lb (375 g) each, trimmed of excess fat

2 tablespoons olive oil

2 cups (16 fl oz/500 ml) Chicken Stock (page 314)

1/3 cup (2 oz/ 60 g) Niçoise or Kalamata olives, pitted

Fresh thyme sprigs for garnish

Pork Tenderloin with Corn, Mushrooms, and Carrots

White or cremini mushrooms, cut into thin slices, can replace the oyster mushrooms. Serve as a main dish accompanied with your favorite type of noodle or Steamed White Rice (page 317).

2 cloves garlic, minced

1 tablespoon soy sauce

2 tablespoons sake

1 tablespoon cornstarch (cornflour)

1 lb (500 g) pork tenderloin, cut into thin strips about 2 inches (5 cm) long and ¹/₂ inch (12 mm) wide

3 tablespoons peanut oil

2 small carrots

¹/₂ lb (250 g) oyster mushrooms, tough stem bottoms removed, cut into thin strips about 2 inches (5 cm) long and ¹/₄ inch (6 mm) wide

1 cup (6 oz/185 g) corn kernels (about 2 ears)

¹/₃ cup (3 fl oz/80 ml) Beef Stock (page 314)

Salt and freshly ground pepper

¹/₂ teaspoon Chili Oil (page 17), or to taste

1 tablespoon minced fresh cilantro (fresh coriander)

In a nonaluminum bowl, combine the garlic, soy sauce, sake, and cornstarch and stir to dissolve the cornstarch. Add the pork strips and toss to coat well. Cover and marinate in the refrigerator for 15 minutes to 1 hour.

In a wok or frying pan over high heat, heat 1 tablespoon of the oil, swirling to coat the bottom and sides of the pan. When the oil is almost smoking, using a slotted spoon, remove half of the pork from the marinade and add it to the pan. Stir-fry until golden brown, 3–4 minutes. Be sure to distribute the meat evenly in the pan so it comes into maximum contact with the heat and cooks evenly. Transfer to a dish. Add another 1 tablespoon oil to the pan and cook the remaining pork in the same manner. Transfer to the dish.

Peel the carrots and cut into thin strips 2 inches (5 cm) long and ¹/₂ inch (12 mm) wide. Add the remaining 1 tablespoon oil to the pan over high heat, again swirling to coat the pan. When the oil is almost smoking, add the carrots and mushrooms and stir-fry until just slightly softened, 2–3 minutes. Add the corn kernels and stir-fry 1 minute longer. Add the reserved pork and accumulated juices, the stock, ¹/₂ teaspoon salt, ¹/₂ teaspoon pepper, the chili oil, and cilantro and stir-fry until heated through, about 1 minute. Taste and adjust the seasoning. Serve immediately.

Serves 4

Pork Tenderloins with Guacamole

Pork today is quite lean, which means it can sometimes be dry. Tenderloins, though, are tender and juicy when soaked in a light marinade and served with fresh guacamole.

In a bowl, stir together the wine, vinegar, olive oil, thyme, 1/2 teaspoon salt, and 1/4 teaspoon pepper. Reserve 1/4 cup (2 fl oz/60 ml) of the mixture. Place the tenderloins in a nonaluminum baking dish just large enough to hold them comfortably in one layer. Pour the wine mixture evenly over the pork. Cover and refrigerate for at least 2 hours, turning occasionally.

Peel and pit the avocados and place them in a bowl. Using a fork, mash them coarsely, leaving a few small lumps. Add the tomato, garlic, and cilantro, then mix in the lime juice, Tabasco sauce, jalapeño (if using), and salt and pepper to taste. Press a piece of plastic wrap directly onto the surface of the guacamole and refrigerate until serving.

Prepare a fire in a charcoal grill, or preheat a gas grill. Remove the tenderloins from the marinade, reserving the marinade, and pat them dry with paper towels. Place the marinade in a saucepan, bring to a boil, and boil for 5 minutes. Place the meat on the grill rack. Grill 4–6 inches (10–15 cm) from the heat source for about 25 minutes, brushing the meat occasionally with the marinade and turning it frequently so it browns evenly. It is done when slightly pink in the center and an instant-read thermometer inserted into the thickest part registers 150°F (66°C). Remove the meat from the grill and cover loosely with aluminum foil. Let rest for 5 minutes before carving. Cut on the diagonal into thin slices. Serve with the guacamole and tortillas.

Serves 4–6

1/2 cup (4 fl oz/125 ml) dry red or white wine

2 tablespoons balsamic vinegar

2 tablespoons olive oil

2 teaspoons minced fresh thyme

Salt and freshly ground pepper

About 2 lb (1 kg) pork tenderloin, trimmed of excess fat

FOR THE GUACAMOLE:

2 or 3 large ripe avocados

1 large ripe tomato, peeled and seeded (page 329), then chopped

1 clove garlic, minced

2 tablespoons chopped fresh cilantro (fresh coriander)

2 tablespoons fresh lime juice

1/4 teaspoon Tabasco, or to taste

1 teaspoon minced jalapeño chile (optional)

Warm tortillas

Grilled Pork Tenderloin with Dried-Fruit Chutney

Chutney and pork are natural partners. Try using dried apples, cherries, or figs in place of any of the dried fruits in this recipe. Serve with Steamed White Rice (page 317) and grilled vegetables or simply garnish with strips of orange peel.

FOR THE DRIED-FRUIT CHUTNEY:

6 tablespoons (3 fl oz/90 ml) balsamic vinegar

1/2 cup (3 1/2 oz/105 g) firmly packed golden brown sugar

1/4 lb (125 g) dried apricots

1/4 lb (125 g) dried pitted prunes

1/4 lb (125 g) dried cranberries

1 teaspoon grated orange zest

Juice of 1 orange

1/2 cup (4 fl oz/125 ml) brewed orange-spice tea

1/4 teaspoon ground cinnamon

1/4 teaspoon ground allspice

3 pork tenderloins, about 3/4 lb (375 g) each, trimmed of excess fat

2 tablespoons olive oil

Salt and freshly ground pepper

To make the chutney, in a saucepan, combine the vinegar, brown sugar, dried fruits, orange zest and juice, tea, cinnamon, and allspice. Bring to a boil over medium heat, stirring occasionally, then reduce the heat to low. Simmer gently, uncovered, until thick, 1–2 hours, adding water as necessary to prevent sticking. Remove from the heat and let cool to room temperature.

Prepare a fire in a charcoal grill, or preheat a gas grill or broiler (grill).

Brush the pork tenderloins with the olive oil and sprinkle with salt and pepper to taste. Place the tenderloins on the grill rack and grill 4–6 inches (10–15 cm) from the heat source, turning occasionally, until golden brown on all sides and an instant-read thermometer inserted into the thickest part registers 150°F (66°C), or the meat is pale pink when cut in the thickest portion, about 12 minutes.

Remove the tenderloins from the grill and cover loosely with aluminum foil. Let rest for 2–3 minutes before carving.

Cut crosswise into slices 1/2 inch (12 mm) thick. Place 4 or 5 slices on each plate along with a spoonful of chutney. Serve immediately.

Serves 6

Apricot-Glazed Pork Kabobs with Wild Rice

Apricot preserves and dried apricots lend a mild and fruity sweetness to this savory dish. Wild rice rounds out the flavors, providing a nutty counterpoint. Garnish with fresh flat-leaf (Italian) parsley, if you like.

To make the apricot glaze, in a small saucepan, combine the butter, orange juice, ginger, and apricot preserves. Cook over medium heat until the butter and preserves melt and the mixture begins to bubble around the edges, 3–4 minutes. Transfer to a small bowl and let cool for 10 minutes. Reserve ¹/₄ cup (2 fl oz/60 ml) of the glaze.

Sprinkle the pork cubes with salt and pepper and add them to the remaining apricot glaze. Stir to coat evenly. Let stand at room temperature for 30 minutes.

If using wooden skewers, soak 12 long ones in water to cover for 30 minutes. In a saucepan, combine the wild rice, water, and ³/₄ teaspoon salt. Bring to a boil, reduce the heat to low, cover, and cook for 20 minutes. Uncover, stir in the dried apricots, re-cover, and continue to cook until the rice is tender, about 25 minutes longer. Check from time to time and, if necessary to prevent sticking, add a little water. When the rice is ready, fluff it with a fork.

While the rice is cooking, prepare a fire in a charcoal grill, or preheat a gas grill or broiler (grill). Thread the pork cubes on 12 skewers, dividing evenly. Fifteen minutes before the rice is ready, place the skewers on the grill rack or on a broiler pan. Grill or broil 4 inches (10 cm) from the heat source, turning occasionally and basting with the reserved glaze, until the pork is browned on the outside and firm to the touch, about 10–12 minutes.

To serve, place 2 skewers on each plate and accompany with the wild rice.

Serves 6

FOR THE APRICOT GLAZE:

¹/₄ cup (2 oz/60 g) unsalted butter

6 tablespoons (6 fl oz/90 ml) fresh orange juice

1 tablespoon peeled and grated fresh ginger

1 jar (10 oz/315 g) apricot preserves

1¹/₂ lb (750 g) pork tenderloin, trimmed of excess fat and cut into 1-inch (2.5-cm) cubes

Salt and freshly ground pepper

1¹/₄ cups (7¹/₂ oz/235 g) wild rice, rinsed and drained

4 cups (32 fl oz/1 l) water

¹/₂ cup (3 oz/90 g) dried apricot halves

Salad of Grilled Pork, Pears, and Toasted Pecans

1/2 cup (2 oz/60 g) pecans

1 tablespoon peanut oil

Salt and freshly ground pepper

Pinch of sugar

2 pork tenderloins, about
3/4 lb (375 g) each, trimmed
of excess fat

1 tablespoon olive oil

FOR THE DRESSING:

6 tablespoons (3 fl oz/90 ml)
olive oil

2 tablespoons sherry vinegar

1 tablespoon hazelnut
(filbert) oil

Salt and freshly ground pepper

2 firm but ripe pears,
preferably Bosc, halved and
cored

6 handfuls (about 6 oz/185 g)
mixed salad greens

Prepare a fire in a charcoal grill, or preheat a gas grill or broiler (grill). Preheat the oven to 350°F (180°C).

In a bowl, combine the pecans, peanut oil, salt and pepper to taste, and sugar and toss well to coat the nuts. Spread the pecans evenly on a baking sheet and bake until lightly golden, 5–7 minutes. Let cool.

Brush the pork tenderloins with the 1 tablespoon olive oil and season to taste with salt and pepper. Place on the grill rack or on a broiler (grill) pan 4 inches (10 cm) from the heat source and cook, turning occasionally to brown evenly, until an instant-read thermometer inserted into the thickest part registers 150°F (66°C) or the pork is pale pink when cut in the thickest portion, about 12 minutes. Transfer to a cutting board, cover loosely with aluminum foil, and let rest for 2–3 minutes before carving. Cut crosswise into slices 1/4 inch (6 mm) thick.

To make the dressing, in a small bowl, whisk together the olive oil, sherry vinegar, hazelnut oil, and salt and pepper to taste.

Cut the pears lengthwise into very thin slices. In a large bowl, combine the pear slices, greens, pork, pecans, and dressing. Toss to mix well. Transfer to a platter and serve immediately.

Serves 6

Pork Tenderloin with Chutney Dressing

The blend of ingredients in the dressing complements the naturally rich flavor of the pork. This dish can be served hot or cold. If serving cold, let the tenderloins cool before slicing, then arrange over a bed of lettuce.

2 tablespoons olive oil

2 teaspoons dried thyme or sage

Salt and freshly ground pepper

2 pork tenderloins, about 6 oz (375 g) each, trimmed of excess fat

FOR THE CHUTNEY DRESSING:

$^{1}/_{2}$ cup (5 oz/155 g) mango chutney

$^{1}/_{2}$ cup (4$^{1}/_{2}$ oz/140 g) applesauce

$^{1}/_{4}$ cup (2 oz/60 g) tomato ketchup

1$^{1}/_{2}$ teaspoons curry powder

Romaine (cos) or butter (Boston) lettuce leaves for serving (optional)

Preheat the oven to 350°F (180°C).

In a bowl, stir together the olive oil, thyme, $^{1}/_{2}$ teaspoon salt, and $^{1}/_{2}$ teaspoon pepper. Rub the herb mixture evenly over the pork. Place the tenderloins in a roasting pan and roast until firm to the touch and pale pink when cut in the thickest portion and an instant-read thermometer inserted into the thickest part of a tenderloin reads 150°F (66°C), about 40 minutes. Remove from the oven and set aside for about 5 minutes before slicing.

Meanwhile, make the chutney dressing: In a small bowl, stir together the chutney, applesauce, ketchup, and curry powder until well blended.

To serve, cut the pork on the diagonal into slices $^{1}/_{4}$–$^{1}/_{2}$ inch (6–12 mm) thick. Arrange the slices, overlapping slightly, on a platter. Serve at once and pass the dressing at the table. Or, let the meat cool before slicing, then arrange over a bed of romaine (cos) or butter (Boston) lettuce.

Serves 6

Thai Pork Satay with Peanut Sauce

Serve this dish with thinly sliced cucumbers and red onion dressed with seasoned rice vinegar. Coconut milk and fish sauce can be found in Asian markets and many supermarkets.

In a bowl, combine the coconut milk, curry powder, salt to taste, and pork. Stir to coat the pork evenly with all the ingredients. Cover and refrigerate for 1 hour.

Meanwhile, soak 18 long wooden skewers in water to cover for 30 minutes. To make the sauce, in a food processor, process the peanuts to a coarse meal. Add the coconut milk, brown sugar, red pepper flakes, fish sauce, vinegar, and salt to taste. Process to combine. Pour into a frying pan and place over medium heat. Bring to a simmer and cook until the sauce is thick, about 10 minutes. Remove from the heat and pour into a small bowl.

Prepare a fire in a charcoal grill, or preheat a gas grill or broiler (grill). Drain the skewers and thread the pork strips onto them. Arrange the skewers on the grill rack or broiler (grill) pan and grill or broil 4 inches (10 cm) from the heat source, turning occasionally, until the pork is cooked through, 2–3 minutes.

Transfer the skewers to a warmed platter, garnish with the cilantro, and spoon the peanut sauce evenly over the top. Serve immediately.

Serves 6

¼ cup (2 fl oz/60 ml) coconut milk

1½ teaspoons curry powder

Salt

1 lb (500 g) boneless pork loin, trimmed of excess fat and cut into strips about 3 inches (7.5 cm) long by 1 inch (2.5 cm) wide by 1 inch (3 mm) thick

FOR THE PEANUT SAUCE:

½ cup (3 oz/90 g) unsalted roasted peanuts

1 cup (8 fl oz/250 ml) coconut milk

1 tablespoon firmly packed golden brown sugar

⅛–¼ teaspoon red pepper flakes

2 teaspoons fish sauce

3 teaspoons rice vinegar or cider vinegar

Salt

Fresh cilantro (fresh coriander) leaves for garnish

Pork Loin with Madeira Marinade

To make the marinade, in a small bowl, whisk together the wine, olive oil, vinegar, salt, allspice, cloves, and pepper. Place the pork in a large lock-top plastic bag and pour in the wine mixture. Press out the air and seal the bag. Massage the bag gently to distribute the marinade evenly. Place in a large bowl and refrigerate, turning and massaging the bag occasionally, for at least 6 hours, or for up to 2 days if you wish.

Prepare a fire for indirect-heat cooking in a charcoal grill with a cover (page 326), or preheat a gas grill.

Remove the pork from the marinade and pat it dry with paper towels.

Place the pork loin on the grill rack over indirect heat, cover the grill, and open the vents halfway. Cook for 45 minutes, then turn the roast. Add fresh coals to replenish the fire; continue to cook, turning once more, until the meat is slightly pink when cut into at the thickest part and an instant-read thermometer inserted into the thickest part registers 150°F (66°C), 50–60 minutes longer.

Remove the pork from the grill and cover loosely with aluminum foil. Let rest for 10 minutes. To serve, remove the twine, carve the meat crosswise into slices about ¹/₄ inch (6 mm) thick, and arrange on a warmed platter.

Serves 8

FOR THE MADEIRA MARINADE:

1¹/₂ cups (12 fl oz/375 ml) Madeira wine

¹/₄ cup (2 fl oz/60 ml) olive oil

¹/₄ cup (2 fl oz/60 ml) red or white wine vinegar

1 teaspoon salt

1 teaspoon ground allspice

¹/₂ teaspoon ground cloves

¹/₂ teaspoon freshly ground pepper

1 boneless pork loin, 3¹/₂–4 lb (1.75–2 kg), trimmed of excess fat and tied at 2-inch (5-cm) intervals for roasting

Roast Loin of Pork with Baked Apples

For a more substantial main course, serve the pork and baked apples alongside one-half recipe Scalloped Potatoes and Ham with Cheddar (page 150), made without the ham, or your favorite green vegetable.

1 boneless pork loin, about 3 lb (1.5 kg), trimmed of excess fat

2 cloves garlic, minced

1 tablespoon minced fresh rosemary

Salt and freshly ground pepper

6 tart green apples such as pippin or Granny Smith

1/4 cup (2 oz/60 g) firmly packed golden brown sugar

2 tablespoons unsalted butter

1/2 cup (4 fl oz/125 ml) water

1/4 teaspoon ground cinnamon

1/2 teaspoon grated lemon zest

Position a rack in the lower third of the oven and preheat to 500°F (260°C).

Place the pork on a rack in a roasting pan. In a small bowl, mix together the garlic, rosemary, 1/2 teaspoon salt, and pepper to taste. Rub the mixture evenly over the surface of the pork. Place in the oven and roast until the pork begins to spatter, about 15 minutes.

Meanwhile, peel the top one-third of each apple and then core the apples. In a small pan, combine the sugar, butter, water, cinnamon, and lemon zest. Place over high heat and bring to a boil, stirring. Remove from the heat and set aside.

Reduce the oven temperature to 350°F (180°C). At the same time, place the apples in an 8-cup (2-l) baking dish and pour the sugar mixture evenly over them. Cover the dish with aluminum foil and place in the oven with the pork. Continue to roast the pork until an instant-read thermometer inserted into the thickest part registers 150°F (66°C) or the meat is pale pink when cut in the thickest portion, about 30 minutes longer. Cook the apples until tender when pierced with a fork, 20–25 minutes. Remove the pork and the apples from the oven. Cover the pork loosely with aluminum foil and let rest for 10 minutes before carving. Keep the apples warm until ready to use.

Slice the pork and arrange on a warmed serving platter with the baked apples. Drizzle the juices from the dish that held the apples over the pork and the apples. Serve immediately.

Serves 6

Orange-and-Ginger-Glazed Pork Roast

The optional dry rub helps bring out the natural flavor of pork, and the orange-ginger mixture gives the meat a dark, spicy glaze. Serve with grilled apple rings or applesauce.

2 tablespoons olive oil, if needed

1 boneless pork loin, 3¹/₂–4 lb (1.75–2 kg), tied for roasting

Dry Rub for pork (page 14) (optional)

¹/₂ cup (5 oz/155 g) orange marmalade

¹/₃ cup (3 oz/90 g) Dijon mustard

1 tablespoon peeled and grated fresh ginger

1 tablespoon Worcestershire sauce

Salt and freshly ground pepper

If using the dry rub, rub the olive oil over the pork, then coat it evenly with the dry rub. Let stand at room temperature for at least 1 hour, or cover and refrigerate for several hours.

Meanwhile, in a small bowl, stir together the marmalade, mustard, ginger, Worcestershire sauce, salt to taste, and ¹/₄–¹/₂ teaspoon pepper.

Prepare a fire for indirect-heat cooking in a charcoal grill with a cover (page 326), or preheat a gas grill. Oil the grill rack and position about 4–6 inches (10–15 cm) above the heat.

Place the pork on the grill rack over indirect heat, cover the grill, and open the vents halfway. Cook for 45 minutes, then turn the roast. Replenish the charcoal fire with fresh coals. Cook, brushing with the marmalade mixture every 10 minutes and turning once or twice, until an instant-read thermometer inserted in the center of the roast registers 150°F (66°C), 40–50 minutes longer.

Remove the pork from the grill, cover loosely with aluminum foil, and let rest for 10 minutes. To serve, remove the twine and cut into slices ¹/₄ inch (6 mm) thick.

Serves 8

Roast Pork with Figs

Pork and fruit are a classic pairing, and are delicious when served together. Black Mission figs work well for this recipe. Garnish the platter with 6–8 thin orange slices, if you like.

Prepare the poached figs (page 316). Drain, reserving the cooking liquid. Cut the figs in half and set aside.

Preheat the oven to 400°F (200°C). Trim the pork loin of visible fat. Rub the pork loin all over with salt and pepper to taste and the 1 teaspoon cinnamon. Place on a rack in a roasting pan.

In a bowl, stir together the 1/2 cup (4 fl oz/125 ml) sherry, orange juice, and honey.

Roast the pork, basting every 10 minutes with the orange juice mixture, until an instant-read thermometer inserted into the center of the loin registers 150°F (66°C), or the meat is pale pink when cut into at the thickest portion, about 1 hour.

Meanwhile, make the sauce: In a sauté pan over medium heat, melt the butter. Add the onion and sauté, stirring often, until softened, 8–10 minutes. Add the garlic and cook for 3 minutes to release its flavor. Add the stock, 1 cup (8 fl oz/250 ml) sherry, almonds, orange zest, 1/2 teaspoon cinnamon, and the cooking liquid from the poached figs. Raise the heat to high and cook until thickened, 8–10 minutes. Taste and add more cinnamon, if desired. Add the figs and heat through. Season to taste with salt and pepper.

Remove the pork from the oven and transfer to a cutting board. Cover loosely with aluminum foil and let rest for 5–10 minutes. Slice the pork and arrange on a platter. Spoon the sauce over the pork and surround with the figs. Serve at once.

Serves 4

Poached Figs (page 316)

1 center-cut boneless pork loin, 3 lb (1.5 kg)

Salt and freshly ground pepper

1 teaspoon ground cinnamon

1/2 cup *each* (4 fl oz/125 ml) dry sherry and fresh orange juice

1/4 cup (3 oz/90 g) honey

FOR THE SAUCE:

3 tablespoons unsalted butter

1 large yellow onion, chopped

3 cloves garlic, minced

1 cup *each* (8 fl oz/250 ml) Chicken Stock (page 314) and dry sherry

1/2 cup (2 oz/60 g) ground toasted almonds (page 326)

1 tablespoon orange zest

1/2 teaspoon ground cinnamon, or to taste

Salt and freshly ground pepper

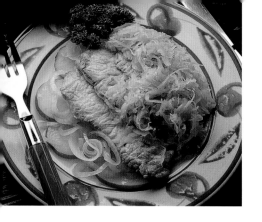

Winter Casserole of Pork, Sauerkraut, and Potatoes

This main-course recipe is inspired by a traditional dish from the Alsatian region of France called *beckenoffe*, or "baker's oven," a slowly baked dish that makes ideal winter fare.

1 can (27 oz/845 g) sauerkraut, drained

1 tart green apple such as Granny Smith or pippin, halved, cored, peeled, and coarsely grated

2 cups (16 fl oz/500 ml) Chicken Stock (page 314)

Salt and freshly ground pepper

1½ lb (750 g) boneless pork loin, trimmed of excess fat and cut into slices ¼ inch (6 mm) thick

3 teaspoons olive oil

2 lb (1 kg) unpeeled red potatoes, cut into slices 1 inch (3 mm) thick

1 yellow onion, thinly sliced

Place the sauerkraut in a colander and rinse under cold running water. Drain well, shaking the colander to remove any excess water.

In a large saucepan over high heat, combine the sauerkraut, the apple, 1½ cups (12 fl oz/375 ml) of the stock, and pepper to taste. Bring to a boil, then immediately reduce the heat to low. Simmer, uncovered, until the sauerkraut softens, about 30 minutes. Remove from the heat and drain in a colander. Set the sauerkraut aside.

Preheat the oven to 350°F (180°C). Place 1 slice of pork between 2 sheets of plastic wrap. Using a meat pounder, pound the pork gently until it is ⅛ inch (3 mm) thick. Repeat with the remaining pork slices. Heat 2 teaspoons of the olive oil in a large frying pan over medium heat. Working in batches if necessary, fry the pork slices, turning once, until white, about 1 minute on each side. Remove from the pan and set aside.

Brush a 13-by-9-inch (33-by-23-cm) baking dish with the remaining 1 teaspoon oil. Layer all the potato slices on the bottom of the dish. Layer evenly with the onion slices and then the pork slices. Pour the remaining ½ cup (4 fl oz/125 ml) stock over the top. Arrange the drained sauerkraut over the pork. Cover with foil and cook until the pork and potatoes are tender when pierced with a fork, 1–1¼ hours.

To serve, season to taste with salt. Spoon onto individual plates and serve at once.

Serves 6

Pecan-Crusted Pork Chops

Any kind of nuts can be substituted for the pecans in this recipe. Try walnuts, hazelnuts (filberts), almonds, or a combination. Serve with Plum and Ginger Chutney or Pear and Mustard Chutney (page 21).

Preheat the oven to 350°F (180°C). Spread the pecans on a baking sheet and bake until lightly golden, 5–7 minutes. Let cool and then chop finely. Place in a shallow bowl and add the 1 teaspoon salt and ¼ teaspoon pepper. Stir to mix well. Raise the oven temperature to 375°F (190°C).

Put the flour in another bowl. In a third bowl, whisk the eggs until well blended.

Coating the pork evenly and completely at each step, dip the pork chops, one at a time, into the flour, shaking off any excess. Dip the chops into the egg and then the finely chopped pecans.

In a large, ovenproof frying pan over medium heat, melt the butter. Add the pork chops in a single layer and cook uncovered, turning once, until golden on each side, 5–6 minutes. Place the frying pan in the oven and continue to cook the pork until firm to the touch and pale pink when cut in the center, 10–12 minutes; do not allow the nut coating to burn.

Transfer the pork chops to a warmed platter and serve immediately.

Serves 6

2 cups (8 oz/250 g) pecans

Salt and freshly ground pepper

½ cup (2½ oz/75 g) all-purpose (plain) flour

3 eggs

6 center-cut pork loin chops, each about 6 oz (185 g) and 1 inch (2.5 cm) thick, trimmed of excess fat

3 tablespoons unsalted butter

Pork Chops with Prune and Apple Stuffing

The basic elements of a stuffing for pork chops are butter, onion, and bread crumbs, but mixed fresh herbs, minced garlic, sautéed chopped wild mushrooms, or chopped cooked bacon can also be added, if you like.

Place the prunes in a bowl and pour in boiling water to cover. Let stand for about 30 minutes. Drain the prunes well and chop finely. Set aside.

In a frying pan over medium heat, melt the butter. Add the onion and sauté, stirring, until very soft, about 10 minutes. Transfer the onion to a bowl and add the prunes, apple, bread crumbs, cinnamon, and salt and pepper to taste. Mix well.

Using a small, sharp knife, cut a horizontal slit 1 inch (2.5 cm) long into the side of each pork chop. With the knife, work inward from the slit, cutting almost to the opposite side of the chop; be careful not to cut through the chop completely. Stuff an equal amount of the stuffing into each chop; flatten the chops slightly.

In a frying pan large enough to hold the chops in a single layer without crowding, warm the olive oil over medium heat. Add the chops and cook, uncovered, for 5 minutes. Turn the chops and season to taste with salt and pepper. Reduce the heat to medium-low and continue to cook uncovered, turning occasionally, until golden and firm to the touch, about 12 minutes longer.

Transfer the chops to warmed plates and serve immediately.

Serves 6

15 pitted prunes

Boiling water, as needed

2 tablespoons unsalted butter

1 yellow onion, minced

1 large firm green apple such as Granny Smith or pippin, peeled, halved, cored and coarsely grated

1 cup (2 oz/60 g) fresh herbed bread crumbs (page 316)

Pinch of ground cinnamon

Salt and freshly ground pepper

6 center-cut pork chops, each about 6 oz (185 g) and 1 inch (2.5 cm) thick, trimmed of excess fat

2 tablespoons olive oil

Southwest Pork Stir-Fry

This quick stir-fry can be used as a filling for tacos or served over white rice (page 317). If you like, add 1 cup (6 oz/185 g) steamed corn kernels with the cherry tomatoes. Yellow cherry tomatoes can be substituted for half of the red ones.

1 *each* green, red, and yellow bell pepper (capsicum), seeded and deribbed

4 tablespoons (2 fl oz/60 ml) olive oil

1 large red onion, cut into small wedges

1/2–1 jalapeño or serrano chile, seeded and minced

2 pork tenderloins, about 1 1/2 lb (750 g) total weight, trimmed of excess fat

1/2 cup (4 fl oz/125 ml) Chicken Stock (page 314)

1 tablespoon cornstarch (cornflour)

2 teaspoons ground cumin

3 cloves garlic, minced

15–20 cherry tomatoes

Salt and freshly ground pepper

Chopped fresh cilantro (fresh coriander) leaves for garnish

Cut the bell peppers lengthwise into strips 1/4 inch (6 mm) wide.

In a wok or a large, deep frying pan over medium-high heat, heat 2 tablespoons of the olive oil. Add the onion, chile, and bell pepper strips and stir-fry until the peppers are crisp-tender, 6–8 minutes. Remove the pan from the heat and transfer the mixture to a bowl. Set the bowl and the pan aside.

Cut the pork tenderloins lengthwise into quarters, then cut them crosswise into pieces 1/4 inch (6 mm) thick. In a large bowl, mix together the pork pieces, chicken stock, cornstarch, cumin, and garlic. Return the wok or frying pan to the stove top over medium-high heat and add the remaining 2 tablespoons oil. Add the pork mixture and stir and toss until the pork is cooked, 3–4 minutes. Return the bell pepper mixture to the pan, along with the cherry tomatoes and salt and pepper to taste. Stir and toss for 1 minute.

Transfer to a warmed platter and garnish with the cilantro. Serve immediately.

Serves 6

Moroccan-Style Grilled Pork Chops

The chermoula marinade in this recipe is used in Moroccan cuisine to enhance the flavors of a variety of foods. Lamb chops can be used in place of the pork chops. Serve with steamed couscous or Steamed White Rice (page 317).

To make the chermoula, in a blender or a food processor fitted with the metal blade, combine the cumin, paprika, turmeric, cayenne, garlic, onion, salt and black pepper to taste, cilantro, parsley, lemon juice, olive oil, and 1 tablespoon water. Process until smooth. Place the pork chops in a single layer in a shallow non-aluminum bowl and pour the chermoula over the top. Turn the chops to coat them evenly on both sides with the chermoula. Cover and refrigerate for 1 hour.

Prepare a fire in a charcoal grill, or preheat a gas grill or broiler (grill). Place the pork chops on the grill rack or a broiler pan. Brush any of the chermoula remaining in the dish over the tops of the chops, distributing it evenly. Grill or broil 3 inches (7.5 cm) from the heat source, turning once, until the pork is golden on the outside, firm to the touch, and pale pink when cut in the center, about 10 minutes per side.

Transfer the chops to a warmed platter or plates. Serve immediately.

Serves 6

FOR THE CHERMOULA MARINADE:

1½ teaspoons ground cumin

1½ teaspoons sweet Hungarian paprika

½ teaspoon ground turmeric

¼ teaspoon cayenne pepper

3 cloves garlic

⅓ cup (2 oz/60 g) finely chopped yellow onion

Salt and freshly ground black pepper

6 tablespoons chopped fresh cilantro (fresh coriander)

6 tablespoons (½ oz/15 g) chopped fresh flat-leaf (Italian) parsley

5 tablespoons (3 fl oz/80 ml) fresh lemon juice

5 tablespoons (3 fl oz/80 ml) extra-virgin olive oil

6 center-cut pork chops, each about ½ lb (250 g) and 1–1½ inches (2.5–4 cm) thick, trimmed of excess fat

Mustard-Glazed Sausages with Sauerkraut Relish

For this recipe, use any type of fresh sausage, including pork, beef, chicken, turkey, or a combination. Whichever type you choose, it is important that you cook them fully.

FOR THE SAUERKRAUT RELISH:

3 cups (1–1¼ lb/500–625 g) sauerkraut

¼ cup (⅓ oz/10 g) minced fresh flat-leaf (Italian) parsley

¼ cup (2 fl oz/60 ml) cider vinegar

3 tablespoons olive oil

4 teaspoons sugar

¼ teaspoon freshly ground pepper

½ cup (4 oz/125 g) Dijon mustard

¼ cup (3 oz/90 g) honey

2 tablespoons cider vinegar or white wine vinegar

2 lb (1 kg) fresh pork sausages, 1–1¼ inches (2.5–3 cm) in diameter

To make the relish, put the sauerkraut in a colander and rinse under cold running water. Drain well, then squeeze to remove the excess water. In a large bowl, combine the sauerkraut, parsley, vinegar, olive oil, sugar, and pepper. Stir and toss with a fork to mix. Cover tightly and refrigerate for at least 2 hours or for up to 3 days, to blend the flavors.

Prepare a fire in a charcoal grill, or preheat a gas grill or broiler (grill).

In a small bowl, whisk together the mustard, honey, and 2 tablespoons vinegar; set aside.

Arrange the sausages on the grill rack or a broiler pan 4 inches (10 cm) from the heat source. Have a spray bottle of water handy to extinguish flare-ups if using a charcoal grill. Grill or broil, turning often, until well browned and fully cooked, 15–18 minutes. During the last 6–8 minutes of grilling, brush the sausages 2 or 3 times with the mustard mixture.

To serve, spread the sauerkraut relish on a warmed platter or individual plates and arrange the sausages on top.

Serves 4–6

Sausage Sandwiches with Red and Yellow Peppers

These delicious sandwiches can also be topped with fresh basil leaves, grilled or broiled eggplant (aubergine) or tomato slices, and melted Fontina or mozzarella cheese.

In a large frying pan or sauté pan over medium heat, heat the olive oil. Add the onion wedges and sauté until they begin to soften, about 5 minutes. Add all the bell peppers and continue to cook uncovered, stirring occasionally, until the peppers are soft, about 10 minutes. Transfer the peppers and onions to a platter and keep warm.

Place the same pan over medium heat and add the water. Add the sausages and cook, turning occasionally, until cooked through, about 12 minutes.

Transfer the sausages to a cutting board and cut on the diagonal into slices 1/4 inch (6 mm) thick.

Rub one side of each toasted bread slice with a whole garlic clove, holding the toast as if it were a flat hand-held grater and moving the garlic back and forth over it. Spread the garlic-rubbed side of half of the bread slices with a thin layer of mayonnaise. Divide the sausage slices, peppers, and onions evenly among the bread slices. Top with the remaining toasted slices, garlic-rubbed side down.

Place the sandwiches on individual plates. Cut them in half on the diagonal and serve immediately.

Serves 6

2 tablespoons olive oil

1 large red onion, cut into wedges 1/2 inch (12 mm) wide

1 yellow and 2 red bell peppers (capsicums), seeded, deribbed, and cut lengthwise into strips 1/2 inch (12 mm) wide

1/4 cup (2 fl oz/60 ml) water

4 spicy pork sausages, about 1 lb (500 g) total weight, pricked with a fork

12 slices country-style bread, toasted

2 cloves garlic

1/4 cup (2 oz/60 g) mayonnaise

Red Onions Stuffed with Pork

Onions become sweet when roasted with a flavorful filling. This stuffing can also be made with lamb, and either stuffing can also be used to fill red, green, or yellow bell peppers (capsicums).

4 cups (14 oz/37 g) pine nuts

6 large red onions, boiled in salted water for 15 minutes

Salt and freshly ground pepper

1/2 lb (250 g) ground (minced) lean pork

1/2 cup (3 1/2 oz/105 g) long-grain white rice, rinsed and drained

1/4 cup (1 1/2 oz/45 g) golden raisins (sultanas)

1 large tomato, peeled and seeded (page 329), then chopped

1 tablespoon tomato paste

1/4 cup (1/3 oz/10 g) minced fresh flat-leaf (Italian) parsley

2 tablespoons chopped fresh mint, plus fresh mint leaves for garnish

1/4 teaspoon ground allspice

2 tablespoons olive oil

1 cup (8 fl oz/250 ml) Chicken Stock, plus more if needed (page 314)

Juice of 1/2 lemon

Preheat the oven to 350°F (180°C). Spread the pine nuts on a baking sheet and toast, shaking the pan occasionally, until lightly golden, 3–5 minutes. Remove from the oven, transfer immediately to a plate, and let cool. Raise the oven temperature to 375°F (190°C).

Drain the onions well and let cool. Cut a 1/2-inch (12-mm) slice off the top of each onion. Trim a slice off the bottom of each onion just thick enough so that it will stand upright; do not trim too much or the onion will fall apart. Using a small knife, cut the center out of each onion, leaving a shell 1/2 inch (12 mm) thick. Discard the removed onion. Season the onion shells with salt and pepper.

In a bowl, combine the pork, toasted pine nuts, rice, raisins, tomato, tomato paste, parsley, chopped mint, allspice, olive oil, 3/4 teaspoon salt, and pepper to taste. Mix well. Stuff the onions with the pork mixture, filling them no more than three-fourths full to allow room for expansion. Place the onions close together in a baking dish. In a small saucepan, bring the 1 cup (8 fl oz/250 ml) stock to a boil and pour it between the onions. Sprinkle the lemon juice evenly over the onion tops. Cover with aluminum foil and bake until the onions are tender when pierced with a knife and the rice is cooked, 45–50 minutes. Add more stock to the baking dish if the dish is drying out.

Carefully transfer the onions to a platter and pour the pan juices over the filling. Let cool slightly, then garnish with the mint leaves. Serve warm.

Serves 6

Polenta with Pork Sausages and Tomatoes

Sautéed red, green, and yellow bell peppers (capsicums) can be added to this recipe to make it even more colorful. Replace the Parmesan cheese with pecorino, if you like.

In a large saucepan over high heat, bring the water to a rolling boil. Add 1 1/2 teaspoons salt. Add the polenta in a slow, steady stream, whisking constantly. As soon as all of the polenta has been added, reduce the heat to low and switch to a wooden spoon. Cook, stirring often, until the polenta is so thick that the spoon can stand upright, about 30 minutes.

Meanwhile, in a large frying pan or sauté pan over medium heat, heat the olive oil. Add the onion and sauté until very soft, about 10 minutes. Add the sausages and cook, turning occasionally, until they are firm to the touch and cooked through, about 10 minutes.

Pour off any excess fat in the pan. Add the tomatoes and raise the heat to high. Cook, uncovered, until the tomatoes thicken, about 10 minutes. Season to taste with salt and pepper.

When the polenta is done, stir in the butter, rosemary, and salt and pepper to taste. To serve, spoon the polenta onto a warmed serving platter or plates and make a well in the center. Cut the sausages in half on the diagonal and spoon the sausages and tomato sauce into the well. Sprinkle with the Parmesan cheese, garnish with the parsley if you like, and serve immediately.

Serves 6

8 cups (64 fl oz/2 l) water

Salt and freshly ground pepper

2 1/2 cups (15 oz/470 g) polenta

3 tablespoons olive oil

1 yellow onion, finely chopped

3 sweet Italian sausages, about 3/4 lb (375 g) total weight, pricked with a fork

3 hot Italian sausages, about 3/4 lb (375 g) total weight, pricked with a fork

3 cups (18 oz/560 g) tomatoes, peeled, seeded (page 329), and chopped, or canned chopped plum (Roma) tomatoes with their juices

3 tablespoons unsalted butter

1 teaspoon minced fresh rosemary

1/2 cup (2 oz/60 g) freshly grated Parmesan cheese

Chopped fresh flat-leaf (Italian) parsley for garnish (optional)

Pork Meat Loaf with Sweet-and-Hot Sauce

Serve this variation on classic beef meat loaf hot with mashed potatoes
and green beans. Leftover meatloaf slices can be tucked into sandwiches
with slices of Cheddar cheese and tomatoes.

12 green (spring) onions

2 tablespoons unsalted butter

1/4 lb (125 g) white or cremini
mushrooms, thinly sliced

1/2 cup (1 oz/30 g) fresh Herbed
Bread Crumbs (page 316)

1 lb (500 g) ground (minced)
lean pork

1/2 lb (250 g) ground (minced)
lean beef

1 egg, lightly beaten

1 clove garlic, minced

3 tablespoons chopped fresh
flat-leaf (Italian) parsley

1/4 cup (2 fl oz/60 ml) Chicken
Stock (page 314)

Salt and freshly ground black
pepper

1/3 cup (3 oz/90 g) tomato
ketchup

1/2 cup (4 oz/125 g) sugar

1/3 cup *each* (3 fl oz/80 ml)
water and white wine vinegar

1 tablespoon soy sauce

1/2 teaspoon cayenne pepper

1 1/2 tablespoons cornstarch
(cornflour)

Preheat the oven to 400°F (200°C).

Thinly slice the green onions. In a frying pan over medium heat, melt the butter.
Add the green onions and sauté until soft, about 8 minutes. Add the mushrooms
and continue to cook, stirring occasionally, until they release their liquid and it
evaporates, about 5 minutes. Remove from the heat and let cool slightly.

Transfer the onion mixture to a bowl and add the bread crumbs, pork, beef, egg,
garlic, parsley, stock, 1 teaspoon salt, and black pepper to taste. Mix well. Pack into
an 8 1/2-by-4 1/2-by-2 1/2-inch (21.5-by-11.5-by-6-cm) loaf pan. Bake until an instant-
read thermometer inserted into the center of the meat loaf reads 155°F (68°C),
45–50 minutes. Or test by cutting into the center; it should be cooked through.

Meanwhile, in a saucepan, combine the ketchup, sugar, water, vinegar, soy sauce,
and cayenne. In a bowl, stir the cornstarch into 3 tablespoons water until dissolved.
Heat the ketchup mixture over medium-high heat, stirring occasionally, until the
mixture comes to a boil, then immediately whisk in the cornstarch mixture. Stir
constantly until thickened, about 30 seconds. Remove from the heat and let cool to
room temperature.

When the meat loaf is done, remove it from the oven, cover to keep warm, and let
stand for 20 minutes before slicing. Pour off any excess fat in the pan. Cut the meat
loaf into slices 1/2 inch (12 mm) thick. Serve immediately, with the sweet-and-hot
sauce on the side.

Serves 6

Pork Verde Burritos

Accompany these burritos with bowls of sour cream, chopped green (spring) onions, fresh cilantro leaves, lime wedges, and store-bought or homemade tomatillo salsa for each person to add as he or she likes.

In a Dutch oven over medium-high heat, heat the olive oil. Working in batches if necessary, add the pork cubes in a single layer (do not crowd the pot) and brown on all sides, about 10–12 minutes per batch. Transfer the pork to a plate. Set aside.

Reduce the heat to medium and add the onions, bell peppers, and chiles. Sauté, stirring occasionally, until the onions are very soft, about 10 minutes. Add the garlic and cumin and continue to sauté, stirring, for 1 minute. Add the tomatillos, cilantro, and water. Return the pork to the pot. Bring to a boil, reduce the heat to low, cover, and simmer until the pork is very tender when pierced with a fork and the mixture is very thick, 1 1/2–2 hours.

Preheat the oven to 300°F (150°C). Wrap the tortillas tightly in aluminum foil. Heat them in the oven until hot, about 15 minutes.

Divide the hot filling among the centers of the warm tortillas and top with the avocado slices. Roll up the tortillas to enclose the filling, leaving the ends open. Place on warmed plates and serve immediately.

Serves 6

2 tablespoons olive oil

2 lb (1 kg) boneless pork shoulder or butt, trimmed of excess fat and cut into 1-inch (2.5-cm) cubes

2 yellow onions, finely chopped

3 large green bell peppers (capsicums), seeded, deribbed, and cut into 1/2-inch (12-mm) dice

1 or 2 jalapeño chiles, seeded, deribbed, and minced

5 cloves garlic, minced

1 1/2 tablespoons ground cumin

4 lb (2 kg) tomatillos, husked, chopped, rinsed, and drained

1 cup (1 oz/30 g) chopped fresh cilantro (fresh coriander)

1 cup (8 fl oz/250 ml) water

6 large flour tortillas

1 avocado, halved, pitted, peeled, and thinly sliced

Curried Pork Satay

Satays are made up of strips or pieces of meat that are soaked in a spicy marinade and then grilled. Serve on a bed of rice along with a tart fruit relish. Lamb may be substituted; it should be cooked for 8–10 minutes.

FOR THE MARINADE:

1/4 cup (2 fl oz/60 ml) soy sauce

1/4 cup (2 fl oz/60 ml) peanut oil

1/4 cup (2 fl oz/60 ml) dry red or white wine

1 tablespoon sugar

2 teaspoons curry powder

1/2–1 teaspoon red pepper flakes

2 1/2 lb (1.25 kg) lean, boneless pork, cut into 1 1/2-inch (4-cm) cubes

To make the marinade, in a large nonaluminum bowl, stir together the soy sauce, oil, wine, sugar, curry powder, and red pepper flakes. Reserve 1/4 cup (2 fl oz/60 ml) of the marinade. Add the pork to the remaining marinade and toss to coat well. Cover tightly and refrigerate for at least 2 hours, tossing occasionally.

If using wooden skewers, soak 6 long skewers in water for 30 minutes. Prepare a fire in a charcoal grill, or preheat a gas grill or broiler (grill).

Remove the pork from the marinade and pat dry with paper towels. Drain the skewers. Thread the pork onto skewers. Arrange the skewers on the grill rack or a broiler (grill) pan 4–6 inches (10–15 cm) from the heat source. Grill or broil, turning frequently and brushing occasionally with the reserved marinade, until well browned on all sides and slightly pink in the center, 15–20 minutes. Serve at once.

Serves 6

Mustard-Glazed Baby Back Ribs

This recipe makes a generous amount of mustard-honey basting sauce, so the leftover sauce can be passed at the table. For a smoky flavor, toss a couple of handfuls of damp hickory chips onto the fire.

In a saucepan over medium heat, heat the olive oil. Add the onion and cook until soft, about 5 minutes. Add the honey, mustard, vinegar, $^1/_2$ teaspoon salt, and the cloves. Stir well and bring to a boil. Reduce the heat and simmer, stirring often, for about 5 minutes. Set aside.

Prepare a fire for indirect-heat cooking in a charcoal grill with a cover (page 326), or preheat a gas grill. Generously sprinkle salt and pepper on both sides of the ribs . Place the ribs on the grill rack over indirect heat, cover the grill, and open the vents halfway. Cook for about 40 minutes, turning once. Add fresh coals to replenish the charcoal fire.

Brush the tops of the ribs evenly with some of the glaze, then cover and cook for 10 minutes. Turn the ribs, brush with a little more sauce, cover, and cook for about 10 minutes longer. The total cooking time is approximately 1 hour. Remove the ribs from the grill and cut into single-rib pieces. Mound on a warmed platter and pass the remaining sauce at the table.

Serves 4–6

2 tablespoons olive oil

1 small yellow onion, chopped

1 cup (12 oz/375 g) honey

1 cup (8 oz/250 g) Dijon mustard

$^1/_2$ cup (4 fl oz/125 ml) cider vinegar

Salt and freshly ground pepper

1 teaspoon ground cloves

About 6 lb (3 kg) baby back ribs, in slabs

Barbecued Spareribs

Finishing the cooking of ribs over a mesquite fire gives them a smoky flavor. While grilling, watch the ribs closely, turning them to ensure even browning and checking to keep them from burning. Serve with corn on the cob and coleslaw.

6 lb (3 kg) pork spareribs in 2 racks, trimmed of excess fat

Salt and freshly ground pepper

FOR THE BARBECUE SAUCE:

1 tablespoon olive oil

1 small yellow onion, finely chopped

1 cup (8 fl oz/250 ml) tomato purée

3 tablespoons Dijon mustard

1/4 cup (2 fl oz/60 ml) fresh lemon juice

1/4 cup (2 oz/60 g) firmly packed golden brown sugar

2 tablespoons Worcestershire sauce

2 tablespoons Tabasco sauce

1/4 teaspoon ground allspice

1/4 teaspoon ground ginger

1/4 cup (2 fl oz/60 ml) water

Salt and freshly ground pepper

Preheat the oven to 350°F (180°C).

Arrange the spareribs in a single layer on a baking sheet. Season well on both sides with salt and pepper and cover with aluminum foil. Bake until tender when pierced with a fork, 1 1/4–1 1/2 hours.

Prepare a fire in a charcoal grill, or preheat a gas grill or broiler (grill).

Meanwhile, make the barbecue sauce: In a saucepan over medium heat, heat the olive oil. Add the onion and sauté until golden, about 10 minutes. Add the tomato purée, mustard, lemon juice, brown sugar, Worcestershire sauce, hot-pepper sauce, allspice, ginger, water, and salt and pepper to taste. Bring to a boil, reduce the heat to low, and simmer gently, uncovered, until the sauce thickens, 5–10 minutes. Remove from the heat.

Remove the ribs from the oven and discard the foil. Place the ribs on the grill rack and brush with the barbecue sauce. Cover the grill partially and cook the ribs until they are browned on the first side, 5–10 minutes. Turn the ribs over, baste them with additional sauce, cover partially, and continue to cook on the second side until golden brown, 5–10 minutes.

Remove the ribs from the grill, cut into serving portions, and serve immediately.

Serves 6

Baked Ham with Maple-Pineapple Glaze

An old-fashioned country ham, punctuated with cloves and glazed to a rich mahogany color, always makes a memorable meal. Choose a ham that has been dry-cured with salt and sugar and then lightly smoked, such as a Virginia ham.

Rinse the ham well in several changes of cold water. Place in a large bowl, add water to cover completely, and refrigerate overnight.

Remove the ham from the water and discard the water. Pat the ham dry. Place in a roasting pan. Using a sharp knife, remove the skin and slice off enough fat so that a layer only $1/2$ inch (12 mm) thick remains. Score the ham fat with crisscrosses to form a diamond pattern. Stick a clove in each diamond.

Preheat the oven to 325°F (165°C).

In a small saucepan, combine the pineapple juice, maple syrup, and brown sugar. Cook over medium heat, stirring, until the sugar dissolves, about 1 minute. Brush the surface of the ham with some of the glaze and bake, basting every 30 minutes with the remaining glaze, until the ham is golden brown and a thick glaze has formed on the surface, $2-2^{1}/2$ hours. Remove the ham from the oven, cover loosely with aluminum foil, and let rest for about 30 minutes before carving.

To serve, cut the ham into slices and arrange on a warmed platter or individual plates. Serve at once.

Serves 8–10

$1/2$ partially boned country-style cured ham, 6–7 lb (3–3.5 kg)

About 30 whole cloves

$1/2$ cup (4 fl oz/125 ml) pineapple juice

3 tablespoons pure maple syrup

3 tablespoons firmly packed golden brown sugar

Scalloped Potatoes and Ham with Cheddar

1¹/₂ lb (750 g) ham steak, about ¹/₄ inch (6 mm) thick, trimmed of visible fat and cut into 1-inch (2.5-cm) cubes

3¹/₂ lb (1.75 kg) baking potatoes, peeled and cut crosswise into slices ¹/₈ inch (3 mm) thick

6 tablespoons (3 oz/90 g) unsalted butter

6 tablespoons (2 oz/60 g) all-purpose (plain) flour

3 cups (24 fl oz/750 ml) warm milk

3 cups (12 oz/375 g) shredded extra-sharp Cheddar cheese

1 tablespoon Dijon mustard

Pinch of cayenne pepper

Salt and freshly ground black pepper

Simmer the ham in a saucepan of boiling water for 30 seconds. Remove from the heat, drain well, and discard the water. Set the ham aside.

Oil a 13-by-9-inch (33-by-23-cm) baking dish. Layer one-fourth of the potatoes on the bottom of the dish. Distribute one-third of the ham over the potatoes. Repeat the layers in the same manner until all of the potatoes and ham have been used, ending with potatoes.

Preheat the oven to 350°F (180°C).

In a saucepan over medium heat, melt the butter. Add the flour and cook, stirring constantly, for 2 minutes. Gradually add the milk and cook, stirring, until the mixture thickens, 4–5 minutes longer. Remove from the heat and stir in the cheese, mustard, cayenne pepper, and salt and black pepper to taste. Return the pan to low heat and stir constantly just until the cheese melts, 1–2 minutes. Pour the cheese sauce evenly over the potatoes and ham.

Bake, uncovered, until the potatoes can be easily pierced with a skewer and are golden brown on top, about 1 hour.

Spoon the casserole onto warmed plates and serve at once.

Serves 6–8

Lamb

Lamb Stew with Eggplant Purée

2 tablespoons unsalted butter

1 tablespoon olive oil

3 lb (1.5 kg) boneless lamb shoulder, trimmed of excess fat and cut into 1½-inch (4-cm) cubes

2 yellow onions, chopped

Salt and freshly ground pepper

½ teaspoon ground allspice

2 teaspoons *each* minced fresh thyme and garlic

2 cups (12 oz/375 g) tomatoes, peeled and seeded (page 329), then chopped

1 cup (8 fl oz/250 ml) Chicken Stock (page 314), or as needed

FOR THE EGGPLANT PURÉE:

3 eggplants (aubergines), about 1 lb (500 g) each

2 tablespoons unsalted butter

2 tablespoons all-purpose (plain) flour

1 cup (8 fl oz/250 ml) heavy (double) cream, warmed

Salt and freshly ground pepper

½ teaspoon freshly grated nutmeg

½ cup (2 oz/60 g) freshly grated Parmesan cheese

Minced fresh flat-leaf (Italian) parsley for garnish

To prepare the lamb, in a heavy pot over medium-high heat, melt the butter with the olive oil. Working in batches if necessary, add the lamb and brown well on all sides, 8–10 minutes per batch. Add the onions and salt and pepper to taste and sauté until the onions are soft and pale gold, about 10 minutes. Add the allspice, thyme, garlic, and tomatoes and cook for 5 minutes to combine. Add the 1 cup (8 fl oz/250 ml) stock, reduce the heat to low, cover, and simmer until the lamb is tender, 45–60 minutes. Stir from time to time and add more stock if needed; when the lamb is done, there should be enough sauce to coat the meat and spill over onto the eggplant. Taste and adjust the seasoning.

Meanwhile, make the eggplant purée: Preheat the oven to 450°F (230°C). Prick each eggplant in a few places with a fork. Place the eggplants in a baking pan and bake, turning occasionally so they cook evenly, until very soft, 45–60 minutes. Remove from the oven and, when the eggplants are cool enough to handle, peel them and place the flesh in a colander. Let stand for 15 minutes to drain off the bitter juices. Transfer the flesh to a food processor and process until puréed. Set aside.

In a small saucepan over medium-low heat, melt the butter. Add the flour and cook, stirring constantly, until thickened but not browned, about 5 minutes. Add the warm cream and whisk until thickened, 3–5 minutes. Season the cream sauce to taste with salt and pepper and add the nutmeg. Add the puréed eggplant and Parmesan cheese to the cream sauce, mixing well.

To serve, mound the warm eggplant purée on a platter or individual plates. Place the lamb stew around the purée. Garnish with the parsley and serve at once.

Serves 4–6

Lamb and Lentil Soup

This soup is so thick that it is almost a stew. It can be made up to 3 days in advance and reheated for serving. Dried beans such as kidney or cannellini, presoaked and cooked until almost tender, can be used in place of the lentils.

In a soup pot, combine the lamb, olive oil, cumin, paprika, bay leaves, lemon zest, red pepper flakes, and 2 cups (16 fl oz/500 ml) of the water. Bring to a boil, reduce the heat to low, cover, and simmer gently until the lamb is tender, 1 1/2–2 hours.

Add the remaining 6 cups (48 fl oz/1.5 l) water, lentils, onion, and carrot and simmer, uncovered, over low heat until the lentils are just tender, 20–30 minutes.

Discard the bay leaves and lemon zest. Stir in the cilantro and salt and pepper to taste. Ladle into warmed bowls and serve immediately.

Serves 6

1 1/2 lb (750 g) boneless lamb stew meat, trimmed of excess fat and cut into small cubes

2 tablespoons olive oil

1/2 teaspoon ground cumin

1/2 teaspoon sweet Hungarian paprika

2 bay leaves

1 strip lemon zest, about 1/2 inch (12 mm) wide and 2 inches (5 cm) long

1/8–1/4 teaspoon red pepper flakes

8 cups (64 fl oz/2 l) water

1 1/4 cups (9 oz/280 g) dried lentils

1 yellow onion, cut into 1/2-inch (12-mm) dice

1 large carrot, peeled and cut into 1/2-inch (12-mm) dice

3/4 cup (3/4 oz/20 g) chopped fresh cilantro (fresh coriander)

Salt and freshly ground pepper

Lamb Stew with Artichokes

Juice of 1 lemon

6 artichokes

4 tablespoons (2 fl oz/60 ml) olive oil

2 yellow onions, coarsely chopped

2 tablespoons all-purpose (plain) flour

Salt and freshly ground pepper

2½–3 lb (1.25–1.5 kg) lamb stew meat, cut into 2-inch (5-cm) chunks

1 bay leaf

½ teaspoon minced fresh thyme

6 fresh flat-leaf (Italian) parsley sprigs, plus fresh parsley leaves for garnish

½ teaspoon minced fresh rosemary

3 cloves garlic, minced

1 cup (8 fl oz/250 ml) dry white wine

2 large tomatoes, peeled, seeded, and coarsely chopped (page 329)

1–2 cups (8–16 fl oz/250–500 ml) Chicken Stock (page 314)

Fill a bowl with cold water and add the lemon juice. Cut off the top half of each artichoke, then remove the tough outer leaves until only light green leaves remain. As the artichokes are trimmed, immerse them in the lemon water. Quarter each trimmed artichoke and scrape away the prickly chokes. Drain the artichokes and blot dry. In a frying pan over low heat, heat 2 tablespoons of the olive oil. Add the artichokes and cook, stirring, until tender, 20–30 minutes. Set aside.

In a Dutch oven over medium heat, heat the remaining 2 tablespoons oil. Add the onions and sauté until golden, about 15 minutes. Transfer to a bowl.

Meanwhile, in a shallow bowl, combine the flour and salt and pepper to taste. Stir to blend. Add the lamb chunks and toss to coat. Working in batches, add the lamb to the pot over medium-high heat and brown on all sides, 10–12 minutes per batch. Place the bay leaf, thyme, and parsley sprigs on a square of cheesecloth (muslin), bring the corners together, and tie securely with kitchen twine to form a bouquet garni. When the lamb is browned, return the onions to the pan, along with the rosemary, garlic, and bouquet garni. Raise the heat to high, add the wine, and deglaze the pot by stirring with a wooden spoon to dislodge any browned bits on the bottom. Add the tomatoes and enough stock to cover the meat. Bring to a boil, reduce the heat to low, cover, and simmer until the meat is easily pierced with a skewer, about 1½ hours.

Using a slotted spoon, transfer the lamb to a bowl. Pour the liquid through a fine-mesh sieve into a clean container; discard the solids. Skim off the fat on the surface of the strained liquid and return to the pot. Bring to a simmer over medium-low heat. Simmer until slightly thickened, 5–10 minutes. Return the lamb to the pot and add the artichokes and salt and pepper to taste. Simmer to heat the artichokes through, 2 minutes. Ladle into warmed bowls and garnish with the parsley leaves.

Serves 6

Lamb and Black Bean Chili

This especially tasty Southwestern variation on chili substitutes lamb for beef and black beans for the customary kidney or pinto beans. Serve warm flour tortillas or corn tortilla chips on the side.

Pick over the beans and discard any stones; rinse well. Place in a bowl and add water to cover by 2 inches (5 cm). Soak for at least 4 hours or as long as overnight.

Drain the beans and place them in a large saucepan. Add water to cover by 2 inches (5 cm). Bring to a boil, reduce the heat to low, and simmer, uncovered, for 30 minutes. Remove from the heat. Drain, reserving the cooking liquid. Set the beans and liquid aside.

In a large soup pot over medium-high heat, heat the olive oil. Working in batches if necessary, add the lamb cubes in a single layer (do not crowd the pot) and brown on all sides, 10 minutes per batch. Transfer the lamb to a plate.

Reduce the heat to low and add the onions, bell pepper, chiles, chili powder, and cumin to the pot. Sauté until the onions are soft, about 10 minutes. Add the garlic and sauté for 2 minutes. Return the lamb to the pot and add the beans and their liquid, the tomatoes, and the beer. Simmer gently, uncovered, until the beans and lamb are tender, $2^{1}/_{2}$–3 hours, adding a little water if the mixture becomes too dry.

Season to taste with salt and pepper. Ladle into warmed bowls and serve at once.

Serves 6

$1^{1}/_{2}$ cups ($10^{1}/_{2}$ oz/330 g) dried black beans

$^{1}/_{4}$ cup (2 fl oz/60 ml) olive oil

2 lb (1 kg) boneless lamb cut from the leg or shoulder, trimmed of excess fat and cut into 1-inch (2.5-cm) cubes

2 yellow onions, chopped

1 green bell pepper (capsicum), seeded, deribbed, and cut into $^{1}/_{2}$-inch (12-mm) dice

2 or 3 serrano or jalapeño chiles, minced

6 tablespoons chili powder

3 tablespoons ground cumin

5 large cloves garlic, minced

4 cups ($1^{1}/_{2}$ lb/750 g) tomatoes, peeled, seeded (page 329), and chopped

2 cups (16 fl oz/500 ml) beer or water

Salt and freshly ground pepper

Lamb Stew with Caramelized Onions

Richly browned lamb and caramelized onions lend color and richness to this substantial dish. Be careful not to brown the meat too much, however, or it will impart a burned taste to the other ingredients.

2 tablespoons olive oil

2 lb (1 kg) boneless lamb shoulder, trimmed of excess fat and cut into 1-inch (2.5-cm) cubes

4 sweet white onions, halved lengthwise and then cut crosswise into slices ¼ inch (6 mm) thick

2 leeks, white parts only, washed and finely chopped

2 cups (16 fl oz/500 ml) Vegetable Stock (page 315) or water

6 white boiling potatoes, peeled and cut into 1-inch (2.5-cm) pieces

4 carrots, peeled and cut into 1-inch (2.5-cm) pieces

½ teaspoon dried thyme

1 bay leaf

Salt and freshly ground pepper

In a large Dutch oven over medium-high heat, heat the olive oil. Working in batches if necessary, add the lamb cubes and brown well on all sides, about 5 minutes per batch. Transfer the lamb to a dish.

Add the onions and leeks to the pot and sauté until well browned, 10–12 minutes. Stir in 2–3 tablespoons of the stock if needed to keep the vegetables from sticking or scorching. They should be dark brown but not black; watch them carefully.

Add the remaining stock and bring to a simmer. Reduce the heat to medium-low, cover, and simmer gently for 1 hour.

Add the lamb, potatoes, carrots, thyme, and bay leaf. Cover and continue to simmer gently until the meat is tender when pierced with a fork, about 1 hour longer. Discard the bay leaf and season to taste with salt and pepper.

Spoon into warmed bowls and serve.

Serves 4

Greek Meatball Stew with Brussels Sprouts

Peel the pearl onions (page 326) and set aside.

In a large bowl, combine the yellow onion, lamb, rice, mint, and $^{1}/_{4}$ teaspoon pepper. Mix well. Form spoonfuls of the mixture into thumb-shaped meatballs. In a large Dutch oven over medium-high heat, heat the olive oil. Add the meatballs and brown on all sides, 3–4 minutes per batch. Transfer the meatballs to a dish, then wipe the pot clean.

In the same pot over medium heat, melt the butter. Whisk in the flour and cook, whisking constantly, for 2 minutes; do not allow to brown. Slowly pour in the stock and lemon juice, whisking constantly, and cook until smooth and slightly thickened, 2–3 minutes.

Return the meatballs to the pot. Add the Brussels sprouts and the pearl onions. Reduce the heat to medium-low, cover, and simmer gently until the vegetables are tender and the meatballs are cooked through, 15–20 minutes. Season to taste with salt and pepper.

Spoon into warmed bowls and serve.

Serves 4–6

1 lb (500 g) pearl onions

$^{1}/_{2}$ cup ($2^{1}/_{2}$ oz/75 g) finely chopped yellow onion

1 lb (500 g) ground (minced) lamb shoulder

$^{2}/_{3}$ cup (3 oz/90 g) Steamed White Rice (page 317), cooled

3 tablespoons finely chopped fresh mint

Salt and freshly ground pepper

2 teaspoons olive oil

$^{1}/_{4}$ cup ($1^{1}/_{2}$ oz/60 g) unsalted butter

$^{1}/_{4}$ cup (12 oz/45 g) all-purpose (plain) flour

$1^{1}/_{2}$ cups ($1^{1}/_{2}$ fl oz/375 ml) Chicken Stock (page 314)

$^{1}/_{4}$ cup (2 fl oz/60 ml) fresh lemon juice

$^{3}/_{4}$ lb (375 g) small fresh Brussels sprouts, trimmed, or 1 package (10 oz/315 g) frozen Brussels sprouts

Irish Stew

This country-style lamb and vegetable stew simmers for 2 hours, yielding especially tender results. Serve thick slices of Irish soda bread alongside. Garnish with parsley sprigs, if you like.

2 lb (1 kg) boneless lamb shoulder, trimmed of excess fat and cut into 1-inch (2.5-cm) cubes

4 white boiling potatoes, peeled and cut crosswise into slices ½ inch (12 mm) thick

2 yellow onions, cut in half lengthwise and then crosswise into slices ½ inch (12 mm) thick

1 large turnip, peeled and cut crosswise into slices ¼ inch (6 mm) thick

2 fresh thyme sprigs, or 4 teaspoons dried thyme

3 fresh flat-leaf (Italian) parsley sprigs, plus extra for garnish

Salt and freshly ground pepper

In a Dutch oven, rinse the meat by combining the lamb cubes with water to cover. Drain off the water and add fresh water to cover by 1 inch (2.5 cm). Bring to a boil over high heat and boil for 5 minutes. Transfer the lamb to a dish. Pour the broth into a separate bowl and set aside.

Layer half of the potato slices in the bottom of the same pot. Cover with half of the onion slices and then top with all of the turnip slices. Distribute the lamb evenly over the turnips and top with the thyme, 3 parsley sprigs, 1 teaspoon salt, and 4 teaspoons pepper. Top with the remaining onions and finally the remaining potatoes. Strain the lamb broth through a fine-mesh sieve over the potatoes.

Bring to a low boil over high heat. Reduce the heat to medium-low, cover, and simmer gently until the lamb is tender when pierced, about 2 hours.

Spoon into warmed bowls, discarding the thyme and parsley sprigs. Garnish with fresh parsley sprigs and serve.

Serves 4–6

Sweet-and-Spicy Lamb Curry

Garnish this highly aromatic dish with toasted coconut, sliced bananas, toasted almonds or peanuts, dried currants, chopped green (spring) onions, or fruit chuntey. Use tart apples such as Granny Smith or pippin.

Trim the lamb of excess fat and cut into 1-inch (2.5 cm) pieces.

In a bowl, toss the lamb pieces with the flour to coat evenly. In a Dutch oven over medium-high heat, melt the butter. Working in batches if necessary, add the lamb and brown on all sides, about 10 minutes per batch; do not crowd the pan. Transfer the lamb to a plate. Chop the celery into small dice. Add the onions, celery, and chile to the pot. Reduce the heat to medium and sauté for about 10 minutes. Add the garlic and sauté for 2 minutes. Return the lamb to the pot and add the stock, curry powder, and ginger. Stir well, cover, and simmer over low heat until the meat is tender, 1 1/2–2 hours.

About 20 minutes before the curry is done, in a heavy saucepan over high heat, bring 2 1/2 cups (20 fl oz/625 ml) water to a boil. Rinse and drain the rice. Add 1/2 teaspoon salt and the rice, reduce the heat to low, cover, and cook for 20 minutes without removing the lid. After 20 minutes, uncover the rice; the water should be absorbed and the rice should be tender. If the rice is not ready, re-cover and cook 2–3 minutes longer. Remove from the heat, fluff the grains with a fork, and keep warm. While the rice is cooking, drain the raisins and add them to the curry, along with the apples and coconut milk. Simmer, uncovered, over low heat until the sauce thickens, about 15 minutes. Season to taste with salt and pepper.

Mound the rice on a serving platter. Make a well in the center and spoon the curried lamb into the well. Serve immediately.

Serves 6

2–2 1/2 lb (1–1.25 kg) lamb stew meat, cut from the leg or shoulder

3 tablespoons all-purpose (plain) flour

3 tablespoons unsalted butter

1 celery stalk

2 yellow onions, chopped

1 jalapeño chile, minced

4 cloves garlic, minced

2 cups (16 fl oz/500 ml) Chicken Stock (page 314)

3 tablespoons curry powder

1 1/2 tablespoons peeled and grated fresh ginger

1 cup (7 oz/220 g) basmati rice

Salt and freshly ground pepper

1/2 cup (4 fl oz/125 ml) golden raisins (sultanas), soaked in very hot water for 30 minutes

2 tart green apples, peeled, halved, cored, and cut into small dice

1/4 cup (2 fl oz/60 ml) coconut milk or heavy (double) cream

Lamb and Potato Skewers

Meat and potatoes can share the same skewer as long as they will cook in about the same amount of time. Sturdy branches of fresh rosemary, about 8 inches (20 cm) long, make aromatic and unusual skewers.

Prepare a fire in a charcoal grill, or preheat a gas grill or broiler (grill). Soak wooden skewers or sturdy fresh rosemary branches in water to cover for 30 minutes.

Bring a large pot of salted water to a boil. Add the potatoes and cook until they are barely tender when pierced with a knife, about 10 minutes. Drain well and cover with cold water. Let stand for about 2 minutes, then drain again and pat dry with paper towels. Drain the skewers. Thread the potatoes alternately with the lamb onto the skewers.

In a small bowl, whisk together the olive oil, rosemary, lemon juice, $^1/_4$ teaspoon salt, and $^1/_4$ teaspoon pepper. Arrange the skewers on the grill rack or on a broiler (grill) pan. Grill or broil 4 inches (10 cm) from the heat source, turning 2 or 3 times and brushing with the olive oil mixture, 6–8 minutes. Take care not to overcook the lamb; it should remain pink in the center.

Serves 4–6

12 small boiling potatoes

2 lb (1 kg) lean boneless lamb, cut into 1$^1/_2$-inch (4-cm) cubes

$^1/_2$ cup (4 fl oz/125 ml) olive oil

1 tablespoon minced fresh rosemary

1 tablespoon fresh lemon juice

Salt and freshly ground pepper

Saffron Lamb Kabobs

Tender cubes of lamb cut from the leg work well for kabobs. Serve on a bed of rice pilaf. Although saffron is expensive, its special flavor is worth the cost. You will extract more essence from a small amount if you first steep it in hot water or stock.

FOR THE MARINADE:

1/2 teaspoon saffron threads

1/2 cup (4 fl oz/125 ml) Beef Stock (page 314), boiling

1/2 cup (4 fl oz/125 ml) dry red or white wine

2 tablespoons olive oil

1/2 teaspoon ground cardamom

Salt and freshly ground pepper

2 lb (1 kg) lean boneless lamb, cut into 1½-inch (4-cm) cubes

To make the marinade, in a large nonaluminum bowl, stir together the saffron and beef stock. Let stand for at least 30 minutes. Add the wine, olive oil, cardamom, $^1/_2$ teaspoon salt, and $^1/_4$ teaspoon pepper. Reserve $^1/_4$ cup (2 fl oz/60 ml) of the marinade. Add the lamb cubes to the bowl with the remaining marinade and toss to combine. Cover and refrigerate for at least 3 hours, tossing occasionally.

Prepare a fire in a charcoal grill, or preheat a gas grill. If using wooden skewers, soak them in water to cover for 30 minutes. Drain the skewers. Oil a grill rack and position about 4–6 inches (10–15 cm) above the heat source. Remove the lamb from the marinade. Pat the meat dry with paper towels, then thread it onto the skewers. Arrange the skewers on the grill rack. Grill, turning frequently and brushing occasionally with the reserved marinade, until browned on the outside but still pink in the center, 6–8 minutes.

Serve at once, either on or off the skewers.

Serves 4–6

Crusted Rack of Lamb

Have your butcher french the racks of lamb by trimming the meat from the last 2 inches (5 cm) of the end of each rib. Accompany with roasted new potatoes and seasonal fresh vegetables, such as asparagus, sugar snap peas, and carrots.

Position a rack in the middle of the oven and preheat the oven to 400°F (200°C).

In a small bowl, whisk together the mustard, olive oil, lemon juice, $1/2$ teaspoon salt, and $1/2$ teaspoon pepper. Set aside.

In a food processor, combine the bread crumbs, garlic, mint, and salt and pepper to taste. Process until well mixed. Set aside.

Lay the racks of lamb in a roasting pan, side by side and fat side up. Roast for about 10 minutes. Remove from the oven and immediately rub the mustard mixture on the top of the lamb. Spread the bread-crumb mixture evenly on top of the mustard. Drizzle the melted butter over the bread crumbs and return the lamb to the oven.

Continue to roast the lamb until the crumbs are golden and an instant-read thermometer inserted into the thickest portion of a rack away from the bone registers 130°–135°F (54°–57°C) for medium-rare or the meat is pink when cut with a knife, about 20 minutes longer. Transfer the lamb to a cutting board and cover loosely with aluminum foil. Let rest for 10 minutes before carving.

Cut the lamb between the ribs and arrange 2 or 3 ribs on each warmed plate.

Serves 6

2 tablespoons Dijon mustard

2 tablespoons olive oil

2 tablespoons fresh lemon juice

Salt and freshly ground pepper

3 cups (6 oz/185 g) fresh Herbed Bread Crumbs (page 316)

3 cloves garlic, minced

$1/3$ cup ($1/3$ oz/10 g) minced fresh mint

3 racks of lamb, about $1\frac{1}{2}$ lb (750 g) each, frenched (see note)

$1/4$ cup (2 oz/60 g) unsalted butter, melted

Herbed Rack of Lamb

For a neater presentation, ask your butcher to french the ribs (page 173). Round out the meal with simple grilled side dishes, such as grilled eggplant (aubergine) or other vegetables and polenta.

1 rack of lamb, about 2 lb (1 kg), with 8 ribs, frenched if desired

1 clove garlic, cut into slivers

Olive oil for coating

2 tablespoons Dry Rub for lamb (page 14)

Prepare a fire in a charcoal grill, or preheat a gas grill.

Trim the excess fat from the rack of lamb. Make a small slit between each rib and insert a sliver of garlic. Coat the meat lightly with olive oil, then rub it with the dry rub. If the ribs are frenched, cover the exposed rib tips with a strip of aluminum foil so that they do not burn.

Place the lamb on the rack. Grill 4–6 inches (10–15 cm) from the heat source, turning several times, until an instant-read thermometer inserted in the center of the rack away from the bone registers 130°–135°F (54°–57°C) for medium-rare, 20–25 minutes. Cut the ribs apart into individual chops to serve.

Serves 2 or 3

Stuffed Leg of Lamb

This recipe is a natural with steamed spinach and creamy mashed potatoes flavored with roasted garlic. Have your butcher bone the leg of lamb for stuffing.

3 cloves garlic, minced

¼ cup (2 oz/60 g) drained oil-packed sun-dried tomatoes, thinly sliced

2 tablespoons chopped, pitted cured black olives

5 tablespoons (½ oz/10 g) chopped fresh flat-leaf (Italian) parsley

1½ teaspoons minced fresh rosemary

½ teaspoon minced fresh sage (optional)

1 cup (4 oz/125 g) dried Herbed Bread Crumbs (page 316)

¼ cup (2 oz/60 g) unsalted butter, melted

Salt and freshly ground pepper

1 boneless leg of lamb, 5–6 lb (2.5–3 kg), trimmed of excess fat and butterflied (page 323)

1 tablespoon olive oil

Fresh rosemary and/or thyme sprigs for garnish

In a bowl, combine the garlic, sun-dried tomatoes, olives, parsley, minced rosemary, sage (if using), bread crumbs, melted butter, and salt and pepper to taste. Mix well.

Lay the lamb flat on a work surface, with the outside surface facing down. Season with salt and pepper. Spread the crumb mixture evenly over the lamb. Roll up the lamb into a bundle resembling its original shape, completely enclosing the stuffing. Using kitchen twine, tie the roast like a package. Sprinkle with salt and pepper.

Position a rack in the lower third of the oven and preheat to 450°F (230°C).

In a large frying pan or sauté pan over medium heat, heat the olive oil. Add the lamb and brown on all sides, about 10 minutes.

Transfer the lamb to a rack in a roasting pan. Roast for 30 minutes. Turn the lamb over and reduce the heat to 325°F (165°C). Continue to roast until an instant-read thermometer inserted into the thickest portion registers 130°–135°F (54°–57°C) for medium-rare or the meat is pink when cut with a knife, about 45 minutes. Transfer to a cutting board, cover loosely with aluminum foil, and let rest for 10 minutes before carving.

To serve, remove the twine. Cut the lamb crosswise into thin slices and arrange on a warmed platter. Garnish with the herb sprigs and serve immediately.

Serves 6–8

Roast Leg of Lamb with Vegetables

When properly cooked, a simple roast leg of lamb is one of the most satisfying dishes you can serve. Here, potatoes and carrots roasted alongside the lamb round out the meal.

In a small bowl, mix together the garlic, minced mint, rosemary, and salt and pepper to taste. Using a sharp paring knife, make incisions 1 inch (2.5 cm) deep all over the meat surface and insert the garlic mixture into the slits. Rub the meat evenly with the olive oil.

Position a rack in the lower third of the oven and preheat to 450°F (230°C).

Place the lamb on a rack in a large roasting pan. Sprinkle with salt and pepper. Roast the lamb for 15 minutes. Add the potatoes and carrots to the pan and roast for 15 minutes longer. Turn the lamb over and reduce the oven temperature to 325°F (165°C). Continue to roast until an instant-read thermometer inserted into the thickest portion and not touching the bone registers 130°–135°F (54°–57°C) for medium-rare or the meat is pink when cut with a knife, about 45 minutes.

Transfer the lamb to a cutting board, cover loosely with aluminum foil, and let rest for about 10 minutes before carving. Pierce the potatoes and carrots with a knife to test for doneness. If they are tender, remove them from the oven as well. If not, leave them in the oven while the lamb is resting.

To serve, cut the lamb crosswise into thin slices (or leave it whole to slice at the table) and arrange on a warmed platter with the potatoes and carrots. Garnish with the mint sprigs and serve immediately.

Serves 6–8

6 cloves garlic, thinly sliced

1 tablespoon minced fresh mint, plus fresh mint sprigs for garnish

2 teaspoons minced fresh rosemary

Salt and freshly ground pepper

1 boneless leg of lamb, 5–6 lb (2.5–3 kg), trimmed of excess fat

2 tablespoons olive oil

2 1/2–3 lb (1.25–1.5 kg) unpeeled small red potatoes, well scrubbed

8 carrots, peeled, cut into 2-inch (5-cm) lengths, boiled for 5 minutes, and drained

Wine-Scented Leg of Lamb

A butterflied leg of lamb is one that is boned and spread out flat; as a result it cooks more evenly and is easier to carve than a bone-in leg. Ask your butcher to prepare it for you. Serve with Grill-Roasted Garlic (page 316) and pilaf or mashed potatoes.

FOR THE MARINADE:

2/3 cup (5 fl oz/160 ml) dry red or white wine

1/4 cup (2 fl oz/60 ml) olive oil

3 tablespoons soy sauce

2 tablespoons minced fresh thyme or rosemary, or 2 teaspoons dried thyme or rosemary

2 teaspoons finely grated lemon zest

2 cloves garlic, minced

Salt and freshly ground pepper

1 leg of lamb, 6–7 lb (3–3.5 kg), trimmed of excess fat and boned and butterflied (page 323)

To make the marinade, in a bowl, whisk together the wine, olive oil, soy sauce, thyme, lemon zest, garlic, 1/2 teaspoon salt, and 1/2 teaspoon pepper. Reserve 1/4 cup (2 fl oz/60 ml) of the marinade.

Place the lamb in a large lock-top plastic bag and pour in the remaining marinade. Press out the air and seal the bag. Massage the bag gently to distribute the marinade evenly. Place in a bowl and refrigerate, turning and massaging the bag occasionally, for at least 3 hours, or all day if you wish.

Prepare a fire in a charcoal grill, or preheat a gas grill. Oil the grill rack and position 4–6 inches (10–15 cm) above the heat.

Remove the lamb from the marinade and pat it dry with paper towels. Place the lamb on the grill rack and grill, turning several times and brushing with the reserved marinade, until an instant-read thermometer inserted into the thickest part of the leg registers 130°–135°F (54°–57°C) for medium-rare or the meat is slightly pink when cut with a knife, about 15 minutes on each side.

Transfer the lamb to a cutting board. Cover loosely with aluminum foil and let rest for 5 minutes. To serve, carve into thin slices and arrange on a warmed platter or individual plates.

Serves 6–8

Lamb and Eggplant Brochettes with Provençal Dressing

Add chunks of red, yellow, or green bell pepper (capsicum); yellow or red cherry tomatoes; or blanched pearl onions to these skewers, if you like. Serve with couscous or Steamed White Rice (page 317).

1¹/₂ lb (750 g) boneless leg of lamb, trimmed of excess fat and cut into 1-inch (2.5 cm) cubes

8 slender (Asian) eggplants (aubergines), cut into 1-inch (2.5-cm) pieces

3 tablespoons olive oil

Salt and freshly ground pepper

FOR THE PROVENÇAL DRESSING:

6 tablespoons (3 fl oz/90 ml) olive oil

2 tablespoons red wine vinegar

1 tablespoon tomato paste

1 clove garlic, minced

4 teaspoons minced fresh rosemary

4 teaspoons minced fresh thyme

4 teaspoons minced fresh oregano

Salt and freshly ground pepper

Soak 12 wooden skewers in water to cover for 30 minutes. Meanwhile, place the lamb and eggplants in a bowl. Add the olive oil and salt and pepper to taste and toss well. Let stand at room temperature until ready to cook.

Prepare a fire in a charcoal grill, or preheat a gas grill or broiler (grill).

To make the dressing, in a small bowl, whisk together the olive oil, vinegar, tomato paste, garlic, rosemary, thyme, oregano, and salt and pepper to taste. Set aside.

Drain the skewers. Alternate equal amounts of lamb and eggplant on each skewer. Place the skewers on the grill rack or on a broiler (grill) pan and grill or broil 4–6 inches (10–15 cm) from the heat source, turning occasionally, until the lamb is still pink inside and the eggplant is golden and cooked through, 6–8 minutes total.

Transfer the skewers to a warmed platter. Quickly whisk the dressing and drizzle it over the skewers. Serve at once.

Serves 6

Lamb Sandwiches with Feta and Cucumber Salad

For added color, flavor, and texture, tuck a few tomato slices, some lettuce leaves, or several pitted Kalamata olives into this delicious Middle Eastern–style sandwich.

Prepare a fire in a charcoal grill, or preheat a gas grill or broiler (grill).

Crumble the feta into a bowl and add 1 tablespoon of the olive oil, the lemon juice, and salt and pepper to taste. Using a fork, mash together to mix thoroughly. Stir in the cucumber, onion, mint, parsley, and dill. Set aside.

Brush the lamb with the remaining 1 tablespoon olive oil. Place on the grill rack or broiler (grill) pan. Grill or broil 4–6 inches (10–15 cm) from the heat source until golden brown and an instant-read thermometer inserted into the thickest portion registers 130°–135°F (54°–57°C) for medium-rare or the meat is slightly pink when cut with a knife, 15 minutes on each side. Transfer the lamb to a cutting board, cover loosely with aluminum foil, and let rest for about 10 minutes before carving.

Slice the meat across the grain on the diagonal. Sprinkle with salt and pepper. Open the pita pockets and evenly distribute the lamb and feta and cucumber salad among the halves. Place 2 halves on each plate and serve immediately.

Serves 6

6 oz (185 g) feta cheese

2 tablespoons olive oil

2 tablespoons fresh lemon juice

Salt and freshly ground pepper

1 cucumber, peeled, halved lengthwise, seeded, and cut into 1/2-inch (12-mm) dice

2 small red onions, cut into 1/4-inch (6-mm) dice

1 tablespoon *each* minced fresh mint and flat-leaf (Italian) parsley

1 tablespoon chopped fresh dill

1 piece boneless leg of lamb, 1 1/2–2 lb (750 g–1 kg), trimmed of excess fat and butterflied (page 323)

Salt and freshly ground pepper

6 pita breads, cut into halves, warmed

Grilled Butterflied Leg of Lamb with Mint Mustard

1/4 cup (2 fl oz/60 ml) olive oil

3 cloves garlic, minced

Salt and freshly ground pepper

1 leg of lamb, 5–6 lb
(2.5–3 kg), trimmed of excess
fat and boned and butterflied
(page 323)

FOR THE MINT MUSTARD:

6 tablespoons (1/3 oz/10 g)
minced fresh mint

3 tablespoons mayonnaise

3/4 cup (6 oz/185 g) Dijon
mustard

1 clove garlic, minced

1 teaspoon fresh lemon juice

Fresh mint sprigs for garnish
(optional)

In a bowl, whisk together the olive oil, garlic, and salt and pepper to taste. Put the lamb in a shallow nonaluminum dish and rub the oil mixture over the entire surface. Let stand at room temperature for 1 hour, or cover and refrigerate overnight.

Prepare a fire in a charcoal grill, or preheat a gas grill or broiler (grill).

To make the mint mustard, in a small bowl, stir together the mint, mayonnaise, mustard, garlic, and lemon juice. Set aside.

Place the lamb on the grill rack or a broiler (grill) pan. Grill or broil 4–6 inches (10–15 cm) from the heat source until an instant-read thermometer inserted into the thickest portion registers 130°–135°F (54°–57°C) for medium-rare or the lamb is golden on the outside and pink in the center, about 15 minutes on each side. Transfer to a cutting board and cover loosely with aluminum foil. Let rest for 10 minutes before carving.

Cut the lamb across the grain into thin slices and arrange on a warmed platter. Garnish with the mint sprigs, if using, and serve the mint mustard alongside.

Serves 6–8

Salad of Grilled Lamb, Potatoes, and Garlic Mayonnaise

Preheat the oven to 375°F (190°C). Prepare a fire in a charcoal grill, or preheat a gas grill or broiler (grill).

Place the potatoes in a single layer in a baking dish. Add the oil and salt and pepper to taste and turn the potatoes to coat them evenly. Cover with aluminum foil and bake until tender, 40–50 minutes. Remove from the oven and remove the foil.

Meanwhile, make the garlic mayonnaise: In a bowl, whisk together the egg yolk, the mustard, and 1 tablespoon of the olive oil until an emulsion forms. In a cup, combine the remaining olive oil and the vegetable oil. Whisking constantly, gradually add the oils to the egg yolk mixture until the emulsion thickens. Add the lemon juice, garlic, and salt and pepper to taste. Whisk in the warm water to make the mayonnaise barely fluid. Cover and refrigerate.

Rub the lamb with the olive oil and salt and pepper to taste. About 10 minutes after placing the potatoes in the oven, place the lamb on the grill rack or a broiler (grill) pan. Grill or broil 4–6 inches (10–15 cm) from the heat source until an instant-read thermometer inserted into the thickest portion registers 130°–135°F (54°–57°C) for medium-rare or the lamb is golden brown on the outside and pink in the center, about 15 minutes on each side. Transfer to a cutting board and cover loosely with aluminum foil. Let rest for 10 minutes before carving.

Meanwhile, place the potatoes on the grill rack or broiler pan and grill or broil, turning occasionally, until hot and well marked, about 10 minutes.

Cut the lamb across the grain into thin slices and arrange on a platter with the potatoes and the roasted bell peppers, if using. Serve the garlic mayonnaise on the side.

Serves 6

2 lb (1 kg) unpeeled small red potatoes, well scrubbed

2 tablespoons olive oil

Salt and freshly ground pepper

FOR THE GARLIC MAYONNAISE:

1 egg yolk

1 teaspoon Dijon mustard

1/3 cup (3 fl oz/80 ml) *each* olive oil and vegetable oil

Juice of 1/2 lemon

2 or 3 cloves garlic, minced

Salt and freshly ground pepper

2 tablespoons warm water

3–3 1/4 lb (1.5–1.65 kg) leg of lamb, trimmed of excess fat and boned and butterflied (page 323)

2 tablespoons olive oil

Salt and freshly ground pepper

3 red bell peppers (capsicums), roasted (page 326) and cut lengthwise into strips 1 inch (2.5 cm) wide (optional)

Stir-Fried Lamb Salad with Sesame-Lemon Dressing

If you like, garnish this dish with toasted sesame seeds, green (spring) onions, or fresh cilantro (fresh coriander) sprigs. This salad makes a nice light main course for lunch or a great first course for a Chinese dinner.

In a small bowl, whisk together 2 tablespoons of the peanut oil and the sesame oil, soy sauce, lemon juice, rice wine vinegar, and salt and pepper to taste to make a dressing. Set aside.

In a large, deep frying pan or a wok over medium-high heat, warm the remaining 2 tablespoons peanut oil. Add the onion and stir and toss until it begins to soften, about 7 minutes. Add the jalapeño and garlic and stir and toss until the garlic is soft, about 1 minute.

Raise the heat to high, add the lamb, and continue to stir and toss until the lamb is cooked through, about 3 minutes. Season to taste with salt and pepper.

Transfer to a bowl and add the romaine lettuce, radicchio, and reserved dressing. Toss gently to mix well. Place on a warmed platter and garnish with the lemon wedges. Serve immediately.

Serves 6

4 tablespoons peanut oil

1 tablespoon Asian sesame oil

2 tablespoons dark soy sauce

2 tablespoons fresh lemon juice

2 tablespoons rice wine vinegar

Salt and freshly ground pepper

1 large red onion, cut into small wedges

1 fresh jalapeño chile, seeded and minced

4 cloves garlic, minced

2$1/2$ lb (1.25 kg) leg of lamb, trimmed of excess fat, boned (page 323), then cut into thin strips 1$1/2$ inches (4 cm) long, $1/2$ inch (12 mm) wide, and $1/4$ inch (6 mm) thick

1 large head romaine (cos) lettuce, leaves carefully washed and dried, then cut crosswise into strips 1 inch (2.5 cm) wide

1 head radicchio, leaves separated, then cut crosswise into strips $1/2$ inch (12 mm) wide

Lemon wedges

Lamb with Eggplant and Green Onions

FOR THE MARINADE:

1 egg white

2 tablespoons soy sauce

1 tablespoon cornstarch (cornflour)

1 lb (500 g) lamb leg meat

FOR THE SAUCE:

3 tablespoons *each* rice wine vinegar and hoisin sauce

2 tablespoons chile paste with garlic

1 teaspoon Asian sesame oil

2 tablespoons Chicken Stock or Beef Stock (page 314), or water

3–4 tablespoons (1½–2 fl oz/ 45–60 ml) peanut oil

4 unpeeled Asian (slender) eggplants (aubergines), cut into strips 2 inches (5 cm) long, ¾ inch (2 cm) wide, and ½ inch (12 mm) thick

4 green (spring) onions, including tender green tops, cut on the diagonal into 1-inch (2.5-cm) pieces

Steamed White Rice (page 317) for serving (optional)

To make the marinade, in a bowl, combine the egg white, soy sauce, and cornstarch and stir to dissolve the cornstarch. Cut the lamb into strips 2 inches (5 cm) long, ¾ inch (2 cm) wide, and ½ inch (12 mm) thick. Add the lamb to the marinade and toss to coat. Cover and marinate for 15 minutes to 1 hour in the refrigerator.

To make the sauce, in a small bowl, combine the vinegar, hoisin sauce, chile paste, sesame oil, and stock and stir to mix well. Set aside.

In a wok or frying pan over high heat, heat 2 tablespoons of the oil, swirling to coat the bottom and sides of the pan. When the oil is almost smoking, add the eggplants and stir-fry until slightly softened, 3–4 minutes. Add the green onions and stir-fry for 1 minute longer. Transfer the vegetables to a bowl.

Add another 1 tablespoon oil to the pan over high heat, again swirling to coat the pan. When the oil is almost smoking, add half of the lamb and stir-fry until browned, 3–4 minutes. Be sure to distribute the lamb evenly in the pan so that it comes into maximum contact with the heat and cooks evenly. Transfer to the bowl holding the vegetables. Add the remaining 1 tablespoon oil, if needed, and cook the remaining lamb in the same manner.

Quickly stir the sauce and add it to the pan over medium-high heat along with the eggplant, green onions, and lamb. Cook, stirring to coat the ingredients evenly with the sauce, until the sauce thickens slightly, about 2 minutes longer. Spoon on top of steamed rice if you like. Serve immediately.

Serves 4

Leg of Lamb with Yogurt Sauce

Using a sharp knife, make incisions 1/2 inch (12 mm) deep all over the surface of the leg of lamb. Insert the garlic slivers into the slits.

To make the marinade, in a bowl, whisk together the minced garlic, oregano, lemon juice, olive oil, wine, and salt and plenty of pepper to taste. Reserve about 1/2 cup (4 fl oz/125 ml) of the marinade. Place the lamb in a nonaluminum container and pour the remaining marinade over it. Turn the lamb in the marinade to coat evenly. Cover and refrigerate overnight.

To start the yogurt sauce, line a sieve with cheesecloth (muslin) and place over a bowl. Spoon the yogurt into the sieve, cover, and refrigerate for at least 4–6 hours or as long as overnight.

Preheat the oven to 375°F (190°C).

Remove the meat from the marinade. Sprinkle the lamb with salt and pepper and place in a roasting pan. Roast, basting occasionally with the reserved marinade, until an instant-read thermometer inserted into the thickest portion and not touching the bone registers 130°–135°F (54°–57°C) for medium-rare or the meat is slightly pink when cut into with a knife, 1–1 1/4 hours.

Meanwhile, finish making the sauce: Place the grated cucumber in a sieve set over a bowl, sprinkle with salt, and let drain for 30 minutes. Rinse off the salt and squeeze the cucumber dry. In a bowl, combine the drained yogurt, garlic, and olive oil. Fold in the cucumber. Stir in the lemon juice and minced mint and season to taste with salt and pepper. Cover and refrigerate until serving.

When the lamb is done, transfer it to a cutting board, cover loosely with aluminum foil, and let rest for 5–10 minutes before carving. Slice, arrange on a warmed platter, and garnish with the mint sprigs, if desired. Serve at once with the sauce.

Serves 6

1 bone-in leg of lamb, 5–6 lbs (2.5–3 kg), trimmed of excess fat

4 cloves garlic, cut into slivers

Salt and freshly ground pepper

FOR THE MARINADE:

1 tablespoon minced garlic

3 tablespoons dried oregano

Juice of 2 lemons

1/2 cup (4 fl oz/125 ml) olive oil

1 cup (8 fl oz/250 ml) dry red wine

Salt and freshly ground pepper

FOR THE YOGURT SAUCE:

1 small cucumber, peeled, halved lengthwise, seeded, and grated

2 cups (16 oz/500 g) plain yogurt

Salt and freshly ground pepper

2 large cloves garlic, minced

2 tablespoons olive oil

2 tablespoons fresh lemon juice

3 tablespoons minced fresh mint

Fresh mint sprigs for garnish (optional)

Fillet of Lamb
with Roasted Peppers and Onions

To make this dish, the fillet must be removed from each lamb rack. Bone the racks yourself by cutting around the fillets with a sharp boning knife, or ask your butcher to do it.

¼ cup (2 fl oz/60 ml) olive oil

1 tablespoon minced fresh rosemary

Salt and freshly ground pepper

3 racks of lamb, 1½–2 lb (750 g–1 kg) each, boned and trimmed of excess fat

2 red and 2 yellow bell peppers (capsicums), quartered lengthwise, seeded, and deribbed

3 large red onions, cut into slices ¾ inch (2 cm) thick

FOR THE HERB DRESSING:

¼ cup (2 fl oz/60 ml) olive oil

1 tablespoon red wine vinegar

2 teaspoons mixed minced fresh herbs such as rosemary, oregano, mint, chives, and/or thyme

Salt and freshly ground pepper

Fresh rosemary sprigs for garnish

In a large bowl, whisk together the olive oil, rosemary, and a pinch each of salt and pepper. Reserve half of the mixture. Add the lamb fillets to the bowl and turn to coat completely. Marinate for 1 hour at room temperature.

Meanwhile, prepare a fire in a charcoal grill, or preheat a gas grill. Oil a grill rack and position 4–6 inches (10–15 cm) above the heat.

When the lamb has marinated for 1 hour, put the bell peppers and onion slices on a plate and brush them with the reserved marinade.

To make the dressing, in a bowl, whisk together the olive oil, vinegar, and mixed herbs. Season to taste with salt and pepper. Set aside.

Place the lamb fillets on the grill rack. Grill, turning the lamb every 5 minutes, until an instant-read thermometer inserted into the thickest part of the leg registers 130°–135°F (54°–57°C) for medium-rare or the lamb is well browned on the outside and pink when cut with a knife, 20–25 minutes total. When the lamb has been on the grill 10 minutes, place the onion slices on the grill and cook until soft on one side, 5–7 minutes. Carefully turn the onions and, at the same time, place the bell peppers, skin side down, on the grill rack. Continue to cook the onions and peppers, turning the peppers once, until soft, 5–10 minutes longer.

When the lamb and vegetables are cooked, transfer them to a warmed platter. Quickly whisk the dressing and drizzle evenly over the top. Garnish with the rosemary sprigs and serve at once.

Serves 6

Grilled Lamb Burgers with Mint, Tomatoes, and Garlic

This is a terrific dish for lamb and garlic lovers. Serve these open-face burgers during summer when tomatoes and mint are at their peak of season and the weather is perfect for outdoor grilling.

In a bowl, combine the lamb, the onion, the minced garlic, 2 tablespoons of the minced mint, the cumin, 1 teaspoon salt, and 2 teaspoons pepper. Mix well and form lightly into 6 patties each about 1/2 inch (12 mm) thick. Cover and refrigerate for 1 hour.

Prepare a fire in a charcoal grill, or preheat a gas grill or broiler (grill).

Bring a small saucepan of water to a simmer, add the garlic cloves, and cook, uncovered, until just soft, 10–15 minutes. Drain and reserve the garlic.

In a frying pan or sauté pan over medium heat, heat 2 tablespoons of the olive oil. Add the tomatoes, the remaining minced mint, the garlic cloves, and salt and pepper to taste. Cook until the juices evaporate and the sauce thickens slightly, about 5–10 minutes. Remove from the heat, cover, and keep warm.

Brush the bread slices with the remaining 2 tablespoons olive oil and place on the grill rack or on a broiler (grill) pan. Grill or broil 4–6 inches (10–15 cm) from the heat source, until golden, about 5 minutes on each side. Grill or broil (grill) the lamb burgers at the same time until medium-rare, or pink when cut in the thickest portion, 4–5 minutes on each side.

To serve, place 1 slice of grilled bread on each plate and top with a lamb burger. Spoon the warm sauce on top and garnish with the mint sprigs. Serve immediately.

Serves 6

2 lb (1 kg) ground (minced) lamb

1/4 cup (1 1/2 oz/45 g) minced red onion

2 cloves garlic, minced

6 tablespoons (1/3 oz/10 g) fresh mint, plus fresh mint sprigs for garnish

1/2 teaspoon ground cumin

Salt and freshly ground pepper

24 whole cloves garlic

4 tablespoons (2 fl oz/60 ml) olive oil

4 tomatoes, peeled and seeded (page 329), then chopped

6 slices country-style bread

Lamb and Eggplant Burgers

Eggplant slices replace buns for these burgers, which are eaten with a fork and knife. Serve lettuce leaves, tomato slices, raw or grilled onion slices, and garlic mayonnaise as condiments.

Line a baking sheet with paper towels. Trim the eggplant and then cut it crosswise into slices about $1/2$ inch (12 mm) thick. You should have 12 good-sized slices in all. Sprinkle both sides of each slice lightly with salt. Spread the slices out on the towel-lined baking sheet and cover with more paper towels. Let stand for about 1 hour.

Prepare a fire in a charcoal grill, or preheat a gas grill. Oil the grill rack and position 4–6 inches (10–15 cm) above the heat.

Rinse the eggplant slices and pat them dry with paper towels. Set aside.

In a bowl, combine the lamb, $1\,1/2$ teaspoons salt, $1/2$ teaspoon pepper, and garlic. Mix gently to combine, handling the meat as lightly as possible. Shape the mixture into 6 patties, each about $3\,1/2$ inches (8.5 cm) in diameter and 1 inch (2.5 cm) thick.

Arrange the eggplant slices and the lamb patties on the grill rack. Grill, turning both the burgers and the eggplant slices every 2–3 minutes and brushing the eggplant slices with the olive oil each time you turn them. Grill the eggplant until lightly browned on both sides, about 8 minutes total. Grill the lamb until medium-rare, or pink when cut in the thickest portion, 4–5 minutes on each side.

To serve, slip each lamb burger between 2 eggplant slices and place on warmed individual plates. Serve at once.

Serves 6

1 large eggplant (aubergine), 3–4 inches (7.5–10 cm) in diameter and 6–7 inches (15–18 cm) long

Salt and freshly ground pepper

2 lb (1 kg) ground (minced) lamb

2 cloves garlic, minced

$1/2$ cup (4 fl oz/125 ml) olive oil

Penne with Lamb, Zucchini, Tomatoes, and Basil

Other dried pasta shapes such as bow ties, rigatoni, fettuccine, or linguine also go well with this sauce. Serve this dish with a hearty red wine such as a Cabernet Sauvignon and plenty of crusty Italian bread.

2 tablespoons olive oil

1 small yellow onion, cut into 8 wedges

2 cloves garlic, minced

3/4 lb (375 g) small zucchini (courgettes), cut into pieces 1/2 inch (12 mm) thick on a sharp diagonal and each piece halved lengthwise to make sticks

1 lb (500 g) ground (minced) lean lamb

Salt and freshly ground pepper

3/4 lb (375 g) dried penne pasta

4 large tomatoes, chopped

1/2 cup (4 fl oz/125 ml) Chicken Stock (page 314)

1/2 cup (1/2 oz/15 g) fresh basil leaves, cut into thin strips

1/2 cup (2 oz/60 g) freshly grated Parmesan cheese

In a large frying pan or sauté pan over medium heat, heat the olive oil. Add the onion and sauté until soft, about 10 minutes. Add the garlic and continue to sauté for 2 minutes. Add the zucchini sticks and cook, stirring occasionally, until they begin to soften, about 5 minutes.

Crumble the lamb into the pan and cook, stirring occasionally, until the lamb loses its pinkness, about 5 minutes. Remove the pan from the heat and pour off the fat. Bring a pot of salted water to a boil. Add the pasta and cook, stirring occasionally, until al dente (tender but firm to the bite), about 13 minutes, or according to the package directions.

Return the pan with the lamb to medium-high heat. Add the tomatoes, stock, and salt and pepper to taste. Cook until the lamb and zucchini are heated through, about 5 minutes.

Drain the pasta and pour into a large warmed serving bowl. Add the lamb mixture, basil, and Parmesan cheese and toss well. Serve immediately.

Serves 6

Moussaka

Preheat the oven to 400°F (200°C). Lightly sprinkle the eggplant slices on both sides with salt, place in a colander, and let stand for 30 minutes. Rinse the eggplant slices with cold water and blot dry with paper towels.

Oil 2 baking sheets and place the eggplant slices in a single layer on the baking sheets. Brush the tops of the slices with 3 tablespoons of the olive oil. Bake until golden, turning occasionally, for 10–15 minutes. Remove from the oven; let cool. Reduce the oven temperature to 350°F (180°C).

In a frying pan over medium heat, heat the remaining 2 tablespoons oil. Add the onion and sauté until very soft, about 10 minutes. Add the garlic and sauté for 1 minute. Raise the heat to high, add the lamb, and cook, stirring often, until browned, about 5 minutes. Add the tomatoes, wine, oregano, cinnamon, and salt and pepper to taste. Bring to a boil, reduce the heat to low, cover, and simmer until very thick, 30–40 minutes.

In a saucepan over medium heat, melt the butter. Add the flour and whisk constantly for 2 minutes. Gradually whisk in the milk, then bring to a boil, stirring constantly. Reduce the heat to low and simmer, stirring occasionally, until thickened, about 1 minute. Remove from the heat. Stir in the nutmeg, 1 tablespoon of the Parmesan cheese, and salt and pepper to taste.

Oil a 13-by-9-inch (33-by-23-cm) baking dish. Place one-third of the eggplant slices in a single layer on the bottom, then spread with half of the lamb sauce. Top with half of the remaining eggplant, then the remaining lamb sauce, and finish with a layer of the remaining eggplant. Whisk the egg into the milk mixture and spread evenly on top. Sprinkle with the remaining cheese.

Bake until golden, 50–60 minutes. Let cool slightly, then cut into squares.

Serves 6–8

2 large eggplants (aubergines), 1 lb (500 g) each, cut crosswise into slices 1/4 inch (6 mm) thick

Salt and freshly ground pepper

5 tablespoons (3 fl oz/80 ml) olive oil, plus extra for greasing

1 large yellow onion, chopped

4 cloves garlic, minced

2 lb (1 kg) ground (minced) lamb, crumbled

2 cups (12 oz/375 g) peeled, seeded (page 329), and chopped fresh tomatoes or canned diced tomatoes

1/2 cup (4 fl oz/125 ml) dry white wine

1 teaspoon dried oregano

1/4 teaspoon ground cinnamon

3 tablespoons unsalted butter

1/4 cup (1 1/2 oz/45 g) all-purpose (plain) flour

2 cups (16 fl oz/500 ml) milk

1 teaspoon freshly ground nutmeg

6 tablespoons (1 1/2 oz/45 g) freshly grated Parmesan cheese

1 egg, lightly beaten

Turkish Spiced Lamb and Tomato Pizza

Use purchased dough or your own favorite pizza dough recipe for this spice-infused, Turkish-inspired pie. Fontina cheese or an equal combination of Fontina and mozzarella can be used in place of the mozzarella for added flavor.

FOR THE TOPPING:

2 tablespoons olive oil

1 small yellow onion, finely chopped

6 oz (185 g) ground (minced) lamb

2 small tomatoes, finely chopped

1½ tablespoons tomato paste

1½ tablespoons minced fresh flat-leaf (Italian) parsley

3 tablespoons pine nuts

¼ teaspoon ground cinnamon

¼ teaspoon ground allspice

¼ teaspoon cayenne pepper

Salt and freshly ground black pepper

1 partially baked 12-inch (30-cm) pizza crust or ½ lb (250 g) pizza dough

1½ cups (6 oz/185 g) shredded mozzarella cheese

Preheat the oven to 500°F (260°C).

To make the topping, in a large frying pan or sauté pan over low heat, heat the olive oil. Add the onion and sauté until soft, about 10 minutes. Crumble the lamb into the pan and add the tomatoes, tomato paste, parsley, pine nuts, cinnamon, allspice, cayenne pepper, and salt and black pepper to taste. Cook gently, uncovered, until the mixture is almost dry, about 10 minutes.

Place the pizza crust on a baking sheet. If using pizza dough, roll it out on a floured work surface into a 12-inch (30-cm) round and transfer it to an oiled baking sheet.

Scatter the mozzarella on top of the pizza round, leaving a 1-inch (2.5-cm) border uncovered around the edge. Distribute the lamb mixture evenly over the cheese. Bake until the cheese melts and the crust is crisp and golden, 6–8 minutes if using a partially baked crust or 10–12 minutes if using pizza dough.

Remove from the oven, cut into wedges, and serve at once.

Serves 6 as an appetizer or 2 as a main course

Spiced Lamb Meatballs with Tomatoes and Cilantro

This fragrant dish is an adaptation of a Moroccan tagine, a slowly simmered stew. Accompany servings of stew with steamed couscous and glasses of full-bodied red wine.

1 lb (500 g) ground (minced) lamb

1 cup (5 oz/155 g) finely chopped yellow onion

4 cloves garlic, minced

¼ cup (⅓ oz/10 g) minced fresh flat-leaf (Italian) parsley

½ cup (⅔ oz/20 g) chopped fresh cilantro (fresh coriander)

1 teaspoon *each* ground cumin and paprika

¾ teaspoon ground ginger

¼ cup (2 oz/60 g) dried Herbed Bread Crumbs (page 316)

Salt and freshly ground black pepper

3 cups (18 oz/560 g) tomatoes, peeled and seeded (page 329)

¼ teaspoon red pepper flakes

Pinch of saffron threads

Preheat the oven to 450°F (230°C).

To make the meatballs, in a bowl, combine the lamb, half of the onion, half of the garlic, the parsley, half of the cilantro, the cumin, paprika, ginger, bread crumbs, 1 teaspoon salt, and ½ teaspoon black pepper. Form into balls about 1 inch (2.5 cm) in diameter. Put the meatballs on an oiled baking sheet and bake until brown, about 10 minutes. Remove from the oven and set aside.

In a blender or food processor, combine the tomatoes, remaining onion, remaining garlic, remaining cilantro, red pepper flakes, saffron, and salt and black pepper to taste. Process until smooth. Pour the tomato sauce into a large frying pan or sauté pan. Bring to a simmer over medium-low heat and cook, uncovered, until the sauce thickens, about 30 minutes.

Add the meatballs to the sauce and continue to simmer gently, uncovered, until no pinkness remains in the center of the meatballs, 10–15 minutes.

To serve, transfer the meatballs and sauce to a large bowl. Serve immediately.

Serves 6

Lamb Chops with Herb Butter

Searing the lamb chops on the stove top first and then finishing them in the oven cooks them to a perfect and juicy medium-rare. Serve with a spring vegetable, such as carrots, and a potato gratin.

Preheat the oven to 400°F (200°C).

Cut the garlic clove in half crosswise and rub the cut surfaces over a large rimmed plate. Pour the olive oil onto the plate. Place the chops on the oil, turning to coat.

Place a heavy, ovenproof frying pan over high heat. When hot, add the chops and brown evenly to seal in the juices, about 1 minute on the first side and 30 seconds on the second side. Sprinkle the tops of the chops with the rosemary and place the pan in the oven.

Cook until medium-rare, about 8 minutes. To test for doneness, press gently on the meat with your finger; the meat should feel springy. Alternatively, cut into a chop; it should be pink. Transfer the chops to warmed individual plates. Sprinkle with salt and pepper.

Add the butter to the pan over high heat and stir with a wooden spoon to dislodge any browned bits from the bottom. Stir in the parsley. Spoon the butter over the chops. Serve immediately.

Serves 2

1 large unpeeled clove garlic

1 tablespoon olive oil

4 loin lamb chops, each about 1¹/₂ inches (4 cm) thick, trimmed of excess fat

1 tablespoon minced fresh rosemary

Salt and freshly ground pepper

2 tablespoons unsalted butter

1 tablespoon minced fresh flat-leaf (Italian) parsley

Rosemary-Smoked Lamb Chops

Rosemary sprigs added to the coals impart a smoky, herbal fragrance to grilled lamb chops. Serve with grilled or roasted potatoes and blanched asparagus on the side for a simple, delicious meal.

Prepare a fire in a charcoal grill, or preheat a gas grill. Oil the grill rack and position 4–6 inches (10–15 cm) above the heat.

Soak the rosemary sprigs in water to cover for about 30 minutes before beginning to grill.

In a small bowl, whisk together the olive oil, minced rosemary, $1/2$ teaspoon salt, and $1/4$ teaspoon pepper. Rub a small amount of this mixture over the surface of each chop. Reserve the remainder to brush on the chops as they cook.

Drop half of the damp rosemary sprigs on the fire. Arrange the chops on the grill rack. Grill, turning 2 or 3 times and brushing lightly with the remaining rosemary mixture, until browned but still pink in the center, about 8 minutes. Drop the remaining rosemary sprigs on the fire midway through the cooking.

Serves 4

6–8 sprigs fresh rosemary, plus 2 tablespoons minced fresh rosemary

$1/4$ cup (2 fl oz/60 ml) olive oil

Salt and freshly ground pepper

8 rib or loin lamb chops, each about 1 inch (2.5 cm) thick, trimmed of excess fat

Broiled Lamb Chops with Coriander-Orange Butter

Broiled lamb chops, classic French bistro fare, are dressed up here with a tart and spicy butter. Oven-roasted potatoes and a glass of good red wine are the ideal accompaniments.

FOR THE CORIANDER-ORANGE BUTTER:

6 tablespoons (3 oz/90 g) unsalted butter, at room temperature

3 tablespoons minced fresh cilantro (fresh coriander)

1/2 teaspoon ground coriander

3/4 teaspoon grated orange zest

Salt and freshly ground pepper

12 lamb chops, about 3 lb (1.5 kg) total weight, each about 1 inch (2.5 cm) thick, trimmed of excess fat

2 tablespoons olive oil

Salt and freshly ground pepper

Fresh cilantro (fresh coriander) sprigs and orange wedges for garnish

To make the butter, in a small bowl and using a fork, mash together the butter, minced cilantro, ground coriander, orange zest, and salt and pepper to taste. Cover and refrigerate for 15 minutes.

Remove the butter from the refrigerator. Place a piece of plastic wrap 10 inches (25 cm) square on a work surface. Using a rubber spatula, mound the butter along the center of the plastic wrap. Drape one side of the plastic wrap over the butter and then roll the butter into a log shape about 1 inch (2.5 cm) in diameter and 3 inches (7.5 cm) long. Twist the ends of the plastic wrap in opposite directions, like a candy wrapper, and refrigerate the butter until firm.

Preheat a broiler (grill).

Brush the lamb chops on both sides with the olive oil and season to taste with salt and pepper. Place on a broiler pan and broil (grill) about 4 inches (10 cm) from the heat source until browned on the outside and pink when cut in the center, about 5 minutes on each side.

Transfer the lamb chops to warmed individual plates. Remove the butter from the refrigerator and discard the plastic wrap. Cut the butter into slices 1/4 inch (6 mm) thick. Place 1 slice of butter on top of each lamb chop. Garnish with the cilantro sprigs and orange wedges and serve immediately.

Serves 6

Chicken

Chicken Stew with Parsley Dumplings

Place the chicken pieces in a deep, heavy pot and add the stock. Bring to a boil over high heat, then reduce the heat to a simmer. Skim any froth and scum that form on the surface. Coarsely chop the celery, turnips, carrots, potatoes, leeks, and tomato and add them to the pot. Simmer gently for 15 minutes, then season to taste with salt and pepper. Lift out the vegetables with a slotted spoon and place in a food processor fitted with the metal blade. Process to form a thick purée. Stir the purée back into the pot with the chicken and simmer for about 10 minutes longer while making the dumplings.

In a bowl stir together the egg, water, paprika, cayenne, and melted butter. Season with salt. In another bowl, mix together the flour and baking powder, then stir into the egg mixture to form a thick, smooth batter. Stir in the 2 tablespoons parsley.

Using a teaspoon, drop the dumpling batter by spoonfuls into the simmering stew. Cover the pot and simmer without raising the lid for 15 minutes. Lift out a dumpling and test to see if it is cooked. If it still tastes floury, re-cover the pot and cook 3–4 minutes longer.

Transfer the chicken, dumplings, and vegetable purée to a deep platter. Sprinkle with the chopped parsley and serve.

Serves 4

4 chicken legs

4 chicken thighs

6 cups (48 fl oz/1.5 l) Chicken Stock (page 314)

3 celery stalks

4 small turnips, peeled

4 carrots, peeled

2 russet potatoes, peeled

2 leeks, white parts only, trimmed and carefully washed

1 tomato, cored

Salt and freshly ground pepper

FOR THE DUMPLINGS:

1 egg

2 tablespoons water

Pinch of sweet Hungarian paprika

Pinch of cayenne pepper

1 teaspoon unsalted butter, melted

Salt

3/4 cup (3 oz/90 g) all-purpose (plain) flour

1 teaspoon baking powder

2 tablespoons finely chopped fresh flat-leaf (Italian) parsley

Chopped fresh flat-leaf (Italian) parsley for garnish

Chicken Salad with Radicchio and Red Onions

4 skinless, boneless chicken breast halves

1/2 cup (2 1/2 oz/75 g) all-purpose (plain) flour

2 eggs

Salt and freshly ground pepper

1/2 cup (2 oz/60 g) freshly grated Parmesan or Romano cheese

1 cup (8 fl oz/250 ml) safflower oil

1 small head radicchio, cored and thinly sliced lengthwise

1 small bunch arugula (rocket), stemmed

1 red onion, thinly sliced

1/2 cup (4 fl oz/125 ml) olive oil

1/4 cup (2 fl oz/60 ml) balsamic vinegar

2 tablespoons fresh lemon juice

Trim any visible fat from the chicken. Place each breast between 2 sheets of waxed paper and, using a rolling pin, flatten until the meat is of an even thickness, about 1/4 inch (6 mm). Lightly dust each breast with flour and shake off the excess. In a bowl, beat together the eggs and salt and pepper to taste. Dip the chicken pieces into the egg mixture to coat both sides thoroughly, then dip into the cheese to coat.

In a large, heavy frying pan over medium heat, heat the safflower oil. Add 2 breast halves and cook until golden brown and opaque throughout, 1–2 minutes on each side. Transfer to paper towels to drain. Repeat with the remaining 2 breast halves.

In a large bowl, combine the radicchio, arugula, and onion, reserving a few onion slices for garnish.

In a small bowl, whisk together the olive oil, vinegar, and lemon juice; season to taste with salt and pepper. Pour over the salad greens and toss well.

Slice each chicken breast lengthwise into thin strips. Place the salad greens on a large serving plate. Top with the chicken strips and remaining onion slices.

Serves 4

Malaysian Chicken Breasts with Endive and Ginger

Subtle flavors permeate this pretty green-and-white chicken dish. Serve with a side dish of wild rice mixed with golden raisins (sultanas) and toasted hazelnuts (filberts).

4 skinless, boneless chicken breast halves

4 cups (32 fl oz/1 l) Chicken Stock (page 314)

1 small piece fresh ginger, peeled and cut crosswise into 4 thin slices

1 bay leaf

2 celery hearts, thinly sliced

4 green (spring) onions, including tender green parts, cut into thin strips on the diagonal

2 heads Belgian endive (chicory/witloof), cut length-wise into quarters

Salt and freshly ground pepper

2 tablespoons chopped fresh chives for garnish

Trim any visible fat from the chicken and set the breasts aside.

Pour the stock into a saucepan and place over medium heat. Bring to a boil, reduce the heat to low, and simmer for 2 minutes to concentrate the flavor. Cut the ginger slices into thin strips and add them to the pan with the bay leaf and celery hearts. Simmer for 5 minutes.

Add the chicken breasts, green onions, and endives and cook until the chicken is opaque throughout, 10–12 minutes. The vegetables should remain green. Season to taste with salt and pepper. Discard the bay leaf.

Place each chicken breast half in a warmed individual bowl. Divide the ginger and vegetables among the bowls and add a few tablespoons of the cooking broth. Garnish with the chives.

Serves 4

Chicken with Mango, Sweet Potatoes, and Cashews

This dish is a flavorful combination of the tastes of the Caribbean. If you like, garnish the stew with toasted coconut or banana chips, available in most well-stocked markets.

In a Dutch oven over medium-high heat, heat 2 tablespoons of the olive oil. Add the chicken pieces and sauté until lightly golden, about 5 minutes. Using a slotted spoon, transfer to a bowl. Add all but 2 tablespoons of the orange juice to the pot and, using a large spoon, deglaze the pot over medium-high heat by stirring to dislodge any browned bits from the bottom. In a small bowl, stir together the cornstarch and the reserved 2 tablespoons orange juice until the cornstarch is dissolved. Add the mixture to the pot and stir until slightly thickened, 2–3 minutes. Pour the liquid over the chicken. Wipe the pot clean.

In the same pot, heat the remaining 1 tablespoon oil over medium heat. Add the garlic, white onion, and sweet potatoes and sauté until the onion is translucent, about 5 minutes. Return the chicken and any accumulated juices to the pot and add the mango slices, stock, and curry powder. Stir well and bring to a simmer. Reduce the heat to medium-low, cover, and simmer until the sweet potatoes are tender and the chicken is opaque throughout, about 30 minutes.

Meanwhile, preheat the oven to 350°F (180°C). Spread the cashews on a baking sheet and bake until lightly toasted, about 5 minutes. Remove from the oven and set aside.

Remove the pot from the heat and stir in the green onions and toasted cashews. Season to taste with salt and pepper. Spoon into warmed shallow bowls and serve.

Serves 4

3 tablespoons olive oil

4 skinless, boneless chicken breast halves, cut into 1-inch (2.5-cm) pieces

1 cup (8 fl oz/250 ml) fresh orange juice

2 teaspoons cornstarch (cornflour)

1 clove garlic, minced

1 large sweet white onion, cut into 1-inch (2.5-cm) pieces

4 sweet potatoes, peeled and cut into 1-inch (2.5-cm) pieces

1 large ripe mango, peeled and cut off the pit into slices about 1/2 inch (12 mm) thick

1 cup (8 fl oz/250 ml) Chicken Stock (page 314)

1/2 teaspoon curry powder

1/2 cup (2 1/2 oz/75 g) cashews

2 green (spring) onions, including tender green tops, finely chopped

Salt and freshly ground pepper

Chicken with Okra

Okra adds a unique flavor and texture to this dish adapted from West African kitchens. Serve it spooned over toasted thick slices of French bread or Steamed White Rice (page 317).

2 tablespoons olive oil

4 skinless, boneless chicken breast halves, cut into 1-inch (2.5-cm) pieces

1 large sweet white onion, cut into wedges 1 inch (2.5 cm) thick

1/2 lb (250 g) okra, trimmed and cut crosswise into slices 1/4 inch (6 mm) thick

1 can (28 oz/875 g) whole plum (Roma) tomatoes in purée

1/2 teaspoon ground coriander

Salt and freshly ground pepper

Minced fresh flat-leaf (Italian) parsley for garnish

In a Dutch oven over medium-high heat, heat the olive oil. Add the chicken pieces and sauté until golden brown, about 8 minutes. Transfer the chicken to a dish.

Reduce the heat to medium and add the onion to the same pot. Sauté, stirring, until soft, about 5 minutes. Add the okra and sauté, stirring, for about 5 minutes longer, scraping the bottom of the pan as necessary to keep the vegetables from sticking.

Add the tomatoes and purée, using a wooden spoon to break the large tomatoes in half. Return the chicken and any accumulated juices to the pot, then add the coriander. Stir well and bring to a simmer. Reduce the heat to medium-low, cover, and simmer gently until the okra has softened and the juices have thickened slightly, about 20 minutes. Season to taste with salt and pepper.

Spoon into warmed shallow bowls, garnish with the parsley, and serve.

Serves 4

Almond-Crusted Chicken Breasts

These flattened chicken breasts cook evenly and remain juicy inside, while the nut crust adds a crisp, flavorful coating. Serve with green beans and new potatoes.

Trim any visible fat from the chicken. Place each breast between 2 sheets of waxed paper and, using a rolling pin, flatten to an even thickness of about ¹/₂ inch (12 mm). In a shallow bowl, lightly beat the egg and season with salt and pepper. In another shallow bowl, mix the Parmesan and almonds together.

In a frying pan over medium heat, melt 2 tablespoons of the butter with the olive oil. Dust the chicken breasts with flour and dip in the egg, then in the Parmesan mixture. Place the breasts in the pan and cook, turning once, until golden brown and opaque throughout, about 3 minutes total. Transfer to a warmed platter. Season lightly with salt and pepper and keep warm.

Pour off all but a light film of fat from the pan. Place over medium heat, add the shallots and parsley, and sauté for 30 seconds. Add the wine and gradually whisk in the remaining 4 tablespoons (2 oz/60 g) butter to form a creamy emulsion. Season to taste with salt and pepper. Spoon the sauce over the chicken breasts and garnish with the lemon wedges. Serve immediately.

Serves 4

4 skinless, boneless chicken breast halves

1 egg

Salt and freshly ground pepper

¹/₂ cup (2 oz/60 g) freshly grated Parmesan cheese

¹/₂ cup (2 oz/60 g) sliced (flaked) almonds, finely chopped

6 tablespoons (3 oz/90 g) unsalted butter, at room temperature

3 tablespoons olive oil

All-purpose (plain) flour for dusting

2 tablespoons minced shallots

¹/₄ cup (¹/₃ oz/10 g) minced fresh flat-leaf (Italian) parsley

¹/₄ cup (2 fl oz/60 ml) dry white wine

Lemon wedges for garnish

Moroccan Chicken

The combination of turmeric, olives, almonds, and ginger gives this North African—inspired dish color and fragrance. If you like, serve it atop couscous and garnish with thinly sliced lemons.

Preheat the oven to 350°F (180°C). Spread the almonds on a baking sheet or in a shallow pan and bake until lightly toasted, about 5 minutes. Set aside.

In a Dutch oven over medium-high heat, heat the olive oil. Add the chicken pieces and sauté until golden brown, 8–10 minutes. Transfer the chicken to a dish.

Add the ginger, onion, and carrots to the same pot and sauté over medium-high heat until the onion is soft, about 5 minutes.

Return the chicken and any accumulated juices to the pot and stir in the bell pepper and turmeric. Add the stock and deglaze the pot by stirring with a large wooden spoon to dislodge any browned bits on the pan bottom. Bring to a simmer, reduce the heat to medium-low, cover, and simmer gently until the chicken is tender and opaque throughout, about 15 minutes.

Add the olives and toasted almonds and stir well. Season to taste with salt and pepper. Spoon into warmed shallow bowls or plates and serve.

Serves 4

1/2 cup (2 oz/60 g) slivered blanched almonds

2 tablespoons olive oil

4 skinless, boneless chicken breast halves, cut into bite-sized pieces

2 teaspoons peeled and minced fresh ginger

1 large sweet white onion, cut into bite-sized pieces

3 large carrots, peeled and cut into 1-inch (2.5-cm) pieces

1 large green bell pepper (capsicum), seeded, deribbed, and cut lengthwise into strips 1/2 inch (12 mm) wide

2 teaspoons ground turmeric

1/2 cup (4 fl oz/125 ml) Chicken Stock (page 314)

1/3 cup (2 oz/60 g) pitted green olives, sliced

Salt and freshly ground pepper

Saffron Chicken with Capers

The saffron and capers provide a unique blend of flavors in this light spring or summer dish. Serve with vegetables such as tender young carrots or haricots verts. Grilled tomato halves are also excellent with this dish.

4 skinless, boneless chicken breast halves

2 tablespoons unsalted butter

2 cloves garlic, halved

Green tops of 4 green (spring) onions, slivered lengthwise and then cut crosswise into 1/2-inch (12-mm) pieces

1/2 cup (4 fl oz/125 ml) dry white wine

1/2 teaspoon saffron threads

Salt and freshly ground pepper

1/4 cup (2 oz/60 g) drained capers, rinsed

Trim any visible fat from the chicken breasts.

In a large sauté pan over medium heat, melt the butter. Add the garlic and sauté until tender, 1–2 minutes. Add the chicken and sauté on each side for 2 minutes; do not brown. Using a slotted spoon, remove the garlic and discard. Using a slotted metal spatula, remove the chicken and set aside.

Add the green onion tops to the pan and sauté for 1 minute. Combine the wine and saffron, stir the mixture into the pan, and simmer for about 2 minutes. Return the chicken and any accumulated juices to the pan and cook until opaque throughout, about 5 minutes. Season to taste with salt and pepper. Place the chicken on a warmed platter. Pour the sauce over the chicken and sprinkle with the capers.

Serves 4

Chicken Breast Sauté with Vinegar-Tarragon Sauce

Cooking tempers the bite of vinegar, which gives this sauce a lively tang. Classic French recipes for this dish call for lots of butter, but it isn't necessary, as you will see in this version. Serve with mashed potatoes, if you like.

In a nonstick frying pan over medium heat, melt the butter with the olive oil. Add the shallots and chicken. Sprinkle with $1/2$ teaspoon salt and $1/4$ teaspoon pepper. Cook the chicken until browned, 2–3 minutes on each side.

Add the water and $1/4$ cup (2 fl oz/60 ml) of the vinegar and bring to a boil. Reduce the heat to low, cover, and simmer until the chicken is opaque throughout, 5–7 minutes. Transfer the chicken to a platter, cover loosely with aluminum foil, and keep warm.

Raise the heat to high and add the tarragon and the remaining $1/4$ cup (2 fl oz/ 60 ml) vinegar to the pan. Boil rapidly to reduce the liquid by about one-third, about 3 minutes. Remove from the heat, add the tomato paste and sugar, and stir until blended. Taste and adjust the seasoning. Pour the sauce over the chicken and sprinkle with the minced parsley. Serve at once, garnished with the parsley sprigs, if desired.

Serves 4

1 tablespoon unsalted butter

1 tablespoon olive oil

3 tablespoons minced shallots

4 skinless, boneless chicken breast halves

Salt and freshly ground pepper

$1/4$ cup (2 fl oz/60 ml) water or Chicken Stock (page 314)

$1/2$ cup (4 fl oz/120 ml) red wine vinegar

2 tablespoons minced fresh tarragon, or 1 teaspoon dried tarragon

1 tablespoon tomato paste

$1/2$ teaspoon sugar

2 tablespoons minced fresh flat-leaf (Italian) parsley, plus 4 sprigs fresh parsley for garnish (optional)

Chicken Breasts with Vermouth

This light, quick, and easy chicken dish is good with a Belgian endive (chicory/witloof) and fennel salad, and in springtime with fresh asparagus tips. Noodles with fresh basil and butter also make a delicious accompaniment.

4 boneless, skinless chicken breast halves

¼ cup (1 oz/30 g) all-purpose (plain) flour

1 teaspoon dried sage

3 tablespoons unsalted butter

½ cup (4 fl oz/125 ml) dry white vermouth

1 tablespoon fresh lemon juice

Salt and freshly ground pepper

Finely shredded zest of 1 lemon for garnish

4 fresh basil leaves for garnish (optional)

Trim off any visible fat from the chicken. Place the breasts between 2 sheets of waxed paper and, using a rolling pin, flatten them slightly and evenly. On a plate, mix the flour and sage together. Dust the breasts lightly with the flour mixture, shaking off the excess.

In a large sauté pan over medium heat, melt the butter. Add the chicken breasts and sauté until golden and opaque throughout, 2–3 minutes on each side. Transfer to a warmed platter; keep warm.

Pour the vermouth into the pan and bring to a boil over high heat. Deglaze the pan by stirring with a wooden spoon to dislodge any browned bits from the bottom. Boil until the sauce is reduced by half, 2–3 minutes. Add the lemon juice and season to taste with salt and pepper.

Divide the chicken among individual plates. Pour the sauce over the chicken breasts, sprinkle with the zest, and garnish with the basil, if desired.

Serves 4

Chicken Sauté Provençale

This aromatic sauté, quick and simple to prepare, is rich with the flavors of garlic, wine, and tomatoes. Serve with crusty country bread. Garnish with fresh marjoram or flat-leaf (Italian) parsley sprigs, if you like.

In a nonstick frying pan over medium heat, heat the olive oil. Add the chicken, onion, garlic, $1/2$ teaspoon salt, and $1/4$ teaspoon pepper and cook until the chicken is lightly browned, 2–3 minutes on each side. Add the wine and bring to a boil. Add the tomatoes and minced marjoram and return to a boil. Reduce the heat to low, cover partially, and cook until the sauce has thickened a little and the chicken is opaque throughout, 5–7 minutes.

Using tongs, transfer the chicken to a warmed platter. Spoon the sauce over the top, sprinkle with the chopped parsley, and garnish with the marjoram sprigs.

Serves 4

2 tablespoons olive oil

4 skinless, boneless chicken breast halves

$1/3$ cup ($1 1/2$ oz/45 g) finely chopped yellow onion

2 large cloves garlic, minced

Salt and freshly ground pepper

$1/2$ cup (4 fl oz/125 ml) dry white wine

2 tomatoes, peeled, seeded, and chopped (page 329)

1 tablespoon minced fresh marjoram or oregano, or 1 teaspoon dried marjoram or oregano

1 tablespoon chopped fresh flat-leaf (Italian) parsley

Fresh marjoram or flat-leaf (Italian) parsley sprigs for garnish

Smothered Chicken with Mushrooms and Onions

Smothered chicken is an old-fashioned dish that commonly appeared in early American cookbooks. Satisfying, filling, and full of flavor, it is delicious served over rice.

1 large carrot, peeled

4 skinless, boneless chicken breast halves

Salt and freshly ground pepper

2 tablespoons olive oil

1 large yellow onion, thinly sliced

3/4 lb (375 g) white or cremini mushrooms, brushed clean and thinly sliced

1/4 cup (1 oz/30 g) all-purpose (plain) flour

2 cups (16 fl oz/500 ml) Chicken Stock (page 314)

2 tablespoons minced fresh tarragon, or 1/2 teaspoon dried tarragon

Quarter the carrot lengthwise and then cut crosswise into pieces 1/2 inch (12 mm) thick. Set aside.

Coat a large nonstick frying pan with nonstick cooking spray and place over medium-high heat. When the pan is almost smoking, add the chicken and sprinkle with the 1/2 teaspoon salt and 1/4 teaspoon pepper. Cook until browned, about 2 minutes on each side. Transfer to a plate and set aside.

Return the pan to medium-high heat and add the olive oil. When almost smoking, add the carrot, onion, and mushrooms and cook, stirring frequently, until the vegetables have softened and are lightly browned, about 7 minutes. Sprinkle with the flour and cook, stirring constantly, until fully blended, about 2 minutes longer.

Add the stock and tarragon, bring to a boil, and cook, stirring frequently, until slightly thickened. Return the chicken breasts and any accumulated juices to the pan, pushing them down into the liquid. Reduce the heat to low, cover, and simmer until the chicken breasts are opaque throughout and the vegetables are tender, about 10 minutes.

Season to taste with salt and pepper and serve.

Serves 4

Chicken and Broccoli Casserole

This dish comes to the table with its sauce golden and bubbling. Make a large green salad and a rich chocolate dessert, and your guests are certain to be content.

Preheat the oven to 350°F (180°C).

Trim any visible fat from the chicken.

In a sturdy paper bag, mix the flour, sage, and paprika together. Drop each chicken piece into the bag one at a time and shake to coat on all sides. Shake off any excess.

In a large sauté pan over medium heat, melt the butter. Add the chicken pieces and sauté, turning as they become golden, about 3–4 minutes on each side. Remove the chicken and set aside.

Arrange the broccoli in a layer in the bottom of a baking dish. Cover with the browned chicken and top each chicken piece with a slice of ham.

Pour off the excess oil from the sauté pan and add the cream. Bring to a boil over high heat. Deglaze the pan by stirring with a wooden spoon to dislodge any browned bits from the bottom. Add the sherry and boil for 2 minutes. Stir in all but 2 tablespoons of the cheese and season to taste with salt and pepper. Remove from the heat. Top each piece of ham with a large spoonful of the cream sauce and pour the remaining sauce around the chicken. Sprinkle the reserved 2 tablespoons cheese over the top.

Place in the oven and bake until the chicken is tender and the sauce is bubbling, 30–40 minutes. Serve directly from the baking dish.

Serves 4–6

6 skinless, boneless chicken breast halves

1/2 cup (2 1/2 oz/75 g) all-purpose (plain) flour

1 tablespoon dried sage

1 teaspoon sweet Hungarian paprika

3 tablespoons unsalted butter

2 cups (6 oz/180 g) chopped broccoli

6 thin slices lean boiled ham

1 cup (8 fl oz/250 ml) heavy (double) cream

1/4 cup (2 fl oz/60 ml) dry sherry

1/2 cup (2 oz/60 g) freshly grated Parmesan or Romano cheese

Salt and freshly ground pepper

Chicken Kabobs

Feel free to use your favorite summer vegetables here, such as yellow summer squash and bell peppers (capsicums). Offer Honey-Mustard Dipping Sauce (page 20) or Red Pepper Sauce (page 19) on the side.

4 boneless, skinless chicken breast halves

1 cup (8 fl oz/250 ml) olive oil

4 cloves garlic, halved

2 tablespoons soy sauce

1/2 cup (3/4 oz/20 g) chopped fresh basil, plus 4 sprigs for garnish (optional)

1 lemon, cut in half

8 large white or cremini mushrooms, brushed clean and thickly sliced

1 red onion, thickly sliced

Salt and freshly ground pepper

Fresh mint sprigs for garnish (optional)

If using wooden skewers, soak 4 of them in water for 30 minutes. Drain and set aside. Prepare a fire in a charcoal grill, or preheat a gas grill or broiler (grill). Trim any visible fat from the chicken. Cut the meat into 2-inch (5-cm) squares; you should have 32 in all.

In a large bowl, stir together the olive oil, garlic, soy sauce, basil, and the juice of one lemon half. Reserve 1/4 cup (2 fl oz/60 ml) of the oil mixture. Add the chicken, mushrooms, and onion to the remaining oil mixture and toss to coat lightly.

Alternately thread eight 12-inch (30-cm) skewers with the chicken pieces, mushrooms, and onion.

Arrange the skewers on the grill rack or on a broiler pan about 4–6 (10–15 cm) from the heat source. Grill or broil, turning the skewers to brown all sides and basting occasionally with the reserved oil mixture, until the chicken and vegetables are tender and the chicken is opaque througout, 10–12 minutes. Season to taste with salt and pepper.

Squeeze the juice from the remaining lemon half over the chicken and vegetables; garnish with the mint sprigs, if desired. Serve immediately.

Serves 4

Lemon Chicken Breasts

Skinless, boneless chicken breast halves cook quickly and are low in calories, especially when flavored with this oil-free marinade. If you wish to enrich them a bit, top each breast with a pat of Lemon Butter (page 15) just before serving.

To make the marinade, in a small bowl, stir together the lemon and orange juices, garlic, ginger, tarragon, $1/2$ teaspoon salt, and $1/4$ teaspoon pepper. Reserve $1/4$ cup (2 fl oz/60 ml) of the marinade. Arrange the chicken breasts in a shallow nonreactive bowl and pour the remaining marinade evenly over them. Marinate, turning occasionally, at room temperature for 1 hour or cover and refrigerate for 2–3 hours.

Prepare a fire in a charcoal grill, or preheat a gas grill or broiler (grill). Remove the chicken from the marinade and pat it dry with paper towels. Arrange the chicken on the grill rack or on a broiler pan 4 inches (10 cm) from the heat source. Grill, turning 2 or 3 times and brushing with the reserved marinade, or broil (grill), brushing first and then turning, until the chicken is browned on the outside and opaque throughout, 15–20 minutes.

Serves 6

FOR THE MARINADE:

$1/2$ cup (4 fl oz/125 ml) fresh lemon juice

$1/2$ cup (4 fl oz/125 ml) fresh orange juice

2 cloves garlic, minced

1 tablespoon peeled and grated fresh ginger

1 tablespoon chopped fresh tarragon, or 1 teaspoon dried tarragon

Salt and freshly ground pepper

6 skinless, boneless chicken breast halves

Chicken Breasts Stuffed with Herbs, Green Peppercorns, and Prosciutto

These rolled chicken breasts are also good the next day, sliced thin and served cold with Green Parsley Sauce (page 19). The mushrooms served with this dish also flavor the chicken while it's cooking.

2 whole boneless, skinless chicken breasts

4 slices prosciutto

1 tablespoon green peppercorns, crushed

1 clove garlic, minced

1/4 cup (2 fl oz/60 ml) olive oil

3 tablespoons minced fresh flat-leaf (Italian) parsley

2 tablespoons minced fresh basil, or 1 tablespoon dried basil

Salt and freshly ground pepper

16 white or cremini mushrooms, brushed clean

1/2 cup (4 fl oz/125 ml) Chicken Stock (page 314), heated

Preheat the oven to 350°F (180°C).

Trim any visible fat from the chicken. Place each breast between 2 sheets of waxed paper and, using a rolling pin, flatten to an even thickness of about 1/4 inch (6 mm). Place 1 prosciutto slice on each breast half.

In a small bowl, combine the crushed green peppercorns, the garlic, the olive oil, 2 tablespoons of the parsley, the basil, and salt and pepper to taste. Stir to mix thoroughly. Place 1 tablespoon of the parsley mixture on each prosciutto slice. Roll up each breast and secure with 2 toothpicks. Arrange the rolled breasts, seam side down, in a baking dish. Surround the rolls with the mushrooms and spoon the remaining herb mixture over the chicken and mushrooms.

Place in the oven and bake for 15 minutes. Pour the hot stock into the dish and baste the chicken and mushrooms. Continue baking, basting frequently with the pan juices, until the chicken is tender and opaque throughout, 20–25 minutes.

Place the chicken breasts and mushrooms on a warmed platter, carefully remove the toothpicks, and spoon the pan juices over the top. Sprinkle with the remaining 1 tablespoon parsley. Cut into slices and serve.

Serves 4

Chicken Fajitas

Traditionally, fajitas are cooked on a grill. Here, a stir-fry of colorful vegetables and chicken provides the filling for warm tortillas. If you can find them, use chicken "tenders," or tenderloins, which are strips of tender breast meat.

In a wok or large frying pan over medium-high heat, heat 2 tablespoons of the olive oil, swirling to coat the bottom and sides of the pan. When the oil is hot, add the chicken strips and stir-fry until lightly browned on the outside and opaque throughout, 3–4 minutes. Be sure to distribute the chicken evenly in the pan so it comes into maximum contact with the heat and cooks evenly. Transfer to a dish and set aside.

Add the remaining 1 tablespoon oil to the pan, again swirling to coat the pan. Add the onion and stir-fry for 1 minute. Add the bell pepper and jalapeños and stir-fry until the onion has softened, 4–6 minutes. Add the garlic and tomato and stir-fry for 1 minute longer. Add the lime juice, cumin, cilantro, and reserved chicken. Stir-fry until the chicken is heated through, 1 minute. Add salt and pepper to taste.

Transfer to a serving bowl and garnish with cilantro leaves. Serve immediately with a basket of warmed tortillas and small bowls of the sour cream, salsa, and diced avocado on the side.

Serves 4

3 tablespoons olive oil

1 lb (500 g) boneless, skinless chicken breasts, cut into strips about 2 inches (5 cm) long, 3/4 inch (2 cm) wide, and 1/4 inch (6 mm) thick

1 red onion, thinly sliced

1 red bell pepper (capsicum), seeded, deribbed, and thinly sliced

2 jalapeño chiles, seeded and minced

2 cloves garlic, minced

1 tomato, peeled and seeded (page 329), then diced

3 tablespoons fresh lime juice

1/2 teaspoon ground cumin

2 tablespoons chopped fresh cilantro (fresh coriander), plus whole leaves for garnish

Salt and freshly ground pepper

FOR SERVING:

Flour or corn tortillas, warmed

1 cup (8 fl oz/250 ml) *each* sour cream and tomato salsa

1 ripe avocado, halved, pitted, peeled, and diced

Chicken with Plum Sauce

Crisp, mild water chestnuts are a good counterpoint to the sweet yet pungent plum sauce in this flavorful dish. Look for plum sauce, which is used as both an ingredient and as a dipping sauce, in Asian markets and well-stocked markets.

1½ lb (750 g) boneless, skinless chicken breasts, cut into 1½-inch (4-cm) chunks

1 tablespoon cornstarch (cornflour)

1 tablespoon rice wine or dry sherry

1 tablespoon soy sauce

2 teaspoons rice vinegar

2 tablespoons peanut oil

¾ cup (3 oz/90 g) canned water chestnuts, rinsed, well drained, and halved

6 green (spring) onions, including tender green tops, cut into 2-inch (5-cm) lengths and then sliced lengthwise

3 tablespoons plum sauce

½ cup (4 fl oz/125 ml) Chinese-Style Chicken Stock (page 315)

Place the chicken pieces in a bowl and sprinkle with the cornstarch. Toss to coat and add the rice wine, soy sauce, and vinegar, tossing again to coat evenly.

In a wok or large frying pan over high heat, heat the oil, swirling to coat the bottom and sides of the pan. When the oil is almost smoking, add the chicken pieces and stir-fry until opaque throughout, 5–6 minutes. Using a wire skimmer or slotted spoon, transfer to a dish.

Add the water chestnuts and green onions to the oil remaining in the pan and stir-fry just until the onions are wilted, 1–2 minutes. Add the plum sauce and chicken stock and bring to a boil. Return the chicken pieces to the pan and stir-fry to heat through, about 1 minute.

Taste and adjust the seasoning. Serve immediately.

Serves 4–6

Chicken with Apples

Calvados, an apple brandy from Normandy, imparts a special flavor to chicken. A good-quality regular brandy may be substituted. Serve this satifsying cold-weather dish with buttered egg noodles.

Trim any visible fat from the chicken.

In a large sauté pan over medium heat, melt the butter. Stir in the thyme and add the chicken. Sauté until golden, 3–4 minutes on each side. Add the apple slices and cook, turning once, until tender, 3–4 minutes. Transfer the apples to a plate and sprinkle with the sugar.

Pour off the excess oil from the pan. Pour the Calvados into a small saucepan and warm gently. Using a long-handled match, ignite the liquor. When the flame dies, pour the liquor over the chicken. Add the apple juice and arrange the leeks around the chicken. Cover and cook over medium-low heat until the chicken is opaque throughout, about 15 minutes.

Using a slotted spoon, transfer the chicken and leeks to a warmed platter, leaving the ends of the platter uncovered.

Pour the cream into the pan and bring to a boil over high heat. Deglaze the pan by stirring with a wooden spoon to dislodge any browned bits from the bottom. Boil to thicken the sauce slightly, about 2 minutes. Season to taste with salt and pepper.

Pour the sauce over the chicken. Place the apple rings around the ends of the platter and serve.

Serves 4

4 skinless, boneless chicken breast halves

1/4 cup (2 oz/60 g) unsalted butter

1 teaspoon dried thyme

3 unpeeled tart green apples such as pippin or Granny Smith cored, and thickly sliced crosswise

2 tablespoons sugar

3 tablespoons Calvados or other brandy

1/2 cup (4 fl oz/125 ml) apple juice

2 leeks, white parts only, trimmed, well washed, and chopped

1/2 cup (4 fl oz/125 ml) heavy (double) cream

Salt and freshly ground pepper

Chicken Breasts with Black Olive Butter

FOR THE BLACK OLIVE BUTTER:

½ cup (4 oz/125 g) unsalted butter, at room temperature

¼ cup (1¼ oz/37 g) chopped black olives

2 tablespoons chopped fresh flat-leaf (Italian) parsley or tarragon

1 tablespoon fresh lemon juice

Pinch of freshly ground pepper

3 whole boneless chicken breasts with skin intact, 10–12 oz (315–375 g) each

4 teaspoons olive oil

Salt and freshly ground pepper

In a small bowl, combine the butter, olives, parsley, lemon juice, and pepper. Using a fork or wooden spoon, beat vigorously until blended. Transfer half of the butter mixture to a sheet of plastic wrap and shape it into a log about 3 inches (7.5 cm) long and 1 inch (2.5 cm) in diameter. Wrap in the plastic wrap and refrigerate until firm, at least 1 hour. Set the remaining butter mixture aside.

Prepare a fire for indirect-heat cooking in a charcoal grill with a cover (page 326), or preheat a gas grill. Oil the grill rack and position 4–6 inches (10–15 cm) above the heat source.

Working with 1 chicken breast at a time, gently slide your fingertips under the skin to make a pocket. Divide the butter mixture in the bowl into 3 equal portions and, using your fingertips, slip a portion under the skin of each breast, distributing it evenly. Tie pieces of kitchen twine crosswise around each breast in 2 places to make a cylindrical roll. Rub the breasts with the olive oil, and sprinkle with salt and pepper to taste.

Place the chicken on the grill rack over indirect heat, cover the grill, and open the vents halfway. Cook for 20 minutes. Turn the chicken and continue to cook until browned on the outside and opaque throughout and an instant-read thermometer inserted into a breast registers 170°F (77°C), about 20 minutes longer. Remove from the grill, cover loosely with aluminum foil, and let rest for 5 minutes.

To serve, remove the twine and cut each breast crosswise into slices ½ inch (12 mm) thick. Arrange on warmed plates. Cut the butter log into 6 slices and place a slice on top of each serving. Serve at once.

Serves 6

Tropical Chicken Breasts

Bring the flavors of Polynesia to your table with this savory-sweet grilled chicken dish. Serve with stir-fried vegetables, such as snow peas (mangetouts). Garnish with thinly sliced lemons and limes.

FOR THE MARINADE:

1 cup (6 oz/185 g) fresh pineapple chunks or drained canned unsweetened pineapple chunks

2/3 cup (5 fl oz/160 ml) canned coconut milk

1 piece fresh ginger, 4–5 inches (10–13 cm) long, peeled and thinly sliced

Salt and freshly ground pepper

6 skinless, boneless chicken breast halves

To make the marinade, in a blender or a food processor, combine the pineapple, coconut milk, ginger, 1/2 teaspoon salt, and 1/4 teaspoon pepper and process until smooth. Reserve 1/3 cup (3 fl oz/80 ml) of the marinade.

Arrange the chicken breasts in a single layer in a shallow, nonaluminum bowl. Pour the remaining marinade over the chicken and turn to coat evenly. Cover and let marinate in the refrigerator for 2–3 hours.

Prepare a fire in a charcoal grill, or preheat a gas grill or broiler (grill).

Remove the chicken from the marinade. Arrange the chicken on the grill rack or on a broiling pan 4–6 inches (10–15 cm) from the heat source. Grill or broil for 5 minutes. Brush with the reserved marinade, turn the chicken, and grill for about 5 minutes longer. Again brush with the marinade and turn. To broil, turn the chicken, then brush. Continue cooking until the chicken is browned on the outside and opaque throughout, 5–10 minutes longer.

Transfer the chicken to warmed plates and serve immediately.

Serves 6

Chicken Paillards

For a light meal, serve these simple, herb-seasoned chicken scallops with skewers of grilled vegetables and offer Honey-Mustard Sauce (page 20) for dipping on the side.

Trim any visible fat from the thighs. Slit the underside of each thigh, if necessary, so that the meat lies flat. Place each thigh between 2 sheets of waxed paper and, using a rolling pin, flatten to an even thickness of about $^1/8$ inch (3 mm).

Trim any visible fat from the breasts. Place each breast between 2 sheets of waxed paper and, using a rolling pin, flatten in the same manner as the thighs.

Brush each chicken piece on both sides with the melted butter. Sprinkle with the sage and thyme.

Heat a heavy, cast-iron frying pan over high heat until very hot. Add the chicken and cook until opaque throughout, 1–2 minutes on each side. Season to taste with salt and pepper, transfer to a warmed platter, and serve at once.

Serve 2–4

2 chicken thighs, skinned and boned (page 318)

2 skinless, boneless chicken breasts

$^1/4$ cup (2 oz/60 g) unsalted butter, melted

1 teaspoon dried sage

1 teaspoon dried thyme

Salt and freshly ground pepper

Paprika Chicken

The Ottoman Turks, who carried back spices from their far-flung conquests, brought this rich dish to Hungary. Serve with noodles tossed with sesame seeds.

8 chicken legs

8 chicken thighs

2 lemons

2 tablespoons unsalted butter

2 tablespoons olive oil

1 yellow onion, chopped

2 tablespoons sweet Hungarian paprika

Pinch of cayenne pepper

$^1/_2$ cup (4 fl oz/125 ml) Chicken Stock (page 314)

2 tomatoes, chopped

$^1/_2$ cup (4 fl oz/125 ml) heavy (double) cream

Salt and freshly ground black pepper

Remove the skin from the chicken pieces, if desired, and then trim off any visible fat. Place the chicken in a single layer in a large dish and squeeze the juice of $^1/_2$ lemon evenly over the top.

In a sauté pan over medium heat, melt the butter with the olive oil. Add the chicken pieces and sauté, turning them as they become golden, 3–4 minutes on each side. Stir in the onion and sauté until soft, 2–3 minutes. Mix in the paprika and cayenne pepper. Add the stock and bring to a boil for a few seconds over high heat. Deglaze the pan by stirring with a wooden spoon to dislodge any browned bits from the bottom. Reduce the heat to low, cover, and simmer for 20 minutes.

Meanwhile, in a small saucepan over medium heat, cook the tomatoes until they are soft and the liquid evaporates, 3–4 minutes. Force them through a sieve with a wooden spoon, then add to the chicken. Continue to cook until the chicken is opaque throughout, about 10 minutes longer.

Transfer the chicken to a warmed platter. Stir the cream into the pan juices and heat thoroughly. Add the juice of the second $^1/_2$ lemon and season to taste with salt and black pepper. Pour over the chicken. Cut the remaining lemon into quarters and serve with the chicken.

Serves 4–6

Chicken Stuffed with Herbs and Cheese

As the stuffed chicken thighs slowly cook, a rich stock-and-wine sauce forms in the pan. Serve with thick slices of warm country-style bread to mop up the delicious juices.

In a small bowl, stir together the parsley, thyme, chives, Parmesan cheese, and 2 tablespoons of the olive oil.

Trim any visible fat from the chicken. Slit the underside of each thigh, if necessary, so the meat lies flat; lay underside up. Place 1 tablespoon of the herb mixture in the center of each thigh and fold in the sides to enclose it. Tightly secure each thigh with 2 toothpicks.

In a large sauté pan over medium heat, heat the remaining 3 tablespoons oil. Add the thighs, seam side down, and sauté, turning them as they become golden, about 3–4 minutes on each side. Remove and set aside.

Pour the stock into the pan and bring to a boil over high heat. Deglaze the pan by stirring with a wooden spoon to dislodge any browned bits from the bottom. Reduce the heat to low and add the wine, carrots, onion, and leeks. Return the chicken and any accumulated juices to the pan and season to taste with salt and pepper. Cover and simmer until the vegetables are tender and the chicken is opaque throughout, 30 minutes.

Place the vegetables and sauce on a warmed platter. Carefully remove the toothpicks and arrange the chicken thighs on top. Garnish with the herb sprigs.

Serves 4–6

2 tablespoons chopped fresh flat-leaf (Italian) parsley

1 tablespoon chopped fresh thyme, or 1 teaspoon dried thyme

1 tablespoon minced fresh chives

1/4 cup (1 oz/30 g) freshly grated Parmesan cheese

5 tablespoons (3 fl oz/80 ml) olive oil

8 chicken thighs, skinned and boned (page 318)

1 cup (8 fl oz/250 ml) Chicken Stock (page 314)

1/2 cup (4 fl oz/125 ml) dry white wine

2 carrots, peeled and sliced

1 yellow onion, sliced

2 leeks, white parts only, trimmed, carefully washed, and sliced

Salt and freshly ground pepper

Fresh herb sprigs for garnish

Skewered Chicken Provençal

These kabobs comprise the flavors of Provence: rosemary, thyme, eggplant (aubergine), and tomato. If you use wooden skewers, soak them in water for 30 minutes before grilling.

FOR THE MARINADE:

2 cloves garlic, halved

1/2 cup (4 fl oz/125 ml) olive oil

1 teaspoon dried rosemary

1 teaspoon dried thyme

Salt and freshly ground pepper

8 chicken thighs, skinned and boned (page 318)

1 eggplant (aubergine), cut into sixteen 2-inch (5-cm) cubes

8 plum (Roma) tomatoes, halved

Salt and freshly ground pepper

To make the marinade, in a large, shallow bowl, combine the garlic, olive oil, rosemary, thyme, and salt and pepper to taste. Stir to blend. Reserve 1/4 cup (2 fl oz/60 ml) of the marinade.

Trim any visible fat from the chicken. Slit the underside of each thigh, if necessary, so the meat lies flat. Add the chicken to the remaining marinade and turn to coat well. Let stand at room temperature for 1 hour, turning frequently.

Have ready eight 12-inch (30-cm) skewers. Prepare a fire in a charcoal grill, or preheat a gas grill or broiler (grill). Remove the chicken from the marinade. Cut each thigh in half; you should have sixteen 2-inch (5-cm) pieces in all. Thread each of the skewers in the following manner: 1 eggplant cube, 1 chicken piece, 1 tomato half, 1 eggplant cube, 1 chicken piece, 1 tomato half.

Arrange the skewers on the grill rack or on a broiler pan 4–6 inches (10–15 cm) from the heat source. Grill or broil, turning the skewers to brown all sides and basting occasionally with the reserved marinade, until the chicken is opaque througout and the vegetables are tender, 10–13 minutes. Season to taste with salt and pepper.

Slip the vegetables and chicken from the skewers onto a warmed platter.

Serves 4

Chicken Curry

Serve this dish with Steamed White Rice (page 317) and an assortment of condiments such as chutney, chopped cucumber, spiced yogurt, grated coconut, nuts, and raisins.

First, poach the chicken: If the neck and giblets are in the cavity, reserve for another use. Trim any visible fat from the chicken. Truss the chicken (page 318) and place in a large pot. Add enough cold water to cover the chicken. Bring to a boil, skimming the surface regularly. Reduce the heat to low and simmer for 1 hour, skimming the foam as necessary. Remove the chicken from the pot. When the chicken is cool enough to handle, remove the skin and bones. Cut the meat into small cubes and set aside.

In a saucepan over medium heat, melt the butter. Add the green onions and sauté until soft, 2–3 minutes. Stir in the curry powder, mixing it well with the onions and butter. Gradually stir in the coconut milk and 1 cup (8 fl oz/250 ml) of the stock. Bring to a boil, stirring to blend well. Reduce the heat to low and add the ginger, red pepper flakes, and mint. Cover and simmer for 30 minutes. Add the reserved chicken pieces and the remaining 1 cup (8 fl oz/250 ml) stock and simmer for 15 minutes longer. Stir in the raisins, lime juice, and cream and simmer for 5 minutes.

Transfer to a warmed serving bowl and garnish with the lime slices, if desired.

Serves 4–6

1 chicken, about 3½ lb (1.75 kg)

2 tablespoons unsalted butter

4 green (spring) onions, including tender green tops, finely chopped

3 tablespoons curry powder

1 cup (8 fl oz/250 ml) coconut milk

2 cups (16 fl oz/500 ml) Chicken Stock (page 314)

3 tablespoons chopped crystallized ginger

Pinch of red pepper flakes

2 teaspoons chopped fresh mint, or 1 teaspoon crushed dried mint

2 tablespoons raisins

¼ cup (2 fl oz/60 ml) fresh lime juice

½ cup (4 fl oz/124 ml) heavy (double) cream

1 lime, cut into slices (optional)

Chicken Legs with Chutney

Brown rice cooked with thyme, raisins, and sliced bananas nicely complements these well-seasoned drumsticks. Chilled mango slices with lime juice provide the perfect finish. Serve on top of a bed of rice, if desired.

Preheat the oven to 350°F (180°C).

Remove the skin from the chicken legs and trim off any visible fat. Using a sharp knife, score the chicken legs so the chutney mixture can be absorbed. Place the legs in a baking dish and squeeze the juice of 1 lemon half over them.

In a small bowl, mix together the butter, curry powder, mustard, and juice from the remaining lemon half. Stir in the chutney and season to taste with pepper. Coat the chicken with the mixture to cover completely.

Place in the oven and roast for 15 minutes. Pour the warm wine into the dish and baste the chicken with the pan juices. Continue to roast, turning the legs to brown them on both sides and basting occasionally with the pan juices, until tender and opaque throughout, about 30 minutes.

Transfer the chicken to a warmed platter and garnish with the thyme, if desired. Serve at once.

Serves 4

8 chicken legs

1 lemon, halved

5 tablespoons (2½ oz/75 g) unsalted butter, at room temperature

2 teaspoons curry powder

2 tablespoons Dijon mustard

3½ tablespoons mango chutney

Freshly ground pepper

½ cup (4 fl oz/125 ml) dry white wine, heated

Fresh thyme sprigs for garnish (optional)

Basque Chicken

1 chicken, about 3¹/₂ lb
(1.75 kg), cut into 8 serving
pieces (page 319)

3 tablespoons olive oil

¹/₂ teaspoon dried thyme

¹/₂ teaspoon dried oregano

2 shallots, minced

2 tomatoes, sliced

1 cup (8 fl oz/250 ml) Chicken
Stock (page 314)

Salt and freshly ground pepper

¹/₂ cup (2¹/₂ oz/75 g) green
olives, preferably Italian

¹/₂ cup (2¹/₂ oz/75 g) black
olives, preferably Italian

Trim any visible fat from the chicken pieces.

In a large sauté pan over medium heat, heat the olive oil. Stir in the thyme and oregano and add the chicken. Sauté, turning the pieces as they become golden, 3–4 minutes on each side.

Add the shallots and tomatoes and stir until tender, 2–3 minutes. Pour in ¹/₂ cup (4 fl oz/125 ml) of the stock and bring to a boil. Deglaze the pan by stirring with a wooden spoon to dislodge any browned bits from the bottom. Season to taste with salt and pepper. Add the green and black olives, reduce the heat to low, cover, and simmer gently for 30 minutes.

Stir the sauce and then pour in the remaining ¹/₂ cup (4 fl oz/125 ml) stock. Simmer until the chicken is tender and opaque throughout, about 15 minutes.

Transfer the chicken to a warmed platter with the sauce and serve.

Serves 4

Chicken Stuffed with Corn Bread and Sausage

If the neck and giblets are in the chicken cavity, reserve for another use. Trim any visible fat from the chicken. Rinse the chicken and pat dry with paper towels. In a large Dutch oven over medium-high heat, sauté the sausage, stirring and breaking up any lumps, until browned, 3–5 minutes. Using a slotted spoon, transfer to paper towels to drain. Pour off the fat from the pot, but leave any browned bits.

Reduce the heat to medium, add the onions, and sauté until translucent, about 5 minutes. Add 2–3 tablespoons of the stock if the onions begin to stick. Add the remaining stock and deglaze the pot by stirring with a wooden spoon to dislodge any browned bits on the bottom. Remove from the heat and set aside.

In a bowl, mix together the corn bread, water, melted butter, bell pepper, and reserved sausage. Pack loosely into the cavity of the chicken. Place the stuffed chicken in the pot. Bring the liquid to a simmer over medium-low heat, cover, and cook for 1 hour.

Using a large spoon, skim off any fat from the surface of the stock. Add the rosemary, carrots, and potatoes and bring to a simmer. Re-cover and continue to simmer over medium-low heat until an instant-read thermometer inserted into the thickest part of a thigh away from the bone registers 170°F (77°C) and the vegetables are tender, 45–60 minutes longer. Season to taste with salt and pepper.

To serve, carve the chicken meat and place some meat, stuffing, and vegetables on warmed individual plates.

Serves 4

1 stewing chicken, 4–5 lb (2–2.5 kg)

1/2 lb (250 g) bulk pork sausage meat

2 large sweet white onions, cut in half and then into slices 1/2 inch (12 mm) thick

1 cup (8 fl oz/250 ml) Chicken Stock (page 314)

2 cups (4 oz/125 g) crumbled dried corn bread or corn bread stuffing mix

1 cup (8 fl oz/250 ml) water

2 tablespoons unsalted butter, melted

1 green bell pepper (capsicum), seeded, deribbed, and coarsely chopped

3 tablespoons fresh rosemary leaves, or 1 teaspoon dried rosemary

4 carrots, peeled and cut into 1 1/2-inch (4-cm) pieces

6–8 unpeeled small red potatoes

Salt and freshly ground pepper

Turkish Chicken Pilaf

Almonds or pistachios may be substituted for the pine nuts here. Basmati rice, a particularly aromatic grain, makes an excellent pilaf. Garnish with flat-leaf (Italian) parsley sprigs, if you like.

1 chicken, 2½–3 lb
(1.25–1.5 kg)

2 carrots, cut into pieces

2 yellow onions, cut into chunks, plus 1 cup (4 oz/125 g) chopped

3 fresh flat-leaf (Italian) parsley sprigs

6 peppercorns

2 cups (14 oz/440 g) long-grain white rice, preferably basmati

6 tablespoons (3 oz/90 g) unsalted butter

¼ cup (1 oz/30 g) pine nuts

¼ teaspoon ground allspice

Salt and freshly ground pepper

¼ cup (1½ oz/45 g) dried currants

Pinch of saffron threads, crushed and steeped in 2–3 tablespoons water

¼ cup (⅓ oz/10 g) minced fresh flat-leaf (Italian) parsley

In a stockpot, combine the chicken, carrots, onion pieces, parsley sprigs, and peppercorns. Add water to cover and bring to a boil. Skim off any foam on the surface. Reduce the heat to low, cover, and simmer until the chicken is tender and the juices run clear when a thigh is pierced at the thickest part with a knife, about 45 minutes. Transfer the chicken to a plate and let cool. Reserve the stock. Remove the skin and bones and discard. Tear the meat into bite-sized pieces. You should have 1½–2 cups (9–12 oz/280–375 g) meat. Cover and set aside. Strain the stock and set aside 3 cups (24 fl oz/750 ml) for the pilaf.

Place the rice in a fine-mesh sieve, rinse well under cold running water, and drain. Transfer to a bowl and add water to cover; let stand for 15 minutes. Drain well. In a heavy sauté pan over medium heat, melt 3 tablespoons of the butter. Add the nuts and sauté, stirring occasionally, until golden, 4–5 minutes. Transfer to a plate.

Add the remaining 3 tablespoons butter to the pan and place over medium heat. Add the chopped onion and sauté until golden, 8–10 minutes. Stir in the allspice, 2 teaspoons salt, and pepper to taste. Add the rice and stir until it turns opaque, 3–4 minutes. Stir in the currants, reserved 3 cups (24 fl oz/750 ml) stock, and saffron, if using. Bring to a boil over medium-high heat. Reduce the heat to low, cover, and simmer until nearly all of the liquid is absorbed, 10–15 minutes. Fold in the nuts, reserved chicken, and minced parsley. Cover tightly, reduce the heat to very low, and cook until the liquid is absorbed and the rice is tender, 15–20 minutes longer. Spoon onto a warmed platter and serve.

Serves 4

Jamaican Jerk Chicken

Jerk is the term used to describe a traditional Jamaican style of grilling that uses a spicy marinade paste of chiles, lime juice, herbs, and spices. Serve with Honey-Mustard Dipping Sauce (page 20).

To make the marinade, in a blender or food processor, combine the jalapeño, lime juice, chopped rosemary, thyme, mustard seed, Dijon, onion, garlic, and 1 teaspoon salt. Process to a thick, smooth paste. Scrape the marinade into a small bowl, cover, and refrigerate for about 2 hours, or for up to 2 days. This allows the marinade to firm up a bit and gives the flavors time to blend.

Pat the chicken pieces dry with paper towels. Rub the pieces with the marinade, coating them completely, and place them on a nonaluminum baking sheet. Cover with plastic wrap and refrigerate for at least 2 hours, or for up to 24 hours.

Prepare a fire for indirect-heat cooking in a charcoal grill with a cover (page 326), or preheat a gas grill. Oil the grill rack and position 4–6 inches (10–15 cm) above the heat source.

Place the chicken, skin side down, over indirect heat. Cover the grill and open the vents slightly less than halfway. Have a spray bottle of water handy to douse any flare-ups for a charcoal fire. Cook slowly, turning the chicken every 15 minutes, until opaque throughout and the juices run clear when a thigh joint is pierced, 60–70 minutes.

To serve, transfer to a warmed platter or individual plates, garnish with the rosemary sprigs, and serve at once.

Serves 4–6

FOR THE MARINADE:

8–10 jalapeño chiles, halved and seeded

¼ cup (2 fl oz/60 ml) fresh lime juice

¼ cup (⅓ oz/10 g) chopped fresh rosemary, or 1 tablespoon dried rosemary, plus fresh rosemary sprigs for garnish

2 tablespoons chopped fresh thyme, or 2 teaspoons dried thyme

2 tablespoons mustard seed

2 tablespoons Dijon mustard

½ yellow onion, cut into chunks

2 large cloves garlic

Salt

4–5 lb (2–2.5 kg) chicken pieces

Fried Chicken with Herbs

Pack this crisp chicken for a picnic, or accompany it with corn on the cob,
a tossed vegetable salad, or a cold soup. Serve Red Pepper Sauce (page 19)
and Tomato-Cranberry Salsa (page 21) alongside.

2 chickens, each about 2½ lb
(1.25 kg) and cut into 8 serving
pieces (page 319)

1 cup (5 oz/155 g) all-purpose
(plain) flour

Salt

1 teaspoon sweet Hungarian
paprika

1 teaspoon dried thyme

1 teaspoon dried sage

10 fresh flat-leaf (Italian)
parsley sprigs

About 2 cups (16 fl oz/500 ml)
peanut oil

2 lemons, cut into quarters,
for garnish

Trim any visible fat from the chicken pieces.

In a sturdy paper bag, combine the flour, salt to taste, paprika, thyme, and sage; shake well to blend thoroughly. Add the chicken pieces to the bag, 3 or 4 at a time, and shake to coat. Shake off the excess and set aside. Add the parsley sprigs to the flour mixture and shake to coat. Remove the parsley sprigs and set aside.

Preheat the oven to 200°F (95°C).

Pour the oil into a deep, heavy saucepan to a depth of 1½ inches (4 cm). Place over medium heat until the oil is almost smoking (350°F/180°C). Carefully add 3 of the chicken pieces to the pan. Do not crowd the pan, or the chicken will not brown evenly. Increase the heat to medium-high and cook, turning to brown on all sides, until golden brown, about 3 minutes. Reduce the heat to low and cook until opaque throughout, 4–5 minutes. Using tongs, transfer to paper towels to drain. Place the chicken in the oven. Repeat with the remaining chicken pieces.

Add the parsley sprigs to the hot oil and fry until golden, 1–2 minutes. Using a large spoon or wire skimmer, transfer to paper towels to drain.

Place the chicken on a warmed platter. Garnish with the fried parsley and lemon quarters and serve.

Serves 4–6

Oven-Braised Chicken with Vegetables

Oven braising makes chicken moist and juicy. This recipe makes almost an entire meal in one pot. Thin noodles or potato pancakes are good with this dish; offer ripe, fragrant melon wedges for dessert.

Preheat the oven to 375°F (190°C).

If the neck and giblets are in the chicken cavity, reserve for another use. Trim any visible fat from the chicken. Rub the body cavity with salt and place the onion halves inside. Set aside.

Cut the leeks in half lengthwise and then thickly slice crosswise. Place the lettuce, carrots, leeks, and bell peppers in the bottom of a heavy, ovenproof pot. Rub the outside of the chicken with the butter and season with salt and pepper. Place it in the pot, breast side up. Add the wine and stock. Cover and braise in the oven for 1 hour. Uncover and continue to cook until an instant-read thermometer inserted into the thickest part of a thigh away from the bone registers 170°F (77°C), about 30 minutes longer.

Transfer the chicken to a warmed deep platter. Arrange the vegetables around the chicken and spoon the pan juices over it and the vegetables. Carve at the table.

Serves 4

1 chicken, 3 1/2–4 lb (1.75–2 kg)

Salt and freshly ground pepper

1 yellow onion, halved

2 leeks, including tender green tops, trimmed and carefully washed

1 head iceberg lettuce, cored and sliced lengthwise

2 carrots, peeled and coarsely chopped

2 green bell peppers (capsicums), seeded, deribbed, and coarsely chopped

2 tablespoons unsalted butter, at room temperature

1/2 cup (4 fl oz/125 ml) dry white wine

1/2 cup (4 fl oz/125 ml) Chicken Stock (page 314)

Chicken with Bell Peppers and Parmesan

Here is the perfect chicken dish: simple to prepare and delicious to eat.
A yellow bell pepper (capsicum) makes a colorful addition. Serve with crusty
bread and braised fennel, or white beans mixed with olive oil.

1 chicken, 3–4 lb (1.5–2 kg), quartered

3 tablespoons olive oil

1 teaspoon dried sage

1 teaspoon dried thyme

3 tomatoes, chopped

2 red bell peppers (capsicums), seeded, deribbed, and cut into long, wide strips

1/2 cup (4 fl oz/125 ml) Chicken Stock (page 314), heated

1/2 cup (4 fl oz/125 ml) dry red wine

1/2 cup (2 oz/60 g) freshly grated Parmesan or Romano cheese

Freshly ground pepper

Position a rack in the upper third of the oven and preheat to 375°F (190°C).

Trim any visible fat from the chicken. Place skin side up in a baking dish; brush the bottom of the dish and the chicken with 2 tablespoons of the olive oil. Turn the chicken quarters skin side down and sprinkle with the sage and thyme.

Place in the oven and bake for 20 minutes. Baste the chicken with the pan juices. Add the tomatoes, bell peppers, stock, and wine. Bake for 20 minutes, basting occasionally. Turn the chicken skin-side up, sprinkle the cheese over the top, and season to taste with pepper. Bake until the chicken is browned and the meat is opaque througout, another 20 minutes longer.

Transfer the chicken to a platter and spoon the pan juices and vegetables around it.

Serves 4

Rosemary Chicken with Potatoes

The chicken and potatoes absorb the rosemary's fragrance as they roast. Serve with a green salad tossed with chopped celery, radishes, and chives. For a large dinner party, roast two birds.

Preheat the oven to 350°F (180°C).

If the neck and giblets are in the chicken cavity, reserve for another use. Trim any visible fat from the chicken. Rinse the chicken and pat dry with paper towels. Rub the chicken inside and out with the cut side of the lemon halves. Place 2 rosemary sprigs in the body cavity. Truss the chicken (page 318) and tuck 1 rosemary sprig under each wing. Place the chicken on its side in a roasting pan and surround with the potatoes. In a small pan, melt the butter and stir in the olive oil. Brush the butter mixture evenly over the chicken and potatoes and then sprinkle with the dried rosemary and thyme.

Place in the oven and roast for 30 minutes. Turn the chicken so it rests on its opposite side. Add the stock to the pan and baste the chicken with the pan juices. Roast for another 30 minutes. Turn the chicken breast side up, baste with the pan juices, and season to taste with salt and pepper. Roast until an instant-read thermometer inserted into the thickest part of a thight away from the bone registers 170°F (77°C), another 20–30 minutes longer.

Transfer the chicken to a warmed platter and surround with the potatoes. Garnish with the remaining 2 rosemary sprigs. Cover loosely with aluminum foil and let rest for about 5 minutes before carving the chicken at the table. Serve the pan juices in a bowl on the side.

Serves 4

1 chicken, about 3½ lb (1.75 kg)

1 lemon, halved

6 fresh rosemary sprigs

4 russet potatoes, peeled and cut into 3-inch (7.5-cm) cubes

3 tablespoons unsalted butter

3 tablespoons olive oil

2 teaspoons dried rosemary

1 teaspoon dried thyme

½ cup (4 fl oz/125 ml) Chicken Stock (page 314)

Salt and freshly ground pepper

Chicken with Garlic

Preheat the oven to 375°F (190°C).

If the neck and giblets are in the chicken cavity, reserve for another use. Trim any visible fat from the chicken. Rinse the chicken and pat dry with paper towels. Rub the body cavity with 1 tablespoon of the butter and then sprinkle the cavity with the sage. Place 8 of the garlic cloves inside.

On the bottom of a roasting pan, rub 1 tablespoon of the butter. Scatter the green onions over the bottom and place the chicken on top of the onions. Rub the entire surface of the chicken with the remaining 1 tablespoon butter. Place the bird on its side and tuck the remaining garlic cloves around the chicken and under the wings.

Place in the oven and roast for 30 minutes. Turn the bird so it rests on its opposite side. Combine the stock and wine and stir 1/2 cup (4 fl oz/125 ml) of the mixture into the pan. Baste the chicken and roast for another 30 minutes.

Add the remaining 1/2 cup (4 fl oz/125 ml) of the stock mixture. Turn the chicken breast side up, baste with the pan juices, and season to taste with salt and pepper. Roast until an instant read thermometer inserted into the thickest part of a thigh away from the bone registers 170°F (77°C), 20–30 minutes longer.

Transfer the chicken to a warmed platter with the garlic cloves. Carve at the table.

Serves 4

1 chicken, about 3 1/2 lb
(1.75 kg)

3 tablespoons unsalted butter,
at room temperature

1 teaspoon dried sage

3 heads garlic, separated into
cloves and peeled

6 green (spring) onions,
including tender green tops,
sliced lengthwise

1/2 cup (4 fl oz/125 ml) Chicken
Stock (page 314)

1/2 cup (4 fl oz/125 ml) dry
white wine

Salt and freshly ground pepper

Roast Chicken with Gravy

Preheat the oven to 375°F (190°C). Remove the neck and giblets from the chicken cavity. Reserve the liver for another use; chop the heart and gizzard and reserve for the gravy, along with the neck. Discard any loose fat from around the body cavity. Rinse the chicken, pat dry with paper towels, and sprinkle the body cavity and the surface with salt and pepper. Strip enough leaves from 1 bunch of thyme to measure 1 tablespoon and reserve for the gravy. Place the remaining thyme sprigs from the bunch in the body cavity. Truss the chicken (page 318). Rub the skin with the butter. Place the bird in a roasting pan, breast side down. Roast for 30 minutes, basting frequently with the pan juices after the first 10 minutes. Turn breast side up, baste, and add the onion to the pan. Continue to roast, basting frequently, until the juices run clear and an instant-read thermometer inserted in the thickest part of the thigh away from the bone registers 170°F (77°C), 30 minutes longer.

In a saucepan, combine the stock, chopped giblets, and neck and bring to a boil. Reduce the heat to low, cover, and simmer for 30 minutes. Strain and set aside. Transfer the chicken to a platter and cover loosely with foil to keep warm.

Meanwhile, make the gravy. Discard the onion from the roasting pan. Pick up the pan and carefully pour off all but 3–5 tablespoons of the pan juices. Place the pan over medium heat. Sprinkle in 1–3 tablespoons all-purpose (plain) flour, stirring rapidly until lightly browned. Raise the heat to high and, stirring vigorously, pour in the stock and bring to a boil. Reduce the heat to medium and simmer, stirring often, about 5 minutes. Stir in more of the stock if needed to achieve the desired consistency. Season to taste with salt and pepper. Pour through a fine-mesh sieve into a warmed gravy boat.

Garnish the chicken with the remaining thyme. Carve at the table and pass the gravy alongside.

Serves 4

1 chicken, 3½–4 lb (1.75–2 kg)

Salt and freshly ground pepper

2 bunches fresh thyme

1 tablespoon unsalted butter, at room temperature

1 yellow onion, quartered

1–3 tablespoons all-purpose (plain) flour

2 cups (16 fl oz/500 ml) Chicken Stock (page 314)

Chicken with Plum Jam and Almonds

This Chinese-inspired dish combines plums and chicken in a sweet-and-sour sauce with ginger and almonds. Serve with Steamed White Rice (page 317) and green beans and celery cut on the diagonal and cooked briefly in chicken stock.

1 chicken, about 3½ lb (1.75 kg), cut into 8 serving pieces (page 319)

2 tablespoons Asian sesame oil

½ cup (5 oz/150 g) plum jam

2 tablespoons peeled and grated fresh ginger

1 tablespoon fresh lemon juice

2 tablespoons dry sherry

2 tablespoons red wine vinegar

½ cup (4 fl oz/125 ml) Chicken Stock (page 314), heated

½ cup (2 oz/60 g) chopped almonds

Fresh cilantro (fresh coriander) sprigs for garnish

Preheat the oven to 325°F (165°C).

Trim off any visible fat from the chicken pieces.

In a large sauté pan over medium heat, heat the oil. Add the chicken and sauté, turning the pieces as they become golden, 3–4 minutes on each side. Transfer to a baking dish and set aside.

In a small bowl, combine the jam, ginger, lemon juice, sherry, and vinegar. Stir to mix well. Spoon some of the jam mixture over each chicken piece and turn to coat both sides.

Place in the oven and bake for 25–30 minutes. Add the hot stock to the pan juices and continue to bake, basting frequently with the pan juices, until the chicken is tender and the juices run clear when a thigh joint is pierced with a knife, another 20–25 minutes longer.

Place the chicken on a warmed serving platter. Dust with the chopped almonds and garnish with the cilantro.

Serves 2 or 3

Greek Chicken with Oregano

The Greeks are fond of using oregano in their cooking, particularly in chicken dishes. A mixed vegetable salad and oven-broiled potato slices are delicious accompaniments to these succulent birds.

Preheat the oven to 400°F (200°C).

Trim any visible fat from the chicken. Rinse the chicken and pat dry with paper towels. In a bowl, combine the olive oil, lemon juice, and oregano and stir to mix well. Brush the mixture over both sides of each chicken half, including under the wings. Place in a roasting pan, skin side down. Tuck the onions and garlic into the hollows of the chicken pieces and sprinkle with salt and pepper.

Place in the oven and roast for 20 minutes. Turn the chicken halves skin side up, stir the 1/2 cup (4 fl oz/125 ml) wine into the pan juices, and baste the chicken. Continue to roast, basting frequently with the pan juices, until the chicken is tender and the juices run clear when a thigh joint is pierced with a knife, 30 minutes longer. Add more wine to the pan if needed to keep the chicken moist.

Arrange a bed of spinach leaves on a warmed platter and place the chicken on top. Strain the pan juices and pour over the chicken. Garnish with the oregano sprigs.

Serves 4

2 chickens, about 2 1/2 lb (1.25 kg) each, halved lengthwise

1/2 cup (4 fl oz/125 ml) olive oil

Juice of 2 lemons

2 tablespoons dried oregano

2 yellow onions, cut into wedges

4 cloves garlic, minced

Salt and freshly ground pepper

1/2 cup (4 fl oz/125 ml) dry white wine, or as needed

1 bunch spinach, stemmed and well washed

4 fresh oregano sprigs

French Chicken with Prunes

A pretty wintertime supper dish with the contrasting colors of carrots and prunes. This dish is excellent served with braised fennel or an orange, onion, and avocado salad, and winter pears for dessert.

2 chickens, about 2¹/₂ lb (1.25 kg) each, quartered

2 tablespoons unsalted butter, at room temperature

1 teaspoon dried thyme

¹/₂ cup (4 fl oz/125 ml) fresh orange juice

¹/₂ cup (4 fl oz/125 ml) dry white wine

12 prunes, pitted

¹/₂ cup (4 fl oz/125 ml) Chicken Stock (page 314), heated

3 carrots, peeled and cut into slices ¹/₄ inch (6 mm) thick

2 tablespoons brandy

Salt and freshly ground pepper

Preheat the oven to 375° (190°C).

Trim any visible fat from the chicken. Butter the chicken pieces on both sides and then sprinkle with the thyme. Arrange in a baking dish, skin side down. Place in the oven and bake for 20 minutes.

Meanwhile, in a saucepan, combine the orange juice and wine and bring to a boil over high heat. Reduce the heat to low, add the prunes, cover, and simmer until soft, 8–10 minutes.

Turn the chicken pieces skin side up, stir the hot stock into the pan juices, and baste the chicken. Using a slotted spoon, transfer the cooked prunes to the baking dish. Add ¹/₂ cup (4 fl oz/125 ml) of the prune cooking liquid to the juices in the dish. Scatter the carrots around the chicken. Bake until the chicken is tender and opaque throughout, 40–50 minutes. During the last 10 minutes of cooking, add the brandy to the juices and season to taste with salt and pepper.

Place the chicken, prunes, and carrots on a warmed platter. Spoon the pan juices over all and serve.

Serves 4

Chicken with Forty Cloves of Garlic

Don't be alarmed at the amount of garlic in this recipe. As it roasts, garlic turns mild and creamy—perfect for spreading on grilled bread. Serve the chicken with green beans, if desired.

4 fresh thyme sprigs

2 bay leaves

4 fresh rosemary sprigs

6 fresh sage leaves

1 chicken, 3–4 lb (1.5–2 kg)

1 lemon, halved

Salt and freshly ground pepper

1/2 cup (4 fl oz/125 ml) olive oil

40 unpeeled cloves garlic

Chicken Stock (page 314), if needed

Preheat the oven to 350°F (180°C). Tie 2 of the thyme sprigs, 1 of the bay leaves, 2 of the rosemary sprigs, and 3 of the sage leaves with kitchen string to form a bouquet garni. Repeat with the remaining herbs. If the giblets and neck are in the chicken cavity, reserve for another use. Trim any visible fat from the chicken. Rub inside and out with the cut side of the lemon halves. Sprinkle inside and out with salt and pepper. Place 1 herb bouquet inside the chicken along with the lemon halves.

In a Dutch oven over medium heat, heat the olive oil. Add the garlic cloves and sauté until they release their fragrance, about 3 minutes. Add the chicken, turn it in the scented oil, and position breast side up. Add the second bouquet garni to the pot and cover tightly. Place in the oven and roast until an instant-read thermometer inserted into the thickest part of the thigh away from the bone registers 170°F (77°C), 1–1 1/2 hours.

Remove the chicken from the oven and transfer to a cutting board. Using a slotted spoon, transfer the garlic cloves to a small bowl and keep warm. Discard the bouquets garni in the pot and from the cavity. Let the chicken rest for about 5 minutes. Carve into serving pieces and arrange on a warmed platter. Add a little stock to the pan juices if they seem scant, reheat, and season with salt and pepper. Drizzle the juices over the chicken. Serve the garlic cloves on the side.

Serves 4

Teriyaki Chicken

The soy-and-ginger marinade is good with flank steak and lamb as well as chicken. Serve this dish with grilled mixed vegetables and Steamed White Rice (page 317).

To make the marinade, in a small bowl, stir together the soy sauce, sherry, oil, sugar, garlic, and ginger. Reserve ¼ cup (2 fl oz/60 ml) of the marinade. Place the chicken in a large lock-top plastic bag and pour in the remaining marinade. Press out the air and seal the bag. Massage the bag gently to distribute the marinade. Set the bag in a large bowl and refrigerate for at least 2 hours, or all day if you wish, turning and massaging the bag occasionally.

Prepare a fire in a charcoal grill, or preheat a gas grill or broiler (grill). Oil the grill rack and position 4–6 inches (10–15 cm) above the fire.

Remove the chicken pieces from the marinade and pat them dry with paper towels. Arrange the chicken pieces on the grill rack, skin side down, or skin side up on a broiler pan. Grill or broil, turning frequently, for 30–35 minutes. During the last 10 minutes of cooking, brush the chicken 2 or 3 times with the reserved marinade. If the chicken starts to get too dark, turn it skin side up and move it to a cooler part of the grill not directly over the fire, or cool the fire a little by covering the grill and opening the vents halfway. If broiling, lower the broiling pan.

Serves 2–4

FOR THE MARINADE:

⅓ cup (3 fl oz/80 ml) soy sauce

⅓ cup (3 fl oz/80 ml) dry sherry or rice wine

¼ cup (2 fl oz/60 ml) peanut oil

2 tablespoons sugar

2 cloves garlic, minced

1 tablespoon peeled and grated fresh ginger

1 frying chicken, about 3½ lb (1.75 kg), cut into serving pieces

Chicken and Eggplant Casserole

Make this casserole in late summer, when peppers, eggplants, and tomatoes are at their peak of season. Serve with hot garlic and herb bread and a salad of shredded celery root (celeriac).

Preheat the oven to 375°F (190°C).

Trim any visible fat from the chicken pieces. Place the chicken skin side up in a 6-cup (48–fl oz/1.5-l) baking dish and brush with the brandy. Add 2 tablespoons of the olive oil and the garlic to the dish and turn the chicken skin side down. Place in the oven for 10 minutes to brown. Turn skin side up and bake 10 minutes longer. Remove from the oven and season to taste with salt and pepper.

In a large frying pan over medium heat, heat the remaining 2 tablespoons olive oil. Add the bell peppers and sauté for 2 minutes. Add the tomatoes and eggplant and cook, stirring occasionally, for 5 minutes. Pour off the oil. Pour in $^1/_2$ cup (4 fl oz/125 ml) of the hot stock and add the thyme and bay leaves. Simmer until the vegetables soften slightly, 3–4 minutes. Remove from the heat.

Spoon the vegetables and herbs around the chicken. Add the remaining $^1/_2$ cup (4 fl oz/125 ml) hot stock and the white wine. Cover, return to the oven, and bake until and the juices run clear when a thigh joint is pierced with a knife, about 40 minutes longer.

Sprinkle the parsley over the top and serve directly from the casserole.

Serves 4–6

2 chickens, about 2$^1/_2$ lb (1.25 kg) each, quartered

3 tablespoons brandy

4 tablespoons (2 fl oz/60 ml) olive oil

2 cloves garlic, halved

Salt and freshly ground pepper

2 cups (10 oz/315 g) chopped red and yellow bell peppers (capsicums)

4 tomatoes, cut into quarters

1 small eggplant (aubergine), cut lengthwise into sticks $^1/_4$ inch (6 mm) thick

1 cup (8 fl oz/350 ml) Chicken Stock (page 314), heated

1 teaspoon dried thyme

2 bay leaves

$^1/_2$ cup (4 fl oz/125 ml) dry white wine

1 tablespoon chopped fresh flat-leaf (Italian) parsley or cilantro (fresh coriander)

Lemon-Rosemary Chicken

Fresh rosemary gives chicken an irresistible flavor, and a handful of sprigs tossed on the fire during the last few minutes of cooking imparts a pleasant smokiness. Rosemary, by the way, is very easy to grow in a garden.

FOR THE MARINADE:

½ cup (4 fl oz/125 ml) fresh lemon juice

⅓ cup (3 fl oz/80 ml) olive oil

2 tablespoons shallots

2 tablespoons chopped fresh rosemary

Salt and freshly ground pepper

1 frying chicken, about 3½ lb (1.75 kg), quartered

Handful of fresh rosemary sprigs

To make the marinade, in a small bowl, combine the lemon juice, olive oil, shallots, rosemary, ½ teaspoon salt, and ½ teaspoon pepper and mix well. Reserve ¼ cup (2 fl oz/60 ml) of the marinade. Place the chicken quarters in a large lock-top plastic bag and pour in the remaining marinade. Press the air out of the bag and seal it tightly. Massage the bag gently to distribute the marinade. Set the bag in a large bowl and refrigerate for at least 2 hours, or all day if you like, turning and massaging the bag occasionally.

Soak the rosemary sprigs in water to cover for about 30 minutes. Prepare a fire in a charcoal grill, or preheat a gas grill or broiler (grill). Oil the grill rack and position 4–6 inches (10–15 cm) above the heat.

Remove the chicken from the marinade and pat dry with paper towels. Arrange the chicken quarters, skin side down, on the grill rack. Grill or broil, turning frequently, for 30–35 minutes. During the last 10 minutes, drop the soaked rosemary sprigs on the fire and brush the chicken 2 or 3 times with the reserved marinade. If the chicken starts to get too dark, turn it skin side up and move it to a cooler part of the rack so it isn't directly over the fire, or cool the fire a little by covering the grill and opening the vents halfway.

Serves 2–4

Grill-Roasted Chicken with Potato Fans

Baking potatoes and a roasting chicken are good grill partners because both will cook in the same amount of time. Serve the chicken atop a bed of fresh herb sprigs, to hint at the flavors that await.

Prepare a fire for indirect-heat cooking in a charcoal grill with a cover (page 326), or preheat a gas grill. Oil the grill rack and position about 4–6 inches (10–15 cm) above the heat source.

If the neck and giblets are in the chicken cavity, reserve for another use. Trim any visible fat from the chicken. Rinse and pat dry with paper towels. Rub inside and out with the cut sides of the lemon. Sprinkle inside and out with salt and pepper. Tuck the herb sprigs in the cavity. Rub the skin with the olive oil. Truss the chicken (page 318) and set aside.

Slice each potato crosswise at $^1/_4$-inch (6-mm) intervals, cutting only three-fourths of the way through; the slices must remain attached. In a bowl, turn the potatoes in the butter and season with the salt and pepper to taste.

Place the chicken, breast side down, over indirect heat. Place the fanned potatoes, cut side up, alongside the bird. Cover the grill and open the vents halfway. After 30 minutes, turn the chicken breast side up and turn the potatoes cut side down. Cook the chicken until the juices run clear when a thigh joint is pierced and an instant-read thermometer inserted into the thickest part of the thigh away from the bone registers 170°F (77°C), about 1 hour total. The potatoes will be tender in about the same amount of time.

Transfer the chicken to a warmed platter and let rest for 10 minutes; keep the potatoes warm on the grill. To serve, remove the twine and carve the chicken. Arrange the potatoes alongside.

Serves 4

1 roasting chicken, 5–6 lb (2.5–3 kg)

1 lemon, halved

Salt and freshly ground pepper

Several sprigs of fresh rosemary, thyme, sage, or flat-leaf (Italian) parsley

1–2 tablespoons olive oil

4 baking potatoes, about $^1/_2$ lb (250 g) each, peeled

3 tablespoons unsalted butter, melted

Fettuccine with Sausage, Garlic, and Mushrooms

3/4 lb (375 g) cooked low-fat smoked chicken sausages

1 tablespoon olive oil

2 large cloves garlic, minced

1 lb (500 g) white or cremini mushrooms, brushed clean and thinly sliced

1 cup (8 fl oz/250 ml) dry white wine

1/4 cup (1/3 oz/10 g) minced fresh flat-leaf (Italian) parsley

Salt and freshly ground pepper

1 lb (500 g) dried fettuccine

Slice the sausages into rounds about 1/4 inch (6 mm) thick. In a large, nonstick frying pan over medium heat, heat the olive oil. When it is hot, add the sausage slices. Cook, stirring often, until lightly browned, about 3–4 minutes. Add the garlic and mushrooms and stir until the mushrooms have softened and released some of their liquid, about 3 minutes. Add the wine, bring to a boil over medium heat, and cook until the mushrooms are tender, about 3 minutes longer. Stir in the parsley and season to taste with salt and pepper.

While the sauce is cooking, bring a pot of salted water to a boil. Add the fettuccine, stir well, and cook until al dente (tender but firm to the bite), 8–10 minutes, or according to the package directions.

Drain the fettuccine and place in a warmed shallow serving bowl. Pour the sauce over the top and toss briefly to combine. Serve at once.

Serves 6

Hickory-Smoked Chicken

Adding aromatic hickory chips to the fire gives this chicken a smoky taste. It is good served hot or cold. Accompany it with a rice or pasta salad and crusty bread.

1 roasting chicken, 5–6 lb (2.5–3 kg)

1 lemon, cut in half

Salt and freshly ground pepper

Several sprigs of fresh rosemary or flat-leaf (Italian) parsley

Several slices of fresh ginger

1 tablespoon olive oil

Soak 3 handfuls (about 5 oz/155 g) hickory chips in water to cover for about 1 hour.

Prepare a fire for indirect-heat cooking in a charcoal grill with a cover (page 326), or preheat a gas grill. Oil the grill rack and position 4–6 inches (10–15 cm) above the fire.

If the neck and giblets are in the chicken cavity, reserve for another use. Trim any visible fat from the chicken. Rinse and pat dry with paper towels. Rub the outside of the chicken with the cut sides of the lemon. Sprinkle inside and out with salt and pepper. Tuck the rosemary sprigs and ginger slices in the cavity. Rub the skin with the olive oil; truss the bird (page 318) with kitchen twine.

Sprinkle half of the soaked wood chips on the fire. Place the chicken, breast side down, on the grill rack away from the heat and cover the grill. If using a gas grill, place half the chips in an aluminum-foil packet, punch holes in the bottom, and set on the lava rocks. After about 40 minutes, turn the bird breast side up and sprinkle the remaining wood chips on the fire. Cook until a thermometer inserted into the thickest part of a thigh away from the bone registers 170°F (77°C), about 1 hour, adding fresh coals to the fire if necessary to maintain a constant temperature. Remove the chicken from the grill and let rest for about 10 minutes before carving.

Serves 4

Broiled Chicken with Vinaigrette

These golden chickens are served on a bed of lettuce and topped with a mint vinaigrette, which provides a cool contrast to the crisp breaded chicken.

Preheat a broiler (grill). Trim any visible fat from the chicken.

In a small bowl, stir together the sesame and olive oils, mustard, and vermouth. Brush the chicken halves with some of the mixture and place, skin side down, in a shallow baking dish. Slip in the broiler about 4 inches (10 cm) from the heat and broil (grill) for 15 minutes. Turn the chicken, baste with the dish juices, and broil for 15 minutes longer.

Meanwhile, spread the bread crumbs on a sheet of waxed paper and season to taste with salt and pepper. Remove the chicken from the broiler, brush the skin side with the remaining oil-mustard mixture, and roll the skin side in the bread crumbs. Return the chicken to the dish, skin side up, and return to the broiler. Broil until dark golden brown and an instant-read thermometer inserted into the thickest part of a thigh away from the bone registers 170°F (77°C), 4–5 minutes.

Meanwhile, arrange the lettuce leaves on a platter; use only the small inner leaves and save the others for another use. To make the vinaigrette, in a small bowl, stir together the oil, vinegar, mint, soy sauce, and coriander. Drizzle about 1/4 cup (2 fl oz/60 ml) over the lettuce. Place the chicken pieces on the lettuce and spoon about 2 tablespoons of the vinaigrette over each piece.

Serves 4–6

2 chickens, about 2 1/2 lb (1.25 kg) each, halved lengthwise (page 319)

1/4 cup (2 fl oz/60 ml) sesame oil

1/4 cup (2 fl oz/60 ml) olive oil

1 tablespoon Dijon mustard

1/4 cup (2 fl oz/60 ml) dry vermouth

1 cup (4 oz/125 g) dried bread crumbs

Salt and freshly ground pepper

1 head butter (Boston) lettuce, separated into leaves

FOR THE MINT VINAIGRETTE:

1/2 cup (4 fl oz/125 ml) sesame oil

1/4 cup (2 fl oz/60 ml) red wine vinegar

2 tablespoons finely chopped fresh mint

1 tablespoon soy sauce

1/2 teaspoon ground coriander

Broiled Chicken with Herb-Stuffed Breast

For a springtime dish, serve these herb-infused chickens with your choice
of young, tender vegetables. Offer both Horseradish-Mustard Sauce (page 19)
and Green Parsley Sauce (page 19) on the side.

2 young chickens, about 2 lb
(1 kg) each, halved lengthwise

1/2 cup (4 oz/125 g) unsalted
butter, at room temperature

1/2 cup (3/4 oz/20 g) chopped
fresh flat-leaf (Italian) parsley

1/4 cup (1/3 oz/10 g) chopped
fresh chives

1 teaspoon dried tarragon

Salt and freshly ground pepper

4 slices toast, buttered

4 tablespoons (3 oz/90 g)
apricot or peach chutney

Preheat a broiler (grill). Trim any visible fat from the chicken.

In a small bowl, combine the butter, parsley, chives, tarragon, and salt and pepper
to taste. Stir until well mixed. Loosen the skin covering the breast on each chicken
half. Spread 1 tablespoon of the butter-herb mixture evenly over the breast meat of
each chicken half.

Melt the remaining butter-herb mixture. Brush some of it on both sides of the
chicken halves and place the chicken, skin side down, in a shallow baking dish.
Place under the hot broiler (grill) about 3 inches (7.5 cm) from the heat source and
broil (grill) for about 15 minutes.

Turn the chicken skin side up and brush with the remaining melted butter mixture
and the pan juices. Broil until golden brown on the outside and an instant-read
thermometer inserted into the thickest part of a thigh away from the bone registers
170°F (77°C), about 12 minutes longer. Season to taste with salt and pepper.

Place the buttered toasts on a platter and spoon 1 tablespoon of chutney on each
slice. Arrange a chicken half atop each toast. Serve at once.

Serves 4

All-American Barbecued Chicken

Use whole fryers, cut up, or buy any other chicken parts you like, such as thighs, breasts, and/or legs. Brush the sauce on for just the last few minutes of cooking so it doesn't burn. Serve with garlic bread, grilled corn, and potato salad or coleslaw.

Prepare a fire for indirect-heat cooking in a charcoal grill with a cover (page 326), or preheat a gas grill. Oil the grill rack and position 4–6 inches (10–15 cm) above the heat.

Sprinkle the chicken pieces on both sides with salt and pepper. Place them, skin side down, directly above the heat. Grill, uncovered, turning frequently, until well browned, 10–15 minutes. Watch the chicken constantly, and have a spray bottle of water handy to douse flare-ups for a charcoal fire. Move the chicken pieces—you may overlap them slightly—so that they are no longer directly over the heat.

Cover the grill and open the vents halfway. Cook for 10 minutes. Brush the chicken with the sauce, turn, re-cover, and cook for 5 minutes longer. Brush again with the sauce, then cover and cook until the chicken pieces are opaque throughout, about 5 minutes longer. Pass the remaining sauce at the table.

Serves 4–6

5–6 lb (2.5–3 kg) chicken pieces

Salt and freshly ground pepper

Basic Barbecue Sauce (page 17)

Buffalo Wings

Spicy chicken wings, served with celery sticks and blue cheese sauce for dipping, are good hot or cold, and are a perfect finger food. Make them spicier or milder by altering the amounts of chili powder and Tabasco sauce.

FOR THE MARINADE:

1 cup (8 fl oz/250 ml) cider vinegar

2 tablespoons *each* vegetable oil and Worcestershire sauce

2 tablespoons chili powder

1 teaspoon red pepper flakes

Salt and freshly ground pepper

1 tablespoon Tabasco sauce

4 lb (2 kg) chicken wings

FOR THE BLUE CHEESE SAUCE:

$^3/_4$ cup (6 oz/185 g) sour cream

$^1/_2$ cup (4 fl oz/125 ml) mayonnaise

1 large clove garlic, minced

2 teaspoons Worcestershire sauce

1 cup (4 oz/125 g) crumbled blue cheese

Salt and freshly ground pepper

About 2 tablespoons milk

Celery sticks for serving

To make the marinade, in a bowl, stir together the vinegar, oil, Worcestershire sauce, chili powder, red pepper flakes, 1 teaspoon salt, 1 teaspoon pepper, and the Tabasco. Reserve $^1/_4$ cup (2 fl oz/60 ml) of the marinade. Put the chicken wings in a large lock-top plastic bag and pour in the remaining marinade. Press out the air and seal the bag. Massage the bag gently to distribute the marinade. Set in a large bowl and refrigerate for 2–3 hours, turning and massaging the bag occasionally.

To make the blue cheese sauce, in a small bowl, whisk together the sour cream, mayonnaise, garlic, Worcestershire sauce, and blue cheese. Season to taste with salt and pepper. Add enough milk to make a sauce the consistency of pancake batter. Cover and refrigerate.

Prepare a fire in a charcoal grill, or preheat a gas grill or broiler (grill). Remove the wings from the marinade and pat dry with paper towels. Arrange the wings on the grill rack or on a broiler (grill) pan. Grill or broil 4–6 inches (10–15 cm) from the heat source, brushing with the reserved marinade and turning frequently, until opaque throughout, about 25–30 minutes. Serve with the blue cheese sauce and celery sticks.

Serves 4 as a main course, 6–8 as an appetizer

Mustard-Grilled Chicken

The flavor of mustard pairs wonderfully with chicken, and in this recipe it does double duty as both a marinade and a basting sauce. The mixture is spicy; if you desire milder seasonings, reduce the amount of cayenne to 2 teaspoons.

In a small bowl, stir together $^1/_3$ cup ($2^1/_2$ oz/75 g) of the mustard, 1 tablespoon of the cayenne pepper, the olive oil, and the vinegar. Place the chicken in a large lock-top plastic bag and pour in the mustard mixture. Press out the air and seal. Massage gently to distribute the marinade. Set in a large bowl and refrigerate for 2 hours, or all day if you wish, turning and massaging the bag occasionally.

Prepare a fire for indirect-heat cooking in a charcoal grill with a cover (page 326), or preheat a gas grill. Oil the grill rack and position 4–6 inches (10–15 cm) above the heat.

Combine the remaining $^1/_3$ cup ($2^1/_2$ oz/75 g) mustard with the remaining 1 tablespoon cayenne pepper. Remove the chicken from the marinade, allowing as much marinade as possible to cling to the surface.

Place the chicken, skin side down, on the grill rack away from the heat. Grill, turning frequently, for about 25 minutes; do not worry if some of the marinade sticks to the grill. Have a spray bottle of water handy to douse flare-ups for a charcoal fire. Turn the chicken skin side up and brush with the mustard mixture. Cover the grill, open the vents halfway, and cook until a thermometer inserted into the thickest part of a thigh away from the bone registers 170°F (77°C), about 10 minutes longer.

Serves 2–4

$^2/_3$ cup (5 oz/150 g) Dijon mustard

2 tablespoons cayenne pepper

$^1/_4$ cup (2 fl oz/60 ml) olive oil

2 tablespoons wine vinegar

1 broiler chicken, about $2^1/_2$ lb (1.25 kg), halved lengthwise

Other Poultry

Turkey Breast with Bulgur Stuffing

In a bowl, pour the boiling water over the bulgur, stir, and let stand for 1 hour.

Meanwhile, in a large, nonstick frying pan over medium-low heat, heat the olive oil. Add the onion and celery and sauté until soft, about 5 minutes. Add the spinach and cook, stirring frequently, until the moisture evaporates, about 5 minutes. Transfer to a large bowl and add the bulgur, bread crumbs, sage, stock, 1 teaspoon salt, and 1/2 teaspoon pepper. Stir and toss to combine. Set aside.

Preheat the oven to 325°F (165°C). Coat a roasting pan with nonstick cooking spray.

To butterfly the turkey breast, use a sharp knife to make a horizontal cut along the larger, meatier side of the breast, slicing through to within about 1/2 inch (12 mm) of the other side; be careful not to cut all the way through. Lift the top piece of meat and fold back to make a large, flat surface. Sprinkle lightly with salt and pepper and spread with the stuffing, mounding it slightly in the center. Bring the pieces of meat together to enclose the stuffing. Using kitchen twine, tie the rolled breast in 3 or 4 places around its circumference, then tie around the length to secure both ends and make a cylindrical roll.

Place the turkey in the prepared pan and roast until an instant-read thermometer inserted into the center of the roll registers 170°F (77°C), about 1 1/4 hours. Remove from the oven; cover loosely with aluminum foil and let rest for about 20 minutes.

To serve, snip the twine and discard. Cut the turkey roll crosswise into slices 1/2 inch (12 mm) thick. Arrange on a platter and garnish with watercress.

Serves 6

2/3 cup (5 fl oz/160 ml) boiling water

1/3 cup (2 oz/60 g) bulgur wheat

2 tablespoons olive oil

1/2 cup (2 oz/60 g) chopped yellow onion

1/2 cup (2 oz/60 g) chopped celery

1 cup (7 oz/220 g) cooked, drained, and chopped spinach

1/2 cup (1 oz/30 g) fresh white bread crumbs (page 324)

2 tablespoons minced fresh sage or 1 teaspoon dried sage

1/3 cup (3 fl oz/80 ml) Chicken Stock (page 314) or water

Salt and freshly ground pepper

1 skinless, boneless turkey breast half, about 1 3/4 lb (875 g)

Watercress sprigs for garnish

Turkey Breast, Green Beans, and Toasted Almonds

This quick main course is full of crunch from the almonds and sweetness from the green beans. Select small, tender green beans for the best flavor and texture. Serve with Steamed White Rice (page 317).

½ cup (2½ oz/75 g) slivered almonds

3 tablespoons peanut oil

1 lb (500 g) boneless, skinless turkey breast meat, cut into strips about 2 inches (5 cm) long and ½ inch (12 mm) wide

3 celery stalks, cut into thin strips about 2 inches (5 cm) long and ¼ inch (6 mm) wide

½ lb (250 g) green beans, trimmed and cut into 2-inch (5-cm) lengths, parboiled for 3 minutes, drained, rinsed in cold water, and drained again

2 teaspoons cornstarch (cornflour) dissolved in 3 tablespoons water

All-Purpose Stir-Fry Sauce (page 17)

Heat a dry wok or frying pan over medium-high heat. Add the almonds and stir constantly until evenly toasted, 1–2 minutes. Watch carefully so they do not burn. Transfer immediately to a dish and set aside.

Raise the heat to high and add 2 tablespoons of the oil, swirling to coat the bottom and sides of the pan. When the oil is almost smoking, add the turkey strips and stir-fry until lightly browned on the outside and opaque throughout, 4–5 minutes. Be sure to distribute the turkey evenly in the pan so it comes into maximum contact with the heat and cooks evenly. Transfer to another dish.

Add the remaining 1 tablespoon oil to the pan, again swirling to coat the pan. When the oil is hot, add the celery and stir-fry until crisp-tender, 2–3 minutes. Add the green beans and stir-fry for 1 minute longer. Quickly stir the cornstarch mixture and add it to the pan along with the stir-fry sauce and the turkey. Bring the liquid to a simmer and stir until it begins to thicken, 2–3 minutes. Sprinkle on the toasted almonds, stir to mix, and serve immediately.

Serves 4

Grill-Roasted Turkey

This turkey comes out juicy, with a smoky flavor and dark brown skin. To grill-roast a roasting chicken (5—6 lb/2.5—3 kg), halve the ingredients and cook for about 90 minutes.

1 turkey, 10—12 lb (5—6 kg)

2 tablespoons olive oil

2 tablespoons chopped fresh rosemary or 2 teaspoons dried rosemary

Salt and freshly ground pepper

2 lemons, quartered

Large handful of fresh sage, tarragon, or parsley sprigs

1/2 cup (4 oz/125 g) unsalted butter, melted

2 tablespoons fresh lemon juice

Fresh herb sprigs and lemon halves for garnish

Soak 3 handfuls (about 6 oz/185 g) hickory chips in water to cover for 1 hour. Prepare a fire for indirect-heat cooking in a charcoal grill with a cover (page 326), or preheat a gas grill. Oil the grill rack and position about 4—6 inches (10—15 cm) above the heat.

If the neck and giblets are in the turkey cavity, discard or reserve for another use. Trim any visible fat from the turkey. Rinse and pat dry with paper towels and rub with the olive oil and rosemary. Sprinkle inside and out with salt and pepper. Tuck the lemon quarters and herb sprigs inside the cavity; truss the bird (page 318). Sprinkle half of the wood chips on the fire, or for a gas grill, place half the chips in an aluminum-foil packet, poke holes in the bottom, and set directly on the lava rocks. Place the turkey, breast side up, over indirect heat. Cover the grill and cook for about 1 hour.

In a small bowl, stir together the butter and lemon juice. Sprinkle the remaining wood chips on the fire or place a second foil packet on the lava rocks. Brush the turkey with half of the butter mixture, then cover and cook for 45 minutes longer, replenishing the fresh coals for a charcoal grill. Brush with the remaining butter mixture, then cook, covered, until an instant-read thermometer inserted in the thickest part of thigh away from the bone registers 185°F (85°C), 30—45 minutes longer. Total cooking time is about 2 1/2 hours. Remove the turkey from the grill and let it rest for 15—20 minutes before carving.

Serves 10—12

Hickory-Smoked Turkey Thighs

Dropping damp hickory chips onto the fire gives the turkey a subtle, smoky taste. The dry marinade forms a spicy coating and helps bring out the turkey's natural flavor.

Soak a handful (about 2 oz/60 g) of hickory chips in water to cover for 1 hour.

To make the dry rub, in a small bowl, stir together the salt, pepper, sage, thyme, and lemon zest. Pat the turkey thighs dry with paper towels. Rub them with the olive oil, and then rub each one with the dry rub. Let stand at room temperature for 1 hour, or cover and refrigerate for several hours.

Prepare a fire for indirect-heat cooking in a charcoal grill with a cover (page 326), or preheat a gas grill. Oil the grill rack and position 4–6 inches (10–15 cm) above the heat. Scoop the hickory chips out of the water and sprinkle them over the coals.

Place the turkey thighs, skin side down, on the center of the rack. Cover the grill and open the vents halfway. Cook, turning 2 or 3 times, until well browned, opaque throughout, and an instant-read thermometer inserted into the thickest portion of a thigh registers 185°F (85°C), 50–60 minutes.

Remove from the grill, cut each thigh in half along one side of the bone, and arrange on a warmed platter or individual plates. Serve immediately.

Serves 8

FOR THE DRY RUB:

1½ teaspoons salt

1 teaspoon freshly ground pepper

1 teaspoon dried sage

1 teaspoon dried thyme

Finely grated zest of 1 lemon

4 turkey thighs, about 1½ lb (750 g) each

4 teaspoons olive oil

Turkey Burgers with Apple-Mint Relish

A pleasant change from ground-beef burgers, these cheese-laced turkey burgers are complemented by the cool crunch of apple relish. Serve the burgers on hamburger buns, French rolls, or crusty country-style bread.

To make the relish, chop the apples finely or shred them on the large holes of a box grater. Transfer to a large bowl and add the vinegar, mint, sugar, olive oil, celery seed, mustard seed, and 1 teaspoon salt. Stir and toss with a fork to combine, then cover and refrigerate for 2 hours before serving to blend the flavors.

Prepare a fire in a charcoal grill, or preheat a gas grill. Oil the grill rack and position 4–6 inches (10–15 cm) above the heat.

In a large bowl, combine the turkey, cheese, shallots, garlic, 1 1/2 teaspoons salt, and 1/2 teaspoon pepper. Using a fork, mix gently to combine. Shape into 6 patties each about 3 inches (7.5 cm) in diameter and 1 inch (2.5 cm) thick.

Place the patties on the grill rack. Grill, turning 2 or 3 times, until the burgers are well browned on both sides and no longer pink in the center, 16–20 minutes.

To serve, transfer to a warmed platter. Pass the relish at the table.

Serves 6

FOR THE APPLE-MINT RELISH:

2 apples, preferably Golden Delicious, peeled, halved, and cored

1/4 cup (2 fl oz/60 ml) cider vinegar

2 tablespoons minced fresh mint or 1 teaspoon dried mint

1 tablespoon sugar

1 tablespoon olive oil

1/2 teaspoon celery seed

1/2 teaspoon mustard seed

Salt

2 lb (1 kg) ground (minced) turkey

1 cup (4 oz/125 g) shredded Cheddar cheese

1/4 cup (1 oz/30 g) minced shallots

1 clove garlic, minced

Salt and freshly ground pepper

Turkey Kabobs with Peanut Dipping Sauce

Cut the turkey breast into 1 1/2-inch (4-cm) cubes. In a large bowl, whisk together the wine, soy sauce, olive oil, sugar, garlic and 2 teaspoons pepper. Add the turkey and toss to coat evenly. Cover and refrigerate, tossing occasionally, for at least 3 hours, or all day if you wish.

Prepare a fire for direct-heat cooking in a grill (see page 326). Position the grill rack 4–6 inches (10–15 cm) above the fire. If using wooden skewers, soak them in water to cover for 30 minutes, then drain.

Remove the turkey from the marinade and pat dry with paper towels; reserve the marinade. Thread the turkey onto 4–6 skewers.

Arrange the skewers on the rack. Grill, turning frequently and brushing occasionally with the reserved marinade, until the turkey is no longer pink in the center, about 20 minutes. Stop brushing with the marinade 5 minutes before the turkey is done.

To serve, transfer to individual plates and serve immediately with the peanut sauce.

Serves 4–6

1 skinless, boneless turkey breast, 2 lb (1 kg)

1/2 cup (4 fl oz/125 ml) dry white wine

1/4 cup (2 fl oz/60 ml) soy sauce

1/4 cup (2 fl oz/60 ml) olive oil

1 tablespoon sugar

1 large clove garlic, minced

Freshly ground pepper

Peanut Dipping Sauce (page 19)

Turkey Sausages with Chutney Mustard

Sausages are perfect for grilling, and are enlivened here with a spicy mustard. Chicken sausages may be substituted. Serve with slices of fresh mango for a refreshing complement.

2 lb (1 kg) turkey sausages

½ cup (4 oz/125 g) whole-grain mustard

¼ cup (2½ oz/75 g) mango chutney

¼ cup (⅓ oz/10 g) minced fresh cilantro (fresh coriander)

Prepare a fire in a charcoal grill, or preheat a gas grill. Oil the grill rack and position 4–6 inches (10–15 cm) above the heat.

Bring a pot of water to a simmer. Prick the sausages several times with a fork, then blanch in the simmering water for about 5 minutes; drain.

In a small bowl, stir together the mustard, chutney, and cilantro. Cover and refrigerate until serving.

Arrange the sausages on the grill rack. Have a spray bottle of water handy to douse flare-ups for a charcoal grill. Grill, turning every 2 minutes, until the sausages are well browned on the outside and no longer pink in the center, about 15 minutes.

To serve, transfer the sausages to a warmed platter. Pass the chutney mustard in a bowl at the table.

Serves 4–6

Portuguese Stew with Turkey Sausage

Serve this heart-friendly update of a classic pork-sausage recipe with hot, crusty Italian bread. Turkey sausages are available in most well-stocked markets; chicken sausages may also be used.

If using white beans, pick over and discard any damaged beans or stones. Rinse the beans. Place in a bowl, add water to cover by 2 inches (5 cm), and let stand 4 hours or up to overnight. Drain the beans and place in a saucepan with water to cover by 2 inches (5 cm). Bring to a boil, reduce the heat to low, and simmer gently, uncovered, until tender, 1–1¹/₂ hours. Drain the beans and set aside. Alternatively, drain the canned chickpeas and set aside.

In a large Dutch oven over medium-high heat, heat the olive oil. Add the sausages and brown on all sides until golden, about 5 minutes. Using tongs, transfer to a dish and cut crosswise into pieces ¹/₂ inch (12 mm) thick; set aside.

Add the onion slices to the same pot over medium-high heat and sauté, stirring, until tender and the browned bits from the pot bottom begin to cling to the slices, about 8 minutes. Add 2–3 tablespoons of the stock if needed to keep the onion from sticking. Slowly add the remaining stock, stirring with a wooden spoon to dislodge any browned bits from the bottom.

Return the sausage to the pot, along with the bell pepper, squash, tomatoes and purée, thyme, cayenne pepper, bouquet garni, kale, and reserved beans. Stir well and bring to a simmer. Cover and simmer gently over medium-low heat until the kale is tender and the flavors have developed, about 45 minutes. Season to taste with salt and black pepper.

Spoon into warmed bowls and serve.

Serves 4–6

1 cup (7 oz/220 g) dried small white (navy) or cannellini beans, or 1 can (20 oz/625 g) chickpeas (garbanzo beans)

2 tablespoons olive oil

1 lb (500 g) spicy turkey sausages

1 large sweet white onion, cut in half and then into slices ¹/₄ inch (6 mm) thick

2 cups (16 fl oz/500 ml) Chicken Stock (page 314)

1 green bell pepper (capsicum), seeded, deribbed, and cut lengthwise into strips ¹/₂ inch (12 mm) wide

2 cups (10 oz/315 g) peeled and cubed butternut squash

1 can (28 oz/875 g) whole tomatoes in purée

¹/₂ teaspoon dried thyme

¹/₄ teaspoon cayenne pepper

Bouquet Garni (page 316)

1 bunch kale (about 1¹/₄ lb/ 625 g), stemmed

Salt and freshly ground black pepper

Thyme and Mustard Quail

Do not be intimidated by these single-serving birds. Their succulent dark meat will stay moist and delicious if you take extra care not to overcook them. Serve with skewered grilled squash or other grilled vegetables.

⅓ cup (4 oz/125 g) Dijon mustard

½ cup (4 fl oz/125 ml) dry white or red wine

5 tablespoons (3 fl oz/80 ml) olive oil

1 tablespoon chopped fresh thyme or 1 teaspoon dried thyme

8 quail, about 5 oz (155 g) each

Salt and freshly ground pepper

Prepare a fire in a charcoal grill, or preheat a gas grill. Oil the grill rack and position 4–6 inches (10–15 cm) above the heat.

In a small bowl, stir together the mustard, wine, 3 tablespoons of the olive oil, and the thyme; set aside. Rinse the quail and pat dry with paper towels. Rub them with the remaining 2 tablespoons olive oil and sprinkle lightly with salt and pepper.

Place the quail, breast side down, on the grill rack. Grill for 8 minutes, turning them frequently to brown evenly. Brush the mustard mixture on the quail, turn, and cook for 2–3 minutes; repeat to cook the other side. Do not overcook the birds; the meat should remain slightly pink at the bone.

Serves 4

Citrus-Marinated Cornish Hens

First, butterfly the game hens: Place each hen, breast side down, on a work surface. With heavy-duty kitchen scissors, cut from the neck to the tail along both sides of the backbone; lift out the backbone. Turn breast side up and, using the heel of your hand, press down firmly on the breastbone to flatten it. Cut off the tips of the wings and discard. Put the hens in a heavy lock-top plastic bag; set aside.

To make the marinade, in a small bowl, stir together the lemon zest, lemon juice, orange juice, garlic, shallots, jalapeños, and 1/2 teaspoon salt. Reserve 1/4 cup (2 fl oz/ 60 ml) of the marinade. Pour the remaining marinade into the plastic bag with the hens. Press the air from the bag and seal. Set in a bowl and marinate in the refrigerator for at least 2 hours or up to overnight.

Preheat the oven to 425°F (220°C). Coat a roasting pan with nonstick cooking spray.

Remove the hens from the marinade and pat them dry with paper towels. Place 5 of the herb sprigs in the prepared pan and put the hens, breast side up, on top in a single layer, laying them flat. Tuck the remaining 5 herb sprigs around the hens.

Roast for 15 minutes. Brush with some of the reserved marinade, then reduce the heat to 325°F (165°C). Roast for another 15 minutes and brush again with the marinade. Continue roasting until the skin is well browned and the juices run clear when a thigh joint is pierced, about 15 minutes longer. The total cooking time is about 45 minutes.

Transfer the hens to a platter or individual plates and spoon the pan juices over the top. Garnish with the remaining herb sprigs and the lemon, lime, and/or orange slices. Serve at once.

Serves 4

4 Cornish hens, 1 1/2 lb (750 g) each

FOR THE MARINADE:

2 teaspoons finely grated lemon zest

1/2 cup (4 fl oz/125 ml) fresh lemon or lime juice

1/2 cup (4 fl oz/125 ml) fresh orange juice

2 cloves garlic, minced

2 tablespoons minced shallots or green (spring) onions, white part only

2 jalapeño chiles, seeded and minced

Salt

10 fresh thyme or rosemary sprigs, plus extra for garnish

Lemon, lime, and/or orange slices for garnish

Cornish Hens with Green Peppercorns

For a colorful and impressive presentation, serve the hens on a bed of steamed julienned zucchini (courgettes) and yellow squash or another vegetable of your choice and spoon the rice mixture around the edges.

2 Cornish hens, about 1²/₃ lb (815 g) each

2 tablespoons olive oil

1 large sweet white onion, cut into wedges 1 inch (2.5 cm) thick

2 cups (16 fl oz/500 ml) Chicken Stock (page 314)

1 cup (7 oz/220 g) short-grain brown rice

2 or 3 oil-packed sun-dried tomatoes, drained and coarsely chopped

1 tablespoon drained brine-packed green peppercorns, rinsed and crushed with the flat side of a heavy knife blade

4 carrots, peeled and cut into 1-inch (2.5-cm) pieces

Salt and freshly ground pepper

Rinse the Cornish hens well and pat dry with paper towels. In a Dutch oven over medium-high heat, heat the olive oil. Add the hens and brown on all sides until golden, about 8 minutes. Using tongs, transfer the hens to a dish. Pour off the fat from the pot.

Add the onion and 2–3 tablespoons of the stock to the same pot over medium heat. Deglaze the pot by stirring with a wooden spoon to dislodge any browned bits from the bottom. Add the brown rice, sun-dried tomatoes, green peppercorns, carrots, and remaining stock. Bring to a boil over high heat. Reduce the heat to medium-low and return the hens to the pot. Cover and simmer gently until the rice is tender and the meat is opaque throughout when cut into at the thigh joint, 50–60 minutes. Season to taste with salt and pepper.

Place each hen in a warmed shallow bowl and spoon the rice mixture around it.

Serves 2

Herbed Butterflied Squab

Small birds such as squabs and quail grill quickly and are good for a festive dinner because they make ideal single servings. Accompany the squabs with sautéed sliced potatoes on a bed of watercress-and-tomato salad.

Salt and freshly ground pepper

2 tablespoons minced fresh thyme or 2 teaspoons dried thyme

1 teaspoon crushed bay leaf

2 teaspoons crushed juniper berries

4 squabs, about 1 lb (500 g) each, butterflied (page 307)

Olive oil for coating and brushing

Handful of fresh thyme sprigs (optional)

In a small bowl, stir together 1 1/2 teaspoons salt, 1 teaspoon pepper, the thyme, bay leaf, and juniper berries. Rinse the squabs and pat dry with paper towels. Coat each squab lightly with olive oil, then sprinkle each bird with one-fourth of the herb mixture and rub it gently into the skin. Place the birds on a large platter or in a baking dish, laying them flat, and cover with plastic wrap. Marinate in the refrigerator for at least 2 hours; overnight is even better.

If using the thyme sprigs, soak in water to cover for about 30 minutes. Prepare a fire in a charcoal grill, or preheat a gas grill. Oil the grill rack and position 4–6 inches (10–15 cm) above the heat. Arrange the squabs, breast side down, on the grill rack. Grill, turning the birds 2 or 3 times and brushing once or twice with olive oil, until the skin is well browned and the meat is slightly pink when cut to the bone in the thickest part. During the last few minutes of cooking, place a sprig of damp thyme under each bird. The sprigs will smoke gently, giving off a pleasant aroma and flavor.

Remove the squabs from the grill, divide among individual plates, and serve.

Serves 4

Duck in Red Wine
with Apricots and Prunes

The pairing of rich duck and dried fruits makes this stew a perfect winter dish. Try adding dried apples and dried cranberries as well. Serve over mixed wild and white rice.

2 tablespoons unsalted butter

1 duck, 4–5 lb (2–2.5 kg), quartered, skinned, and trimmed of fat

6 shallots, minced

2 cloves garlic, minced

1/2 cup (3 oz/90 g) pitted prunes

1/2 cup (3 oz/90 g) dried apricots

3/4 cup (6 fl oz/180 ml) dry red wine

1 cup (8 fl oz/250 ml) Chicken Stock (page 314)

Salt and freshly ground pepper

In a Dutch oven over medium-high heat, melt the butter. Add the duck pieces, shallots, and garlic and sauté, stirring, until lightly golden, about 10 minutes.

Pour the duck fat from the pot and place the pot over medium-high heat. Add the prunes, apricots, wine, and stock. Deglaze the pot by stirring with a wooden spoon to dislodge any browned bits from the bottom. Reduce the heat to medium-low, cover, and simmer gently for 30 minutes.

Turn the duck pieces, re-cover, and continue to simmer until the duck is tender and opaque throughout, 30 minutes longer. Season to taste with salt and pepper.

Spoon into warmed shallow bowls and serve.

Serves 3 or 4

Orange-Roasted Duck

This orange-infused duck breast makes an elegant meal for two. Serve with puréed parsnips or celery root (celeriac) and a green vegetable such as green beans or asparagus tips.

To make the marinade, in a bowl, whisk together the orange juice, vermouth, marmalade, thyme, and 1 teaspoon salt. Reserve $^{1}/_{4}$ cup (2 fl oz/60 ml) of the marinade. Using a knife, score the duck skin with several crisscross diagonal cuts $^{1}/_{4}$ inch (6 mm) deep. Place the duck breast in a shallow, nonaluminum dish large enough for it to lie flat. Pour the rest of marinade over the breast and turn to coat both sides. Cover and refrigerate, turning occasionally, for at least 1 hour, or all day if you wish.

Prepare a fire in a charcoal grill, or preheat a gas grill. Oil the grill rack and position 4–6 inches (10–15 cm) above the heat.

Remove the duck from the marinade and pat dry with paper towels. Place the duck on the grill rack. Have a spray bottle of water handy to douse flare-ups for a charcoal fire. Grill, turning often and brushing 3 or 4 times with the reserved marinade, until the skin is well browned and the meat is still slightly pink at the bone, 18–20 minutes for medium-rare. For medium to well done, grill for an additional 5–7 minutes. Stop brushing with the marinade 5 minutes before the duck is done.

Remove the duck from the grill, cover loosely with aluminum foil, and let rest for 5 minutes. To serve, cut the meat from the bone into thin slices and arrange on warmed individual plates.

Serves 2

FOR THE MARINADE:

1 cup (8 fl oz/250 ml) fresh orange juice

$^{1}/_{2}$ cup (4 fl oz/125 ml) dry white vermouth

$^{1}/_{4}$ cup (2$^{1}/_{2}$ oz/75 g) orange marmalade

1 tablespoon minced fresh thyme or 1 teaspoon dried thyme

Salt

1 bone-in whole duck breast, 1$^{1}/_{4}$–1$^{1}/_{2}$ lb (625–750 g)

Basic Recipes & Techniques

The following recipes and techniques are found throughout *Meats & Poultry*. Some are components of larger recipes, such as the stocks and carving techniques; others are flavorful side dishes.

Beef Stock

Making stock at home is an all-day task, but the results are well worth the time. You can prepare a large batch of stock and freeze it in small containers for future use.

6 lb (3 kg) meaty beef shanks

Beef scraps or other trimmings, if available

2 onions, coarsely chopped

1 leek, trimmed, carefully washed, and coarsely chopped

2 carrots, peeled and coarsely chopped

1 celery stalk, coarsely chopped

Mushroom stems (optional)

6 cloves garlic

4 fresh parsley sprigs

10 whole peppercorns

3 fresh thyme sprigs

2 small bay leaves

Preheat the oven to 450°F (230°C). Place the beef shanks in a large roasting pan and roast, turning occasionally, until browned but not burned, about 1 1/2 hours.

Transfer the browned shanks to a large stockpot, reserving the juices in the pan, and add cold water to cover by 2 inches. Add the beef scraps, if using.

Bring to a boil over medium-high heat. Reduce the heat to low and simmer, uncovered, for 2 hours. While the stock simmers, using a large spoon, skim off any scum and froth that forms on the surface. Add water as needed to keep the bones generously immersed.

Meanwhile, place the roasting pan on the stove top. Add the onions, leek, carrots, and celery to the fat remaining in the pan. Brown over high heat, stirring often, until the vegetables caramelize but are not scorched, 15–20 minutes.

When the shanks have simmered for 2 hours, add the browned vegetables to the stockpot. Pour 1 cup (8 fl oz/250 ml) hot water into the roasting pan, bring to a simmer, and deglaze the pan by stirring to dislodge any browned bits from the bottom. Add these juices to the stockpot.

Place the mushroom stems (if using), garlic, parsley, peppercorns, thyme, and bay leaves on a square of cheesecloth (muslin) and tie with kitchen string into a small bag. Add to the stockpot. Simmer, over low heat, uncovered, for 6 hours longer (for a total of 8 hours).

Remove from the heat and remove the solids with a slotted spoon or skimmer. Strain the stock through a fine-mesh sieve lined with cheesecloth (muslin)

into a clean pot (if using the stock immediately) or storage container (if saving the stock for future use).

If using the stock immediately, use a large spoon to skim the fat from the surface of the stock. Discard the fat and use the stock in the desired recipe.

If storing the stock, let it cool to room temperature, then cover tightly and refrigerate for up to 5 days, or freeze for up to 6 months. Before using the stock, remove the solidified fat that sits on top of the stock.

Makes 4–5 qt (4–5 l)

Chicken Stock

Any type of chicken can be used for making this stock, although pieces of a stewing chicken (usually a more mature bird) will yield the most flavor.

2 1/2 lb (1.25 kg) chicken pieces, including bones

4 celery stalks with leaves, coarsely chopped

2 carrots, peeled and coarsely chopped

2 yellow onions, coarsely chopped

2 leeks, white part only, carefully washed and coarsely chopped

Bouquet Garni (page 316)

Put the chicken in a large stockpot and add cold water to cover by 2 inches. Bring to a gentle boil over medium-high heat. Reduce the heat to low and simmer for 30 minutes. While the stock simmers, using a large spoon, skim off any scum that forms on the surface.

Add the celery, carrots, onions, leeks, and bouquet garni. Cover partially and boil gently for 30 minutes longer; check periodically, skimming off any scum that forms on the surface.

Remove from the heat and remove the solids with a slotted spoon or skimmer. Strain the stock through a fine-mesh sieve lined with cheesecloth (muslin) into a clean pot (if using the stock immediately) or storage container (if saving the stock for future use).

If using the stock immediately, use a large spoon to skim the fat from the surface of the stock. Discard the fat and use the stock in the desired recipe.

If storing the stock, let it cool to room temperature, then cover tightly and refrigerate for up to 5 days, or freeze for up to 6 months. Before using the stock, remove the solidified fat that sits on top of the stock.

Makes about 5 cups (40 fl oz/1.25 l)

Chinese-Style Chicken Stock

Use this stock, flavored with vegetables and spices common in Chinese cooking, in stir-fries or Asian soups.

2½ lb (1.25 kg) chicken pieces, including bones

1 celery stalk, cut into ½-inch (12-mm) lengths

2 small carrots, peeled and cut into ½-inch (12-mm) lengths

1 leek, including tender green tops, carefully washed and sliced

1 yellow onion, cut in half

2 green (spring) onions, including tender green tops, cut into 2-inch (5-cm) lengths

2 slices fresh ginger, each ⅛ inch (3 mm) thick, peeled

Put the chicken, celery, carrots, leek, yellow onion, green onions, and ginger in a 4-qt (4-l) saucepan. Add enough cold water to fill the pan three-fourths full. Bring to a gentle boil over medium-high heat. Reduce the heat to low and simmer for 2½ hours. While the stock simmers, using a large spoon, skim off any scum that forms on the surface.

Remove from the heat and remove the solids with a slotted spoon or skimmer. Strain the stock through a fine-mesh sieve lined with cheesecloth (muslin) into a clean pot (if using the stock immediately) or storage container (if saving the stock for future use).

If using the stock immediately, use a large spoon to skim the fat from the surface of the stock. Discard the fat and use the stock in the desired recipe.

If storing the stock, let it cool to room temperature, then cover tightly and refrigerate for up to 3 days, or freeze for up to 2 months. Before using the stock, remove the solidified fat that sits on top of the stock.

Makes about 6 cups (48 fl oz/1.5 l)

Vegetable Stock

Sautéing the vegetables before adding water gives this particular stock a special depth of flavor.

2 tablespoons vegetable oil

2 large sweet onions, coarsely chopped

4 celery stalks with leaves, coarsely chopped

3 carrots, peeled and coarsely chopped

1 green bell pepper (capsicum), seeded, deribbed, and coarsely chopped

1 teaspoon salt

Bouquet Garni (page 316)

In a large stockpot over medium heat, warm the vegetable oil. Add the onions, celery, carrots, and bell pepper and sauté, stirring often, until the onions are translucent, about 10 minutes. Add 10 cups (2½ qt/2.5 l) water, the salt, and the bouquet garni. Bring to a gentle boil over medium-high heat. Reduce the heat to low and simmer for 30 minutes.

Remove from the heat and remove the solids with a slotted spoon. Strain the stock through a fine-mesh sieve lined with cheesecloth (muslin) into a clean pot (if using the stock immediately) or storage container (if saving the stock for future use).

If using the stock immediately, proceed with the desired recipe.

If storing the stock, let it cool to room temperature, then cover tightly and refrigerate for up to 5 days, or freeze for up to 12 months.

Makes about 8 cups (64 fl oz/2 l)

Bouquet Garni

6 whole peppercorns

1 bay leaf

1 clove garlic, sliced

3 fresh parsley sprigs

Cut a 6-inch (15-cm) square of cheese-cloth (muslin). Place the peppercorns, bay leaf, garlic, and parsley sprigs on the center of the cheesecloth, bring the corners together, and tie securely with kitchen string. Use as directed in individual recipes.

Herbed Bread Crumbs

The best bread to use here is a coarse-textured white bread that can be purchased sliced in 1- or 1 1/2 -pound (500- or 750-g) loaves. If the recipe calls for dried herbed bread crumbs, make the recipe as directed, then spread the crumbs on a baking sheet. Bake in a 325°F (165°C) oven, stirring often to prevent overbrowning, until golden, about 5 minutes.

4 slices white bread

Pinch of salt

Pinch of freshly ground pepper

1/4 teaspoon chopped fresh thyme or 1/8 teaspoon dried thyme

1/4 teaspoon chopped fresh rosemary

Cut the crusts off the bread and discard. Tear the bread into pieces. In a blender or food processor, combine the bread, salt, and pepper. Process the bread until it forms coarse crumbs.

Add the thyme and rosemary and pulse a few times just until well mixed. Use immediately, or store in an airtight container in the freezer for up to 1 year.

Makes about 1 cup (2 oz/60 g)

Poached Figs

1 lb (500 g) dried figs

1 cup (8 fl oz/250 ml) dry sherry

2 lemon slices

1 cinnamon stick

2 whole cloves

In a saucepan, combine the figs, sherry, lemon slices, cinnamon stick, cloves, and enough hot water to cover the figs. Place over medium heat and bring to a simmer. Cook until the figs are tender, 10–15 minutes. Remove from the heat and set aside for 1–2 hours. Drain the figs, reserving the cooking liquid; discard the lemon slices, cinnamon stick, and cloves.

Serves 4

Grill-Roasted Garlic

4 heads garlic

2 tablespoons olive oil

1 tablespoon chopped fresh thyme or 1/2 teaspoon dried thyme

1/2 teaspoon salt

1/4 teaspoon freshly ground pepper

Prepare a fire for indirect-heat cooking in a covered grill (page 326). Position the grill rack 4–6 inches (10–15 cm) above the fire.

Using a sharp knife, slice off the top 1/4–1/2 inch (6–12 mm) from each garlic head. Rub off some of the loose papery skin covering each head, taking care to keep the heads intact. In a small bowl, combine the garlic heads, olive oil, thyme, salt, and pepper. Toss to combine and coat the garlic evenly.

Place the garlic heads on the center of the rack, cover the grill, and open the vents halfway. Cook, turning the garlic heads 3 or 4 times, until the cloves feel very soft when squeezed gently with tongs or your fingers, 35–40 minutes. Don't worry if the skin chars in spots. Remove from the grill and serve warm.

Serves 4

Old-Fashioned Dumplings

These light and airy dumplings soak up the juices of a stew into their soft interiors. Directions are provided here for cooking the dumplings directly on a plate in a steamer.

2 cups (10 oz/315 g) all-purpose (plain) flour

2 teaspoons baking powder

1/4 teaspoon baking soda (bicarbonate of soda)

1/2 teaspoon salt

1 egg, beaten

3/4 cup (6 fl oz/180 ml) milk

In a bowl, sift together the flour, baking powder, baking soda, and salt. Add the egg and milk and mix with a fork until the flour is absorbed.

Grease a heatproof plate with vegetable oil or butter and place the plate on a rack in a steamer pan filled with water to a depth of about 1 inch (2.5 cm). Bring the water to a boil over high heat. Dip a large metal spoon into cold water, then scoop out spoonfuls of the moist dumpling dough and drop them onto the plate. Cover the steamer and steam until a toothpick inserted into the center of a dumpling comes out clean, about 20 minutes.

Makes about 16 dumplings; serves 4

Steamed White Rice

This recipe is the traditional accompaniment for stir-fries. Its mild taste and whiteness contrast well with the more definite flavors and brighter colors of most stir-fry dishes. Left to cool, the steamed rice can also be used for making fried rice.

1 cup (7 oz/220 g) long-grain white rice

1½ cups (12 fl oz/375 ml) water

Place the rice in a colander and rinse with cold water to remove excess starch. Drain well.

Combine the rice and the water in a saucepan over medium-high heat. Bring to a boil and boil, uncovered, until most of the water evaporates and there are craterlike holes in the surface of the rice, about 10 minutes. Reduce the heat to low, cover tightly, and simmer until the rice is tender, 10–15 minutes longer. Remove from the heat and let stand, covered, for 10 minutes before serving.

Just before serving, fluff the rice with a fork, then serve immediately.

Makes about 3 cups (15 oz/470 g); serves 4–6

Vegetable Fried Rice

You can vary this recipe by using dried mushrooms in place of the fresh: Soak 6 dried shiitake mushrooms in boiling water to cover for 20 minutes; drain, remove and discard the stems, and cut the caps into slices ½ inch (12 mm) thick. Add to the pan with the broccoli.

3 cups (15 oz/470 g) cold Steamed White Rice (left)

2 eggs

4 tablespoons (2 fl oz/60 ml) peanut or vegetable oil

1 cup (2 oz/60 g) small broccoli florets

1 carrot, peeled and cut into 1-inch (2.5-cm) pieces

6 fresh mushrooms, cut into slices ½ inch (12 mm) thick

1 teaspoon dry sherry

2 ears of corn, kernels removed (about 1 cup/60 oz/185 g)

¼ cup (2 fl oz/60 ml) Chinese-Style Chicken Stock (page 315)

2 tablespoons soy sauce

2 tablespoons thinly sliced green (spring) onion, including tender green tops

½ cup (3 oz/90 g) unsalted roasted peanuts (optional)

To separate the rice grains, place in a bowl. Rub the grains between wet fingers until they are separated. Set aside.

In a small bowl, beat the eggs lightly. In a wok or frying pan over medium heat, warm 1 tablespoon of the oil, swirling to coat the bottom and sides of the pan. When the oil is hot, add the eggs and stir continuously until soft curds form, about 1 minute. Transfer to a bowl and set aside.

Add another 1 tablespoon oil to the pan over medium-high heat, again swirling to coat. When hot, add the broccoli, carrot, and mushrooms and stir and toss every 15–20 seconds until the vegetables just begin to soften, 2–3 minutes. Add the sherry and stir and toss for 1 minute. Add the corn and stir and toss for 1 minute longer. Add vegetables to the bowl holding the eggs.

Add the remaining 2 tablespoons oil to the pan over medium-high heat, again swirling to coat the pan. When the oil is hot, add the rice and stir and toss every 20–30 seconds until it is lightly browned, about 5 minutes. Add the stock, soy sauce, and green onion and stir to combine. Add the reserved vegetables and eggs and the peanuts (if using), and stir and toss until the egg is in small pieces and the mixture is heated through, about 1 minute longer. Taste and adjust the seasonings. Serve immediately.

Serves 4–6

TRUSSING

Trussing, or tying whole turkeys or chickens into a compact shape, yields a roast bird that is easier to carve.

There are many different methods for trussing. The method used here is quite simple and requires a single piece of string that is at least long enough to wrap twice lengthwise around the bird; the longer the piece of string you use, the easier it will be to pull tight. Choose a sturdy linen kitchen string, which will not scorch in the heat of the oven.

If you've stuffed the bird, hold the neck flap securely shut as you truss.

1 With the bird breast-side up, slide the center of the string under its tail. Cross

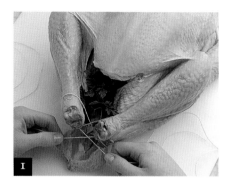

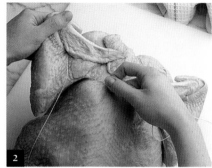

the ends above the tail and loop them around the drumsticks; then cross them again and pull tight to draw together the tail and the ends of the drumsticks.

2 Turn the bird over. Tuck the wing tips across the neck flap to secure them. Pull

one string end along the side, loop it around the nearest wing, pull it tight across the neck flap, and loop it around the other wing. Tie the two string ends tightly together. Cut off excess string.

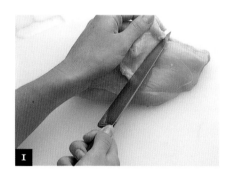

SKINNING & BONING CHICKEN

Start with the breast or thigh portions from a chicken you've already cut up, or with purchased pieces with skin and bones attached. Be sure to save the bones for the stockpot.

1 To skin, place one breast half or thigh, skin side up, on an acrylic cutting board.

Steady the meat with the side of a sturdy knife blade or with your hand; with the other hand, firmly grasp the skin and strip it away from the meat.

2 To bone, starting along the rib side, insert the knife between the bones and meat of the chicken piece. Pressing the knife edge gently against the bones,

gradually cut the bones away from the meat. Neatly trim the edges.

3 Place the chicken piece on the board, bone side up. Starting at the wider end, use a sharp knife to gradually cut the meat away from the bone, keeping the knife edge against the bone.

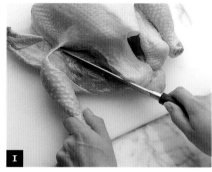

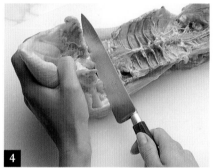

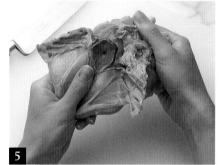

CUTTING UP A CHICKEN

The widespread availability today of ready-to-cook chicken pieces has made disjointing—cutting up a whole, uncooked chicken—an endangered art. If time allows, the techniques involved are fairly simple to master and worth the effort. And a whole chicken will not only cost you significantly less than an equivalent weight of already-cut pieces, but will also yield backbones and other trimmings that can be used for making chicken stock.

A sharp, sturdy knife is essential. Be sure to work on an acrylic cutting board, which provides a safe, slip-proof surface that cleans easily.

I Place the chicken, breast side up and drumsticks toward you, on an acrylic cutting board. With a sharp, sturdy knife, cut through the skin between the thigh and body. Locate the joint by moving the leg, then cut between the thigh and body to remove the leg. Repeat the process on the other side.

2 Move the drumstick to locate the joint connecting it to the thigh. Cut through the joint to separate the two pieces. Repeat with the other leg.

3 Move a wing to locate its joint with the body. Cut through the joint to remove the wing. Repeat with the other wing. If desired, separate the wings at the joints.

4 Starting at the neck opening, cut through both sides of the rib cage, separating the breast section, in one piece, from the remainder of the carcass.

5 Holding the breast skin side down, slit the thin membrane covering the breastbone along its center. Grasp the breast firmly at each end and flex it upward to pop out the breastbone. Pull out the bone, using the knife if necessary to help cut it free.

6 Place the breast skin side down on the cutting board. Cut along the center of the breast to split it, yielding two bone-in breast halves.

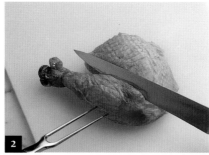

CARVING CHICKEN

1 Position the chicken breast side up. With a sturdy carving knife, cut through the skin between thigh and breast. Move the leg to locate the thigh joint, then cut through the joint to sever the leg. In the same way, remove the wing, cutting

through the shoulder joint where it meets the breast. Repeat the process with the other leg and wing.

2 If the chicken is small, serve the whole leg as an individual portion. If it is larger, cut through the joint to separate the drumstick and thigh into two pieces. You

can also slice a large thigh into two pieces by cutting off the meat on either side of the bone.

3 Starting on one side of the breastbone, cut downward and parallel to the rib cage, carving the meat into long, thin slices. Repeat the process.

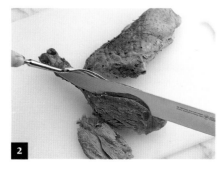

CARVING TURKEY

Turkey offers each guest a choice of dark leg meat and white breast meat. Carve only as needed to serve at one time, completing one side before starting the next.

1 With the turkey breast side up, cut through the skin between the thigh and breast. Move the leg to locate the thigh

joint, then cut through the joint to sever the leg. In the same way, remove the wing (shown at left), cutting through the shoulder joint where it meets the breast. Repeat the process.

2 Next, cut through the joint to separate the drumstick and thigh. Serve them whole or carve them, cutting the meat

into thin slices parallel to their bones.

3 Just above the thigh and shoulder joints, carve a deep horizontal cut toward the bone, creating a base cut on one side of the breast. Starting near the breastbone, carve thin slices vertically, cutting parallel to the rib cage and ending at the base cut.

CARVING HAM

Whether you are carving a whole ham or a butt or shank end, the carving process is basically the same: cutting parallel slices perpendicular to the bone, which are then freed by cutting horizontally along the bone.

1 Place the ham on a carving surface. Starting at its widest end, cut a vertical slice about $1/4$ inch (6 mm) thick and perpendicular to the bone.

2 Continue making cuts of the same width and parallel to the first, cutting as many slices as you wish to serve.

3 To free the slices, cut horizontally through their base, with the knife blade parallel to the bone. When all the meat has been removed from the first side, turn the ham over and repeat the slicing process on the second side.

CARVING BEEF

A prime rib of beef is fairly simple to carve, provided you have a large, sharp knife for slicing and a sturdy fork to steady the roast. You might wish to leave some slices attached to the ribs, for guests who prefer the meat on the bone.

1 Place the roast, ribs down, on a carving surface and steady it by inserting a carving fork. Using a carving knife, cut a vertical slice across the grain from one end of the roast down to the rib bone, cutting along the bone to free the slice.

2 Cutting parallel to the first slice, continue to carve slices of the desired thickness. As individual rib bones are exposed, cut between them to remove them; or leave them attached to slices for guests who request them.

GUIDELINES FOR BUYING MEAT & POULTRY

Beef & Veal: Whatever cut and grade of meat you buy (prime, choice, and select are the three highest USDA ratings), choose a meat that is bright cherry red. Vacuum-packaged meat may appear more purplish. Good-quality veal is fine-grained and creamy pink, with any visible fat a pure milky white. Use uncooked whole cuts of beef or left-over cooked beef within 3 to 4 days, and uncooked veal or ground (minced) beef in 1 to 2 days.

Chicken: First, ask about the source of the chicken and what it was fed on. So-called "free range" chickens tend to be more flavorful. Choose a chicken with a creamy yellow or creamy white skin that looks moist and supple and has well-distributed yellow fat; avoid those that look dried out or discolored. Your nose will tell you if a chicken if fresh. If you must buy a prepackaged bird, check the stamped "sell by" date. Cook the chicken within 2 days.

Lamb: Look for fresh-smelling, firm, pinkish red meat with pure white fat; any cut bones should appear moist, red, and porous. Darker meat or dry, whiter bones could indicate mutton. Store packages of lamb in the coldest part of the refrigerator with any wrappings loosened to allow air to circulate. Cook large pieces of lamb within 3–4 days, and ground (minced) lamb within 2 days of purchase.

Pork: Seek out a good, reliable source for buying pork. The meat should look pale pink and fine in texture, the fat pure and white, and any bones slightly reddish. If you see pork that looks coarse and has hard, white bones, chances are it comes from an older animal and should be avoided. Steer clear, as well, of any meat with an unpleasant odor. Good pork should smell clean and fresh. Use uncooked whole cuts or large pieces of pork within 3–4 days, and uncooked ground (minced) pork within 1–2 days.

CARVING A LEG OF LAMB

Shaped like an irregular, elongated pear, a leg of lamb presents a challenge to the carver. The keys to successful carving lie in cutting parallel to the bone and providing guests with slices from both sides of the leg.

1 Firmly grasp the protruding end of the shank bone with a kitchen towel and tilt it slightly upward. Using a long, sharp, sturdy knife, carve a first slice from the rounded, meaty side of the leg at its widest point, cutting away from you and roughly parallel to the bone.

2 Cutting parallel to the first slice, continue carving the meat in thin slices until you have cut enough to give each guest a slice.

3 Grasping the bone, rotate the leg of lamb to expose its other, flatter side—the inner side of the leg, which is slightly more tender. Still cutting parallel to the bone, carve a slice of this meat for each guest.

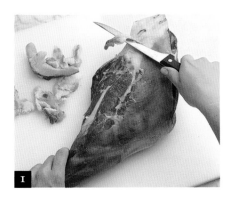

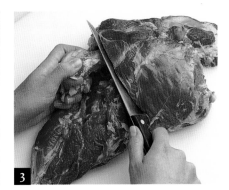

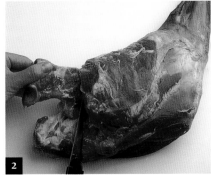

BONING & BUTTERFLYING A LEG OF LAMB

Boning and then butterflying a leg of lamb—that is, cutting it nearly all the way through to a uniform thickness so that, instead of being split into two pieces, it can be opened up to lie almost flat—makes it possible to cook the leg more evenly and quickly. If short on time, a good-quality butcher should be able to do the job for you, but you also might like to try doing it yourself.

Use a good kitchen knife—with a sharp stainless-steel blade and well-attached handle that feels comfortable and secure in your hand—and a good-sized cutting board. These valuable kitchen utensils will make this process much easier.

1 First, trim the leg. Before boning, chill the leg of lamb in the refrigerator for about 3 hours to firm up the meat for easier cutting. Gripping the surrounding white skin with a cloth or paper towel, tear away the outer membrane. Using a knife, carefully trim away the excess fat from the surface of the leg, carefully working parallel to the surface.

2 Locate the pelvic bone in the side rounded end, perpendicular to the length of the leg. With the pelvic bone end closest to you, gradually cut around the bone until you have exposed its ball-and-socket joint with the leg bone. Cut through the ligaments at the joint and pull the pelvic bone free.

3 Grasp the shank bone at the top of the leg and cut through the ligaments around the bone. Then, keeping the knife blade against the bone, carefully cut the meat away from the bone. When you reach the shank bone's joint with the leg bone, cut through the ligaments and remove the shank bone.

4 Cut down to the leg bone through the center of the meat. Cut around the joint at one end and ease the leg bone out of the meat. Holding the free joint, cut and scrape down the length of the bone until it is free from the meat.

5 Holding the knife blade parallel to the work surface, cut into the thickest parts of the leg meat from the center outward toward the edge to open it out in a flap. Take care not to cut completely through the meat. The result should be a large, flat piece of meat of uniform thickness.

Glossary

Armagnac Dry brandy, similar to Cognac, distilled in—and made from wine produced in—the Armagnac region of southwestern France. Other good-quality dry wine-based brandies may be substituted.

Brandy Applies to any spirit distilled from fermented fruit juice, but most specifically to dry grape brandy—the finest of which is generally known to be Cognac, from the French region of the same name.

Bread Crumbs Fresh or dried bread crumbs are sometimes used to add body and texture to ground-beef mixtures. To make bread crumbs, choose a good-quality, rustic-style loaf made of unbleached wheat flour, with a firm, coarse-textured crumb. For fresh crumbs, cut away the crusts and then crumble the bread by hand or in a blender or food processor. For dried crumbs, proceed as for fresh crumbs, then spread the crumbs on a baking pan. Dry slowly, for at least 1 hour, in an oven set at its lowest temperature. Fine dried bread crumbs are also sold prepackaged in supermarkets.

Calvados Dry French brandy that is distilled from apples and bears the

Beef Cuts

Cattle destined for the market are first cut into "primal," or whole-sale cuts—large sections that are then cut by the butcher into single-sized retail cuts purchased by consumers. The illustration shows the standard American primal cuts; individual retail cuts used in this book are described in the text that follows.

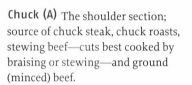

Chuck (A) The shoulder section; source of chuck steak, chuck roasts, stewing beef—cuts best cooked by braising or stewing—and ground (minced) beef.

Foreshank (B) Sold cubed or cut into bone-in slices for stewing, braising, or making stocks.

Rib (C) The rib-cage section—source of tender rib roasts and rib-eye roasts for oven roasting, rib-eye steaks for broiling (grilling) or pan-frying, and short ribs for braising.

Brisket (D) Cut into flat or pointed half briskets, which are often cured and simmered as corned beef. May also be braised.

Plate (E) Source of short ribs and stew beef for braising or stewing, as well as ground (minced) beef. The inner muscle is sometimes sold as skirt steak for braising, broiling, or grilling.

Short Loin (F) Source of T-bone, porterhouse, top loin, tenderloin, fillet, and strip steaks for grilling or broiling; and tenderloin roasts for roasting or broiling (grilling). Tenderloin, the bottom part of the short loin section, is the tenderest beef cut of all.

Flank (G) Source of flank steak for braising or grilling, and ground beef.

Sirloin (H) Source of sirloin steaks for broiling (grilling) or roasting, as well as ground (minced) beef.

Round (I) Source of round (rump) roast for braising or roasting; round steaks for braising, broiling, or grilling; and ground (minced) beef. Top round is the most tender part.

fruit's distinctive aroma and taste. If Calvados is unavailable, dry applejack may be substituted.

Cayenne Pepper Very hot ground spice that is made from dried cayenne chile peppers.

Chili Oil Popular seasoning of olive, sesame, or vegetable oil in which hot chiles have been steeped. Available in gourmet markets, Asian food shops, and the specialty-food aisle at well-stocked markets.

Chives Long, thin green herb with a mild, sweet flavor reminiscent of the onion, to which it is related. Although chives are available dried in the spice section of a supermarket, fresh chives possess the best flavor.

Chutney Refers to any number of spiced East Indian–style relishes served as condiments with meals and used as seasonings in cooking; most common are fruit-based chutneys, particularly mango. Available in ethnic markets, specialty-food stores, and Asian-food sections in supermarkets.

Cilantro Green, leafy herb resembling flat-leaf (Italian) parsley, with a sharp, aromatic, somewhat astringent flavor.

Cognac Dry spirit distilled from wine and produced in the Cognac region of France. Other good-quality, dry, wine-based brandies such as Armagnac may be substituted.

Corned Beef Beef brisket, or sometimes other cuts, cured for about a month in a brine with large crystals ("corns") of salt, sugar, spices, and other seasonings and preservatives. When slowly simmered in water, the meat develops a moist, tender texture, mildly spiced flavor, and bright purplish red color. Best purchased from a butcher shop that corns its own beef.

Cornish Hens Small hybrid bird that usually yields a single serving. Although sometimes available fresh, Cornish hens are most often found in the supermarket freezer section.

Crushing Dried Herbs If using dried herbs, it is best to gently crush them first in the palm of your hand to release their flavor. Alternatively, warm them in a small frying pan and crush them using a mortar and pestle.

Curry Powder A blend of spices commonly used to flavor East Indian–style dishes. Most curry powders will include coriander, cumin, chili powder, fenugreek, and turmeric. Best purchased in

small quantities, because its flavor diminishes rapidly after opening.

Direct–Heat Cooking In grilling, the method of quickly cooking individual servings or relatively thin pieces of food by placing them on the grill rack that is located directly above hot coals.

Eggs, Separating To separate an egg, crack the shell in half by tapping it against the side of a bowl and then breaking it apart with your fingers. Holding the shell halves over the bowl, gently transfer the whole yolk back and forth between them, letting the clear white drop away into the bowl. Take care not to cut into the yolk with the edges of the shell. Transfer the yolk to another bowl.

Filo Tissue-thin sheets of flour-and-water pastry used throughout the Middle East as crisp wrappers for savory or sweet fillings. Usually found in the frozen-food section of well-stocked supermarkets, or purchased fresh in Middle Eastern delicatessens.

Fish Sauce Popular Southeast Asian seasoning made from salted, fermented fish, usually anchovies. Also know as *nuoc mam* (Vietnamese), *nam pla* (Thai), and *patis* (Filipino). Available in Asian markets and specialty-food sections of well-stocked markets.

Garlic Pungent bulb popular worldwide as a flavoring ingredient, raw and cooked. For the best flavor, purchase whole heads of dry garlic, separating individual cloves from the head as needed.

To peel a garlic clove, place on a work surface and carefully cover with the side of a large chef's knife. Press down firmly on the knife to crush the clove slightly; the dry skin will then slip off easily.

Hoisin Sauce Thick, reddish brown sauce of fermented soybeans or wheat, chiles, garlic, vinegar, sesame, and Asian spices; used as a seasoning or sauce ingredient in stir-fries. Sold in bottles in Asian markets and well-stocked markets, it keeps indefinitely in the refrigerator or cupboard.

Horseradish Pungent, hot-tasting root and a member of the mustard family, sold fresh and whole, or already grated and bottled as a prepared sauce. The best prepared horseradish is the freshly grated variety, bottled in a light vinegar and found in the refrigerated sections of supermarkets.

Hot Pepper Sauce Popular bottled commercial cooking and table sauce made from fresh or dried hot red chile peppers. Tabasco is the most commonly known brand.

Indirect-Heat Cooking In grilling, refers to method of cooking larger items that would burn if direct-heat cooking were employed. Glowing coals are pushed to perimeter of the grill's fire pan, and food is placed in the center of the grill rack and usually covered to cook slowly in the radiant heat.

Marinate To flavor and moisturize pieces of meat or poultry by soaking them in a liquid mixture of seasonings known as a marinade. Dry marinade mixtures (dry rubs), which are usually composed of salt, pepper, herbs, or spices, may also be rubbed into meat and poultry.

Marsala Dry or sweet amber Italian wine from the area of Marsala, in Sicily.

Mirin Sweetened Japanese rice wine used as a flavoring ingredient; widely available in Japanese markets and well-stocked food stores. Medium-dry sherry may be substituted.

Mustard, Dijon Spicy mustard, pale in color and made from dark brown mustard seeds. A product of Dijon, France.

Nuts, Toasting To toast nuts, which brings out their full flavor and aroma, preheat an oven to 325°F (165°C). Spread the nuts in a single layer on a baking sheet and toast in the oven until they just begin to change color and are fragrant, 5–10 minutes. Remove from the oven and let cool to room temperature. Toasting such nuts as hazelnuts and walnuts also loosens the skins, which may be removed by wrapping the still-warm nuts in a kitchen towel and rubbing them with the palms of your hands.

Onion, Pearl To peel pearl onions, immerse them in boiling water for about 2 minutes, then drain well. When cool, use a small, sharp knife to trim off their root ends. Slip off the skins by squeezing gently with your fingers. Then use the knife to cut a shallow **X** in each trimmed end, so the onions cook evenly.

Paprika Powdered spice derived from the dried paprika pepper; popular in several European cuisines and available in sweet, mild, and hot forms. Hungarian paprika is the best, but Spanish paprika, which is mild, may also be used.

Peppercorns The most common of all savory spices, best when purchased as whole peppercorns to be ground in a pepper mill or coarsely crushed as needed.

Peppers To prepare a raw pepper, cut it in half lengthwise with a sharp knife. Pull out the stem section from each half, along with the cluster of seeds attached to it.

Remove any remaining seeds along with any thin white membranes, or ribs, to which they are attached.

Carefully cut the pepper halves into quarters, strips, or slices, or as directed in the specific recipe. When handling chiles, wear kitchen gloves to prevent any cuts or abrasions on your hands from contacting the pepper's volatile oils; wash your hands well with warm, soapy water, and take special care not to touch your eyes or any other sensitive areas.

When a recipe calls for roasted and peeled bell peppers, preheat a broiler (grill). Cut the bell peppers in half lengthwise and remove the stem, seeds, and ribs as directed above. Place the pepper halves on a broiler pan, cut side down, and broil until the skins blister and turn black. Transfer to a paper or plastic bag, seal, and let stand until the peppers soften, about 10 minutes. Using your fingertips or a small knife, peel off the blackened skins. Then tear or cut the peppers as directed in the specific recipe.

Pesto Traditional Milanese sauce made of puréed basil, garlic, pine nuts, Parmesan cheese, and olive oil; sometimes used as a seasoning for stews and other dishes. Ready-made pesto can be found in the refrigerated sections of well-stocked markets.

Plum Sauce Sweet-tart bottled Chinese sauce of dried plums and apricots, sugar, vinegar, and spices; used as a condiment. Available in Asian markets and well-stocked markets.

Prosciutto Italian-style raw ham, a specialty of Parma in the Italian region of Emilia-Romagna. It is cured by dry-salting for 1 month, then air-drying in cool curing sheds for half a year or longer. Usually cut into tissue-thin slices.

Pork

Before it is cut into individual retail cuts, pork is first divided into the large "primal" or wholesale cuts shown in the illustration. Individual retail cuts used in this book are discussed in the text that follows; some cuts may not be commonly available and should be sought from a quality butcher.

Shoulder (A) This tough, meaty primal cut yields bone-in and boneless shoulder roasts. The boned meat may also be cut into cubes for grilled or broiled kebabs, or it may be chopped for ground (minced) pork or sausage.

Blade and Center Loin (B) The front blade section of the loin, with its rich, tender meat, is cut into large blade roasts or sliced into bone-in blade chops. Toward the center of the loin, the meat becomes juicier and more tender still. It may be cut into chops for grilling, broiling, or sautéing; and a section with rib bones attached may be shaped and tied into the descriptively named "crown roast." The tender back ribs from this section are excellent for barbecuing.

Sirloin (C) The tenderest pork of all, the tenderloin, comes from this primal cut. The thin tenderloin may be grilled, broiled, or sautéed whole, or cut into thin scallops for sautéing. Loin chops are frequently also cut from this section for grilling, broiling, or sautéing.

Ham (D) The ham section is the source of bone-in, partially boned, and boneless hams. Country-style ham refers to one that has been cured with salt or brine and other seasonings, then smoked; the ham is then cooked partially or completely before it is sold in the market. The fine-grained meat from the center of this section may also be cut to make ham steaks. The top, or butt, portion, which is almost boneless, may also be roasted or braised.

Belly (E) With their very tender meat and generous amounts of fat, the rib bones from the front portion of this primal cut become pork spareribs for baking or grilling. The remainder of the belly yields bacon or salt pork.

Feet (F) Also known as trotters. Used as a rich source of gelatin or for flavoring and thickening soup stocks and stews.

Quail A small game bird—usually a single serving—known for its moist, tender, flavorful meat.

Red Pepper Flakes Coarsely ground flakes of dried red chiles, including seeds, which add moderately hot flavor to the foods they season.

Reduce Simmering or boiling a liquid in order to decrease its quantity through evaporation, while concentrating the flavor and thickening the consistency. A simple way to transform cooking liquid into a sauce.

Roasting Cooking in the dry, radiant heat of an oven, a method well suited to large cuts of meat and whole poultry. Some types of grilling equipment may be used to roast with their lids closed, employing indirect-heat cooking.

Rosemary Popular Mediterranean herb, used either fresh or dried, with a strong aromatic flavor well suited for lamb and veal, as well as poultry and beef dishes.

Saffron Intensely aromatic spice, golden orange in color, made from the dried stigmas of a species of crocus and used to perfume and color many classic Mediterranean and East Indian dishes. Sold either as threads—the whole dried stigmas—or in powdered form. Look for products labeled "pure" saffron.

Sage Pungent herb, used either fresh or dried, that goes particularly well with fresh or cured veal, pork, lamb, or chicken.

Salsa Latin American term for a cooked or fresh, raw sauce—most often one made with tomatoes, tomatillos, or chiles.

Salt, Sea Salt extracted by evaporation from sea water has a more pronounced flavor than regular table salt. Available in coarse and fine grinds in specialty-food stores and well-stocked markets. Coarse or kosher salt may be used in place of coarse sea salt crystals.

Sausages, Italian Fresh Italian sausages are generally made from ground pork, seasoned with salt, pepper, and spices. Those made in the style of northern Italy are usually sweet and mild, sometimes flavored with fennel seed. Southern-style sausages tend to be hotter, often flavored with flakes of dried chile pepper.

Shallot Small member of the onion family with brown skin, white-to-purple flesh, and a flavor resembling a cross between sweet onion and garlic.

Sherry Fortified, cask-aged wine enjoyed as an apertif and often used as a flavoring for sauces and marinades.

Skewer Thin metal or wooden stick upon which small pieces of meat, poultry, or vegetables may be threaded for grilling. The pieces should not be threaded on the skewer too tightly.

Skim To remove impurities—whether scum or fat—from the surface of a liquid during cooking, thereby resulting in a clearer, cleaner-tasting final product. An essential early step in the preparation of chicken stock.

Soy Sauce Asian seasoning and condiment made from soybeans, wheat, salt, and water. Seek out good-quality imported soy sauces; Chinese brands tend to be markedly saltier than Japanese. Those labeled "dark" soy sauce have a fuller, richer flavor.

Squab Delicate-flavored, tender species of pigeon raised specifically for the table. The single-serving birds are available fresh or frozen from well-stocked markets or poultry shops.

Stir-Fry A stove-top technique, Chinese in origin, for quickly cooking small pieces of food in a large pan over moderate to high heat.

Stock Flavorful liquid derived from slowly simmering meat, chicken, or vegetables in water, along with herbs and aromatic vegetables. Used as the primary cooking liquid in stews and braises, as the foundation for sauces and soups, and as a moistening and flavoring agent in other recipes.

Sugars Although thought of as a main dessert ingredient, sugar may be used to flavor marinades and barbecue sauces. It adds a subtle sweetness to grilled meats and, by caramelizing under intense heat, gives a finished dish a rich, deep brown glaze. Sugar-laden sauces burn easily and should be brushed on food during the last 15–20 minutes of cooking.

Sun-Dried Tomatoes When sliced crosswise or halved, then dried in the sun, tomatoes develop an intense, sweet-tart flavor and a pleasantly chewy texture that enhance savory recipes. Available either dry or packed in oil, and with or without herbs and spices. Sold in specialty food stores and well-stocked markets.

Tandoori East Indian style of cooking based on a charcoal-heated tandoor, a clay oven whose intense heat cooks food quickly, lightly charring its surface while keeping it tender and moist within. Tandoori-style marinades, which include yogurt and Indian spices, may be used to flavor foods to achieve a similar effect with any grill.

Tarragon Fragrant, distinctively sweet herb used fresh or dried as a classic seasoning for light meats, and chicken.

Teriyaki Japanese style of grilling in which food is seasoned and basted with a marinade usually based on mirin (sweet rice wine) and soy sauce, to form a rich, shining glaze.

Tequila The best-known Mexican spirit, a powerful, clear or golden liquid distilled from the juice of the blue agave (century) plant.

Thyme Fragrant, clean-tasting, small-leaved herb, popular as a seasoning for light meats, poultry, seafood, or vegetables. Use fresh or dried.

Tomatoes During the summer, when tomatoes are in season, use the best red or yellow sun-ripened tomatoes you can find. At other times of year, plum tomatoes, sometimes called Roma or egg tomatoes, are likely to have the best flavor and texture. For cooking, canned whole, diced, chopped, or puréed plum tomatoes are also good.

To peel fresh tomatoes, bring a saucepan of water to a boil. Using a small, sharp knife, cut out the core from the stem end of the tomato. Then cut a shallow X in the skin at the tomato's base. Submerge for about 20 seconds in the boiling water, then remove and cool in a bowl of cold water. Starting at the X, peel the skin from the tomato, using your fingertips and, if necessary, the knife blade. Cut the tomato in half and turn each half cut-side down. Then cut as directed in the individual recipes.

To seed a tomato, cut it in half crosswise. Squeeze gently to force out the seed sacs.

Turmeric Pungent, earthy-flavored ground spice that, like saffron, adds a vibrant yellow color to any dish.

Vermouth Dry or sweet wine that is commerically enhanced with spices, herbs, and fruits which give it an aromatic flavor.

Worcestershire Sauce Traditional English seasoning or condiment; an intensely flavorful, savory, and aromatic blend of many ingredients, including molasses, soy sauce, garlic, onion, and anchovies. Popular as a marinade ingredient or as a table sauce for grilled foods, especially red meats.

Zest Thin, brightly colored, outermost layer of a citrus fruit's peel, containing most of its aromatic essential oils— a lively source of flavor. Zest may be removed with a simple tool known as a zester, drawn across the fruit's skin to remove the zest in thin strips; with a fine hand-held grater; or with a vegetable peeler or a paring knife that is held away from you. To use, just cut into thin strips taking extra care not to remove any of the bitter white pith. Zest removed with the latter two tools may then be thinly sliced or chopped on a cutting board.

Index

C

cabbage. *See also* sauerkraut
  braised, pork tenderloin with 107
  stuffed 76

caper sauce 19

carrots
  pork tenderloin with corn, mushrooms, and 110
  roast leg of lamb with 177

carving 320–22

cheese
  blue cheese sauce 286
  Cheddar, scalloped potatoes and ham with 150
  chicken stuffed with herbs and 245
  feta and cucumber salad 181
  Roquefort butter 15
  Turkish spiced lamb and tomato pizza 198

chermoula 133

chicken
  all-American barbecued 285
  with apples 239
  Basque 250
  with bell peppers and Parmesan 258
  boning 318
  breasts, almond-crusted 215
  breasts, lemon 231
  breasts, Malaysian, with endive and ginger 212
  breasts, tropical 242
  breast sauté with vinegar-tarragon sauce 221

breasts stuffed with herbs and prosciutto 232
breasts with black olive butter 240
breasts with vermouth 222
and broccoli casserole 227
broiled, with herb-stuffed breast 282
broiled, with vinaigrette 281
buffalo wings 286
buying 322
carving 320
curry 247
cutting up 319
and eggplant casserole 273
fajitas 235
with forty cloves of garlic 270
French, with prunes 268
fried, with herbs 254
with garlic 262
Greek, with oregano 267
grill-roasted 296
grill-roasted, with potato fans 277
hickory-smoked 280
Jamaican jerk 253
kabobs 228
legs with chutney 249
lemon-rosemary 274
with mango, sweet potatoes, and cashews 213
Moroccan 217
mustard-grilled 289
with okra 214
oven-braised, with vegetables 257
paillards 243

paprika 244
pilaf, Turkish 252
with plum jam and almonds 264
with plum sauce 236
Provençal, skewered 246
roast, with gravy 263
rosemary, with potatoes 261
saffron, with capers 218
salad with radicchio and red onions 210
sausage, fettuccine with garlic, mushrooms, and 278
sausages, mustard-glazed, with sauerkraut relish 134
sausages, Portuguese stew with 303
sausages with chutney mustard 302
sauté Provençale 225
smothered, with mushrooms and onions 226
stew with parsley dumplings 209
stir-frying 328
stock 314–15
stock, Chinese-style 315
stuffed with corn bread and sausage 251
stuffed with herbs and cheese 245
teriyaki 271
trussing 318
whole vs. parts 9–10

chili
  lamb and black bean 161
  Texas beef 72

chili oil 17

Chinese beef stew with five-spice powder 26

Chinese-style chicken stock 315

chives
  butter 59
  -mustard butter 16

chutneys. *See also* relishes
  dressing 118
  dried-fruit 112
  pear and mustard 21
  plum and ginger 21

citrus fruits. *See also individual fruits*
  marinade 14
  -marinated Cornish hens 307
  zesting 329

coriander-orange butter 204

corn, pork tenderloin with mushrooms, carrots, and 110

corn bread, chicken stuffed with sausage and 251

corned beef 32

Cornish hens
  citrus-marinated 307
  with green peppercorns 308

cranberries
  dried-fruit chutney 112
  -tomato salsa 21

cucumber and feta salad 181

curries
  chicken 247
  pork satay 142
  sweet-and-spicy lamb 167

stew with eggplant purée 154

and tomato pizza, Turkish spiced 198

Latin American grilled steak with avocado salsa 48

lemons

butter 15

chicken breasts 231

-rosemary chicken 274

lentil and lamb soup 157

M

Madeira marinade 121

Malaysian chicken breasts with endive and ginger 212

mango, chicken with sweet potatoes, cashews, and 213

marinades

chermoula 133

citrus 14

dry 14

jalapeño 84

Madeira 121

mop sauce 18

red or white wine 14

soy-ginger 14–15

marmalade, onion 98

mayonnaise, garlic 183

meatballs

lamb, spiced, with tomatoes and cilantro 200

Moroccan 78

stew, Greek, with Brussels sprouts 165

marinated beef tenderloin with tarragon butter, 63

meat loaf

pork, with sweet-and-hot sauce 138

tomato-glazed 79

Midwestern barbecue sauce 17–18

mint mustard 182

mint vinaigrette 281

mop sauce, spicy 18

Moroccan chicken 217

Moroccan meatballs 78

Moroccan-style grilled pork chops 133

moussaka 197

mushrooms

beef bourguignon 25

beef Stroganoff 52

chicken smothered with onions and 226

fettuccine with sausage, garlic, and 278

grilled veal loin chops with tarragon, cream, and 93

pork tenderloin with corn, carrots, and 110

veal ragout with cream and 91

mustard

butter 15

-chive butter 16

cream sauce 16

-horseradish sauce 19

mint 182

and pear chutney 21

N

nuts, toasting 326

O

oil, chili 17

okra, chicken with 214

olives

butter, black 240

butter, Provençal 15–16

pitting 20

tapenade 20–21

onions

marmalade 98

peeling pearl 326

red, stuffed with pork 136

-stuffed beef kefta 80

oranges

-and-ginger-glazed pork roast 124

-chile sauce, beef with 41

-roasted duck 313

P

papaya and pork 103

paprika chicken 244

paprika veal stew with dumplings 28

parsley sauce 19

parsnips and pork in sherry 101

pasta

fettuccine with sausage, garlic, and mushrooms 278

penne with lamb, zucchini, tomatoes, and basil 194

peanuts

dipping sauce 19

sauce 119

pears

and mustard chutney 21

salad of grilled pork, pecans, and 116

pesto 20

pilaf, Turkish chicken 252

pineapple relish 54

pizza, Turkish spiced lamb and tomato 198

plum and ginger chutney 21

polenta with pork sausages and tomatoes 137

pork. *See also* ham; prosciutto; sausages

baby back ribs, mustard-glazed 145

buying 322

chops, Moroccan-style grilled 133

chops, pecan-crusted 127

chops, stuffed, with prunes and apples 129

cuts of 8, 327

and endive with juniper berries 104

grilled, salad of pears, pecans, and 116

kabobs, apricot-glazed, with wild rice 115

loin, roast, with baked apples 122

loin with Madeira marinade 121

meat loaf with sweet-and-hot sauce 138

medallions with lemon and capers 106

noisettes with peppers and balsamic vinegar 109

and papaya 103

and parsnips in sherry 101

First published in the USA by Time-Life Custom Publishing.

Originally published as Williams-Sonoma Kitchen Library:
Grilling (© 1992 Weldon Owen Inc.)
Beef (© 1993 Weldon Owen Inc.)
Chicken (©1993 Weldon Owen Inc.)
Stir-Fry (© 1994 Weldon Owen Inc.)
Pork & Lamb (©1995 Weldon Owen Inc.)
Stews (©1995 Weldon Owen Inc.)
Cooking Basics (© 1996 Weldon Owen Inc.)
Healthy Cooking (© 1997 Weldon Owen Inc.)
Mediterranean Cooking (© 1997 Weldon Owen Inc.)
Outdoor Cooking (© 1997 Weldon Owen Inc.)

In collaboration with Williams-Sonoma Inc.
3250 Van Ness Avenue, San Francisco, CA 94109

Oxmoor
House®

OXMOOR HOUSE INC.
Oxmoor House books are distributed by Sunset Books
80 Willow Road, Menlo Park, CA 94025
Telephone: 650-321-3600 Fax: 650-324-1532
Vice President/General Manager: Rich Smeby
National Accounts Manager/Special Sales: Brad Moses

Oxmoor House and Sunset Books are divisions of
Southern Progress Corporation

WILLIAMS-SONOMA INC.
Founder and Vice-Chairman: Chuck Williams

WELDON OWEN INC.
Chief Executive Officer: John Owen
President and Chief Operating Officer: Terry Newell
Creative Director: Gaye Allen
Publisher: Hannah Rahill
Associate Creative Director: Leslie Harrington
Senior Designer: Charlene Charles
Assistant Editor: Donita Boles
Editorial Assistant: Juli Vendzules
Production Director: Chris Hemesath
Production Coordinator: Libby Temple
Color Manager: Teri Bell

Williams-Sonoma Meats & Poultry was conceived and
produced by Weldon Owen Inc.
814 Montgomery Street, San Francisco, CA 94133
Copyright © 2004 Weldon Owen Inc.
and Williams-Sonoma Inc.

First printed in 2004.
10 9 8 7 6 5

ISBN 0-8487-2891-2

Printed in China by SNP Leefung Printers Ltd.

CREDITS Lora Brody: Pages 26, 28, 29, 31, 37, 89, 100, 101, 103, 104, 162, 165, 166, 213, 214, 217, 247, 251, 303, 308, 312; Emalee Chapman: Pages 19 (Green Parsley Sauce, Horseradish-Mustard Sauce, Red Pepper Sauce), 21 (Tomato-Cranberry Salsa), 209, 210, 212, 218, 222, 227, 228, 232, 239, 243, 244, 245, 246, 249, 250, 254, 256, 257, 259, 260, 264, 265, 266, 272, 280, 282; Joyce Goldstein: Pages 15 (Roquefort Butter, Provençal Butter), 16 (Mustard-Chive Butter, Cold Horseradish Cream, Mustard Cream Sauce), 18 (Basic Tomato Sauce), 19 (Caper Sauce), 20 (Pesto, Tapenade), 25, 32, 44, 48, 51, 54, 55, 58, 61, 66, 69, 70, 71, 72, 73, 74, 77, 80, 84, 85, 86, 88, 91, 93, 125, 154, 189, 252, 269; Jacqueline Mallorca: Pages 59, 201, 215, 263; John Phillip Carroll: Pages 14, 15, 17 (Basic Barbecue Sauce, Midwestern Barbecue Sauce), 18 (Red or White Wine Barbecue Sauce, Spicy Mop Sauce), 19 (Peanut Dipping Sauce), 20 (Honey-Mustard Dressing, Yogurt and Herb Dressing), 35, 38, 50, 53, 56, 62, 63, 64, 65, 78, 81, 83, 90, 107, 111, 118, 121, 124, 134, 142, 145, 169, 170, 174, 178, 193, 203, 221, 225, 226, 231, 240, 242, 253, 270, 273, 275, 276, 279, 283, 284, 287, 293, 296, 297, 299, 301, 302, 304, 307, 310, 313; Joanne Weir: Pages 21 (Pear and Mustard Chutney, Plum and Ginger Chutney), 97, 98, 106, 109, 112, 115, 116, 119, 122, 126, 127, 129, 130, 133, 135, 136, 137, 138, 141, 146, 149, 150, 157, 158, 161, 167, 173, 176, 177, 180, 181, 182, 183, 185, 190, 191, 194, 197, 198, 200, 204; Diane Rossen Worthington: Pages 17 (All-Purpose Stir-Fry Sauce, Chili Oil), 41, 42, 45, 47, 110, 186, 235, 236, 294.

Photographers: Noel Barnhurst (front cover), and Allan Rosenberg (recipe photography), and Chris Shorten (recipe photography for pages 59, 201, 215).

ACKNOWLEDGMENTS
Weldon Owen would like to thank Carrie Bradley, Kimberly Chun, Ken DellaPenta, Judith Dunham, Arin Hailey, Karen Kemp, Carolyn Miller, and Joan Olson for all their expertise, assistance, and hard work.